Grace Unlimited

Grace Unlimited

CLARK H. PINNOCK, EDITOR

BETHANY FELLOWSHIP, INC.
Minneapolis, Minnesota

Copyright © 1975
Bethany Fellowship, Inc.
All rights reserved
Published by Bethany Fellowship, Inc.
6820 Auto Club Road, Minneapolis, Minnesota 55438
Printed in the United States of America

Library of Congress CIP Data:

Main entry under title:

Grace unlimited.

Includes bibliographical references.
1. Grace (Theology)—Addresses, essays, lectures.
2. Salvation—Addresses, essays, lectures. I. Pinnock, Clark H., 1937-
BT761.2.G7   234   75-22161
ISBN 0-87123-185-9

The saying is sure and worthy of full acceptance, that Christ Jesus came into the world to save sinners. And I am the foremost of sinners; but I received mercy for this reason, that in me, as the foremost, Jesus Christ might display his perfect patience for an example to those who were to believe in him for eternal life. To the King of ages, immortal, invisible, the only God, be honor and glory for ever and ever. Amen.

Saint Paul

33,714

Table of Contents

The Contributors

Dr. Vernon C. Grounds, president of the Conservative Baptist Seminary, Denver, is a noted evangelical scholar, author, and lecturer. After receiving the bachelor of arts degree from Rutgers University, Dr. Grounds received his divinity degree from Faith Seminary, and his doctorate in philosophy from Drew University.

Dr. David J. A. Clines is senior lecturer in biblical studies at the University of Sheffield, England. He holds the B.A. degree in Classics from the University of Sydney, and the M.A. in Semitic Languages from Cambridge University.

Dr. I. Howard Marshall is presently Lecturer in New Testament Exegesis at the University of Aberdeen, in Scotland. He holds a B.A. degree from Cambridge and M.A., B.D. and Ph.D. degrees from Aberdeen.

Dr. Jack W. Cottrell is professor of theology at Cincinnati Christian Seminary. He received a bachelors degree in philosophy from the University of Cincinnati, the M.Div. from Westminster Theological Seminary, and the Ph.D. degree from Princeton University.

Dr. Donald M. Lake is associate professor of theology at Wheaton College. He received his B.A. and M.A. degrees from Wheaton, and his Ph.D. from the University of Iowa in 1967.

Dr. William G. MacDonald is professor of biblical studies at Gordon College. He holds the M.A. degree from Wheaton College, the S.T.M. from Concordia Seminary, and the Th.D. from Southern Baptist Theological Seminary.

Dr. Grant R. Osborne is professor of New Testament at Winnipeg Theological Seminary. He received his M.A. degree from Trinity Evangelical Divinity School and his Ph.D. in New Testament from the University of Aberdeen.

Dr. A. Skevington Wood is senior lecturer in theology at Cliff College in England. He received his B.A. degree from London University and his Ph.D. from Edinburgh.

Dr. James D. Strauss is professor of Christian doctrine and philosophy at Lincoln Christian Seminary in Illinois. He received the B.A. degree from Butler University, the M.Div. degree from Christian Theological Seminary, the Th.M. from the Chicago Graduate School of Theology, and is pursuing doctoral studies at St. Louis University.

Dr. Clark H. Pinnock is associate professor of theology at Regent College, Vancouver, Canada. He holds the B.A. degree in Ancient Near Eastern Studies from the University of Toronto and the Ph.D. degree in New Testament from the University of Manchester.

Introduction

The meaning of our Savior's name Jesus is "Jehovah saves!" It sums up in a single word the central theme of the whole Bible: the triumph of grace in the salvation of sinners, grace unlimited and abounding. It is to this noble subject that the attention of our international symposium is directed. We wish to articulate the doctrine of grace in the most biblical and coherent way possible.[1]

To do that in our day will mean first of all to focus on the *universality* of grace, on all-inclusive scope of God's salvific will. The most important theological presupposition of all of us writing in this volume is our conviction that God is good in an unqualified manner, and that he desires the salvation of all sinners. To each human being God offers forgiveness in Jesus Christ and the gift of sonship. We delight in our Lord's word: "It is not the will of my Father who is in heaven that one of these little ones should perish" (Matt. 18:14). We reject all forms of theology which deny this truth and posit some secret abyss in God's mind where he is not gracious. We consent to Paul's judgment that God "desires all men to be saved and to come to the knowledge of the truth" and to Peter's conviction that God is "not wishing that any should perish, but that all should reach repentance" (1 Tim. 2:4, 2 Pet. 3:9). If it seems controversial to assert this conviction boldly and unashamedly, then it ought at least to be admitted that here is a truth far more deserving of controversy than many which are debated. On it hangs, we believe, the validity of the universal offer of the gospel, and the possibility of Christian assurance. If we do not know that God loves all sinners, we do not know that he loves us, and we do not know that he loves those to whom we take the gospel.[2]

In the cross of Christ we see the will of God for the salvation of all sinners perfectly exemplified. As Paul says, "The love of Christ controls us, because we are convinced that *one* has died for *all*" (2 Cor. 5:14). In Romans the Apostle draws a parallel between Christ and Adam in these words: "As one man's trespass led to condemnation for all men, so one man's act of righteousness leads to acquittal and life *for all men*" (5:18). It is difficult to imagine how the Bible could have made things clearer. Christ's saving work is pertinent to the whole race, as Adam's work was, and is therefore offered to all sinners. Or, again, Paul says, "God was in Christ reconciling the world to himself" (2 Cor. 5:19). According to John, "He is the expiation for our sins, and not for ours only but also for the sins of the whole world" (1 John 2:2). The universal salvific will of the Father has become objectified in the atoning work of the Son according to all these texts so that no sinner can now doubt that God loves him and desires to save him. We take vigorous exception, therefore, to any theology that denies that Jesus, the bread of heaven, means life for the world (John 6:46-51). We are implacably opposed to any attempt to limit grace and the atonement. It is because he died for all that we can claim for ourselves and confidently extend to others the right and title to sonship and salvation through Christ, and live in a state of blessed assurance.[3]

Although the essays are not written in a polemical manner, its thesis gives the book a controversial character in that we are opposing a powerful effort in Protestant orthodoxy to limit the gospel and to cast a dark shadow over its universal availability and intention, manifesting itself most overtly in classical Calvinism. This theology which, in its dreadful doctrine of double predestination, calls into question God's desire to save all sinners and which as a logical consequence denies Christ died to save the world at large, is simply unacceptable exegetically, theologically, and morally, and to it we must say an emphatic "No!"

According to the Westminster Confession of Faith: "By the decree of God, for the manifestation of his glory, some men and angels are predestinated unto everlasting life, and others foreordained to everlasting death." And with particular reference to the nonelect, we read: "The rest of mankind God was pleased, according to the unsearchable counsel of his own will, whereby he extendeth or withholdeth mercy as he pleaseth, for the glory of his sovereign power over his creatures, to pass by, and to ordain them to dishonor and wrath for their sin, to the praise of his glorious justice" (W.C. III). Calvinists themselves have often admitted of course that this is "an unpleasant doctrine."[4] Calvin himself referred to it as a "decretum horribile." Indeed it is so. It is hard to see on the basis of it how the gospel can be preached at all or why in that case it should be called "good" news. It is a theology burdened with extraordinary difficulties of every kind, and we believe it important to show the Christian public that it is not the only way Holy Scripture can be read. Exegetically, it stumbles over the great universal texts of Scripture. Theologically, it impugns the goodness of God and casts a dark shadow over the gospel. Morally, far from glorifying his justice, it calls it into question and raises very serious doubts about it. The theology underlying this volume, on the other hand, exults in the free offer of grace and bears joyous testimony to God's lovingkindness. Truly, "the grace of God has appeared for the salvation of all men" (Titus 2:11).

It is not necessary, strictly speaking, to go any further. If Scripture speaks of the universal salvific will of God, as it does repeatedly, the matter is settled. We need hardly give any theology that limits the gospel a second look. Nevertheless, it is important to probe more deeply, and seek to discover the impetus that lies behind this desire to limit it. Why would a person, a theologian like Augustine or Calvin, conceive of the idea that God does not desire to save all and that Jesus did not die to redeem them? It is because several related scriptural ideas have been seriously misinterpreted, and which, if not corrected, will continue to result in the same theological distortions. Three of the most important of these concepts receive a thorough examination in our symposium: election, faith, and predestination.

With respect to *election*, if a person believed that God has chosen only a limited number of people to be saved out of the larger race, he would have to conclude *either* that the universal texts do not mean what they appear to say, *or* that God has two wills in the matter, one which is well disposed toward all sinners, and another secret will which purposes only to be gracious to a few. So long as the premise regarding election is not corrected, however unsatisfactory the conclusions undoubtedly are, a person would be compelled to select one of them.[5] That is, he would be compelled either to deny the universalistic texts (like 1 Tim. 2:4) outright, or accept the exceedingly paradoxical notion of two divine wills regarding salvation. Therefore, it is imperative that we not only bear witness to the universal grace of God, but also explain this doctrine of election in such a way that the consistency of the Bible's teaching in this area is vindicated.

The contributors to this volume are all convinced that belief in a limited election is mistaken, and does not represent fairly the biblical doctrine. Therefore we present the essay "Conditional Election" by Jack W. Cottrell, which is designed to open up for the reader possibilities of interpretation passed over in the Calvinistic rendering.[6] Like H. H. Rowley, Cottrell points to the emphasis on vocational election, and like biblical theologians in general, to its corporate character in regard to salvation. Beyond that, he defends his own view of the election of individuals to salvation on the basis of the foreknowledge of God. It might be appropriate to add yet another influential interpretation of election, namely, Barth's concept of it. Just like ourselves, Barth found that as he let Scripture speak to him on this subject, he was compelled to break with the Calvinistic understanding of it. In its place he developed a massive exposition of election as "the sum of the gospel," an expression of God's undiluted favor toward sinners and unrestricted grace on their behalf.[7] Election is the divine decision before the foundation of the world to reconcile mankind through Jesus Christ. It is objective and not conditional upon man's decision, as if man really elects himself. Yet it is universal and therefore casts no shadow over the gospel. So long as we stress the importance of man endorsing divine decision for himself, Barth's view of election is yet another option for the evangelical theologian.

Though there remain questions as to emphasis and orientation, and a need to continue the theological discussion, we are convinced that the biblical doctrine of election presents no threat and exists in no tension with the scriptural doctrine of universal grace. God desires to save all peoples and Jesus Christ has died for them all. The path is therefore open for them to return to the Father from whom they have rebelled. Only when it is misrepresented does the doctrine of election suggest any contradiction to this biblical truth.[8]

With respect to *faith*, if a person believed as Augustine did, that saving grace is an irresistible operation of God's Spirit that overwhelms the unbeliever and creates faith in him, he would have to conclude either that all will be saved, or if not, that saving grace is not made universally available. Evangelicals, wanting to take seriously the biblical doctrine of final judgment, will have to opt for the limitation of grace, therefore, if he accepts the Augustinian premise. But, again, it is the premise which is faulty. Augustine's view of irresistible grace was a new theology in the early Christian church. Before that time her teachers such as Irenaeus and Origen had emphasized the universality of grace and the possibility of declining it.[9] We believe this is also the biblical view. Two of our essays in particular explore the dynamic understanding of universal grace: the essay by William G. MacDonald, "The Spirit of Grace," and my own, "Responsible Freedom and the Flow of Biblical History."

Scripture makes it quite clear that the love and grace of God offered to us in the gospel is an overture which can be accepted or rejected, welcomed or repudiated. Although grace is certainly prevenient, it is not coercive. In a comparison of the church with the ancient people of Israel, the writer to the Hebrews declares, "For good news came to us just as to them; but the message which they heard did not benefit them, because it did not meet with faith in the hearers" (Heb. 4:2). God's grace may be genuinely extended to people, but unless it meets the response of faith, the only response that pleases God, it has no saving effect. Stephen declared to the Jews of his day, "You stiff-necked people, uncircumcised in heart and ears, you always resist the Holy Spirit" (Acts 7:51). Personal fellowship of the kind envisioned in the gospel only exists where consummated in a free decision. If we wish to understand God's grace as a personal address to his creatures, we must comprehend it in dynamic, nonmanipulative, non-coercive terms, as the Bible does.

The standard criticism leveled against a theology of this kind is synergism. It is supposed to bring into the event of salvation a decisive human work, and thereby destroy its purely gracious character. But this is simply not the case. Faith is not a work at all (Rom. 4:16). It is not an achievement and has no merit attaching to it. It is simply the surrender of the will to God, the stretching out of an empty hand to receive the gift of grace. In the act of faith, we renounce all our works, and repudiate completely every claim to self-righteousness. Far from encouraging conceit and self-esteem, faith utterly excludes them (Rom. 3:27). Even when we speak of faith as a "condition," let us not misrepresent the meaning of this expression. Faith is not the condition of grace, which originates in the counsels of eternity. Faith is rather the *response* to grace God calls for through which salvation becomes a reality to the individual concerned. We are saved by God's grace *through faith*.

Having expressed appreciation for Barth's doctrine of election, we should now record a dissatisfaction with one of its features. Given Barth's doctrine of the Holy Spirit and his repeated emphasis on the sovereignty of God in the application of salvation, we may well wonder what has been accomplished to ease the problem raised by classical Calvinism. Unless it can be maintained, against Barth's express protests, that he is a universalist who believes that all will finally be saved, then the question *Cur alii, cur alii* (why some and not others?) remains still unresolved. For it seems that in Barth's theology men are saved because of the inscrutable working of the Spirit, and that he has only shifted the mystery from election to the doctrine of the Spirit.[10] If that is true, we can only regret that his revision of classical Calvinism is insufficiently complete, and needs to be carried further into a criticism of the concept of irresistible grace.

The situation seems to be much the same with James Daane's recent book on election which replicates Barth's thesis in both its strengths and weaknesses.[11] Daane affirms God's universal salvific will and rejects vigorously the election/reprobation pattern of classical decretal theology. He points out the weakness in some versions of Arminian theology insofar as election is turned into a human act. But after that Daane's position becomes unclear. Early in the book he criticizes Arminian theology for supposing that the sinner possesses the ability to reject God's elective choice (p. 15), but later on states himself that in his judgment the Bible teaches "he who rejects God, God rejects" (p. 20). Daane really needs to make up his mind. Is the grace that saves sinners irresistible or not? If it is and not all are saved, it must be because it was not universally available, and this in turn raises a doubt about the universal decree of election, as both Daane and Barth want to interpret it. If the grace that saves sinners is resistible as Daane, but not Barth, seems to believe, then he ought to stop criticizing Arminianism which has always stood up for this truth.

The point is this: if God's grace is truly intended for all sinners, and if all sinners are not in the end saved, it must be (there is no other possibility) that the grace of God in the gospel is resistible, or to put it positively and more adequately, personal in character, so that the choice before mankind to choose between life and death is an eternally real one. This is of course the assumption underlying every such exhortation in Scripture.

With regard to *predestination*, if a person believed that the concept of the divine plan and purpose entailed a smothering determinism in which everything that occurs takes place because God has decreed that it should, he would have to conclude that those that are saved and those that are lost are so as the result of God's ordination, and that the glorious message of God's free grace for all sinners is fundamentally misleading. By a faulty understanding of predestination, many have faltered in their convictions about God's universal salvific will, with grievous results of every kind. Therefore, we present two important essays on this subject, one on predestination in the Old Testament by David J. A. Clines, and one on predestination in the New Testament by I. H. Marshall. These essays by two prominent British biblical scholars should do much to correct our thinking on this important matter.

We have referred already to *soteriological* predestination, the view of election first developed by Augustine which is part of a double predestination of human beings either to eternal life or to eternal death. Such a view as we noted contradicts the biblical teaching about universal grace and precludes a sincere offer of the gospel to all men. Moreover, it represents God as unjustly partial and a respecter of persons, and describes him acting in a manner which would never be pleasing to God if we did it. We heartily reject this view of election, and rejoice that such an idea is not to be found in Holy Scripture.

Often associated with soteriological predestination in classical Calvinism is the notion of *cosmic* predestination as well. In an important essay entitled, "Predestination," B. B. Warfield speaks of cosmic and soteriological predestination as the two foci of the idea.[12] Everything that occurs in time and in eternity, from the falling of a stone to the torments of the damned, has been ordered and ordained by God's eternal decree. According to this view, in the words of Hoeksema, the counsel of God is "the eternal reality of all things in God's conception, of which the creatures are but the revelation in time and space."[13] Such a notion, indistinguishable from fatalism, is inconsistent with human freedom and undermines the reality of history and man's moral responsibility. Worse still, it makes God the author of sin, since every act of rebellion, including the fall of Adam and since then was, as every event is, ordained in the secret counsels of God. It is with no small relief that we inform our readers of our conviction that Scripture teaches no such doctrine.

Although we can appreciate the concern of classical Calvinism to call attention to the purpose of God being worked out in all of history, we must also emphasize the reality of the created order, and its relative autonomy. God can create such creatures as he pleases, and he has chosen in fact to give to man the power to love him freely, or to rebel and oppose his plan. Luke says that in their rejection of John's message the Pharisees and the lawyers "rejected the purpose of God for themselves" (Luke 7:30). Does that sound shocking? Men actually have sufficient power and freedom to oppose, and in a measure to frustrate, God's will! In one of Jesus' parables, a question was asked as to why tares appeared in the field alongside the wheat. The Master did not attribute their presence to the sovereign decree of God. He said simply, "An enemy has done this" (Matt. 13:28). By creating a finite world in which there are personal wills other than his own, God made possible relationships between creatures and himself that are freely chosen and fully personal. Possible also is the misuse of freedom that has led historically to the sin of man and the fall of angels. In speaking of an "enemy," Jesus is acknowledging that events occur in the world which God does *not* will and actions which he will eventually punish. It is an understanding of the world completely incompatible with determinism. The idea that God's will is something which is always and infallibly accomplished does not derive from biblical teaching. God's purpose according to Scripture is not a blueprint encompassing all future contingencies. It is a dynamic program for the world, the outworking of which depends in part upon man.

When the term predestination *is* used in relation to salvation, it concerns the believer's future destiny which is to be conformed to Jesus Christ, not to his becoming a Christian. We are "predestined" to be conformed to "the image of his Son" (Rom. 8:29). There is no predestination to salvation or damnation in the Bible. There is only a predestination for those who are already children of God with respect to certain privileges out ahead of them. It means that God's will for those who have been redeemed is that they will one day be conformed to Jesus Christ. It is a pity that a doctrine intended to communicate hope has been turned into such a fearful concept. The two essays by Marshall and Clines should do much to dispel the misconceptions of this doctrine and the fears associated with them as well.[14]

We believe that the majority of Christians recognize and believe the truth about the wideness of God's mercy and the generous offer of grace to all sinners, and do not embrace the malformed theological theories we find it necessary to oppose in this volume. It has become rare to run across "Calvinists without reserve," even in Reformed churches, a development we do not lament. However, we are compelled to admit that the Calvinistic tradition whose theology we are constrained to reject has placed a great value on systematic theological study and learning with the result that it has produced many works of highest quality, far more than those that could be cited in defense of the position developed here. Thus it is that the Reformed position on grace and salvation is better known and defended in evangelical Christian circles than our own. It is the need for scholarly expositions of what we take to be the more biblical position which has called forth this volume, and we hope in turn that its appearance will spark further research and writing until it will be possible for Christian people at large to have a fair opportunity to make an intelligent decision on these matters.

NOTES

1. E. M. B. Green has provided a complete biblical study of the concept of salvation in his book *The Meaning of Salvation* (London: Hodder and Stoughton, 1965), and Samuel J. Mikolaski offers us some reflection on the meaning of grace in his book *The Grace of God* (Grand Rapids, Mich.: Eerdmans, 1966).

2. Admittedly most books which defend double predestination according to which God is said to elect some to salvation, and reprobate the rest to damnation, seek to defend their position against these charges, but we do not think it is possible. Most appropriately then we begin our book with the essay by Vernon C. Grounds, "God's Universal Salvific Grace."

3. In defense of this vital truth, we offer an essay by Donald M. Lake, "He Died for All: The Universal Dimensions of the Atonement." Consult also on this matter Robert P. Lightner, *The Death Christ Died* (Des Plaines, Ill.: Regular Baptist Press, 1967) and Robert Shank, *Elect in the Son* (Springfield, Mo.: Westcott, 1970), ch. 3.

4. Loraine Boettner, *The Reformed Doctrine of Predestination* (Philadelphia, Pa.: Presbyterian and Reformed, 1965), p. 108.

5. Belief in limited election, and what it entails, is as old as Augustine, though no older, and is expounded with characteristic clarity and rigor in B. B. Warfield, *The Plan of Salvation* (Grand Rapids, Mich.. Eerdmans, 1955).

6. We dispute Calvin's bold assertion that there is no other way to handle the biblical doctrine of election than his own. *The Institutes,* Book III, chapter 22, par. 1.

7. Karl Barth, *Church Dogmatics* II/2 (Edinburgh: T. & T. Clark, 1957), pp. 3-506.

8. Ancillary to Cottrell's essay we present one by James D. Strauss, "God's Promise and Universal History" on Romans 9, and two by Grant R. Osborne, "Soteriology in the Epistle to the Hebrews," and "Exegetical Notes on Calvinist Texts."

9. On the novelty of Augustine's theology, see Roger T. Forster and V. Paul Marston, *God's Strategy in Human History* (Wheaton, Ill.: Tyndale House, 1974), pp. 243-296.

10. Geoffrey W. Bromiley registers this criticism in an essay on Barth's theology in Philip E. Hughes, editor, *Creative Minds in Contemporary Theology* (Grand Rapids, Mich.: Eerdmans, 1966), p. 53.

11. James Daane, *The Freedom of God: A Study of Election and the Pulpit* (Grand Rapids, Mich.: Eerdmans, 1973).

12. B. B. Warfield, *Biblical and Theological Studies* (Philadelphia, Pa. Presbyterian and Reformed Publishing Company, 1948), pp. 270-333.

13. Herman Hoeksema, *Reformed Dogmatics* (Grand Rapids, Mich.: Reformed Free Publishing Association, 1966), p. 155. It is amusing to find Boettner as he enumerates how widely spread belief in predetermination is should find satisfaction in the fact that forms of fatalism have been held in heathen countries and deterministic theories in Western lands. For us, these associations are more likely to damn the theory! *Op. cit.,* p. 2.

14. In addition to the ten essays of a theological nature, we have also included three of a historical kind, dealing with figures of great importance

in connection with these subjects: A. Skevington Wood, "The Contribution of John Wesley to the Theology of Grace," Donald M. Lake, "Jacob Arminius' Contribution to a Theology of Grace," and James D. Strauss, "A Puritan in a Post-Puritan World—Jonathan Edwards."

1

God's Universal Salvific Grace

VERNON C. GROUNDS

Behind, beneath, beyond, and yet within the evanescent phenomena of space-time, we Christians believe, is God, the ultimate reality, the eternal, infinite, perfect, self-subsistent being, a trinity of persons all three of whom cohere in an indivisible unity of essence and purpose. God, we believe, is the source and sustainer of whatever exists, the life in all life, the truth in all truth, the goodness in all goodness, the beauty in all beauty, the love in all love. For in that corpus of writings which we call Holy Scripture and which we hold to be God's medium of self-revelation, this being behind and beneath and beyond and yet within all being defines himself as love. Hence we further believe that in the unending process of self-impartation and self-communication of his triune fellowship, God must be the experient of unending beatitude. We believe, moreover, that, because he is love, God freely chooses to expand the orbit of beatitude by creating persons like himself, centers of consciousness and choice whom he wills to share his own eternal fellowship of love according to their finite capacity. This purpose, inexplicable except on the ground of God's free decision, is announced by Paul at the beginning of his Ephesian Letter:

> Grace be to you, and peace, from God our Father, and from the Lord Jesus Christ. Blessed be the God and Father of our Lord Jesus Christ, who hath blessed us with all spiritual blessings in heavenly places in Christ: according as he hath chosen us in him before the foundation of the world, that we should be holy and without blame before him in love; having predestinated us unto the adoption of children by Jesus Christ to himself, according to the good pleasure of his will, to the praise of the glory of his grace, wherein he hath made us accepted in the beloved: in whom we have redemption through

his blood, the forgiveness of sins, according to the riches of his grace; wherein he hath abounded toward us in all wisdom and prudence; having made known unto us the mystery of his will, according to his good pleasure which he hath purposed in himself: that in the dispensation of the fulness of times he might gather together in one all things in Christ, both which are in heaven, and which are on earth; even in him: in whom also we have obtained an inheritance, being predestinated according to the purpose of him who worketh all things after the counsel of his own will: that we should be to the praise of his glory, who first trusted in Christ. (Eph. 1:2-12)

This purpose, explicable solely on the inexplicable ground of God's grace and focusing in Jesus Christ, is the *raison d'être* of everything in nature and history. As Samuel Mikolaski says:

> Put into a real definition, God's purpose is the creation of free men who will experience the bliss of divine fellowship and service. The creation narrative of Genesis teaches that man lost this freedom through sin, but the promise of grace in both Testaments is the restoration of freedom by redemption and forgiveness. God intends that man shall share with Him a common life, spirit, and aim. Grace means that God is determined to accomplish His good and righteous purpose.[1]

Motivated by grace, then, freely electing to share his experience of infinite love with finite experients, God has created *ex nihilo* all that is. Grace is thus the revealed explanation of the whole space-time complex. The act of creation, like everything the triune God does, James Daane reminds us, has grace as its dynamic.

> If we regard it from the point of view of the reality of God, the creation of the world is an amazing decision. God is God alone. Beside him there is none else. He necessarily exists. He needs nothing. The creation of finite, contingent, unnecessary reality, then, in order that man, who is not God, might share in, know, love, and live with God, staggers the human mind. The truth of creation evades man's every rational attempt to comprehend. Philosophy may try to eliminate our sense of wonder at this; science may do the same by dissolving all the mystery of the universe. But true religion begins with wonder and never loses it. For creation is the wonder of God, the new and novel surprise of his freedom to extend and share his love—that is, to share himself.[2]

History, too, which from the biblical perspective pivots on the incarnation of God in Jesus Christ, has grace as its dynamic. In fact, from the biblical perspective, all the events occurring anywhere and everywhere no matter when are teleologically related to the Christ-event. Daane again helps us to appreciate the significance of what we may be in danger of overlooking:

Nowhere is God's freedom more fully expressed than in his resolve to become himself historical, a man existing in space and time in Jesus Christ, and in his Son to become involved in a world of sin and death, and through death to conquer and eliminate sin and death. God is so free that he can, in order to achieve the intention that man know him, love him, and live with him in eternal blessedness, deliver his own Son to the power of sin and death. God is so free that he can elect his own Son for the cross so that, in spite of all man's sin and evil, man may still share God's eternal life, beauty, glory, and joy.[3]

Or in the complementary words of Karl Rahner:

Divine grace is not simply the intermittent chance of salvation of an individualist kind granted to a few only and restricted in time and place, but that it is ultimately the dynamism of all human history everywhere and always, and indeed of the world generally, even though it remains a question put to the free decision of each and every individual.[4]

Yet what is grace, anyway, this dynamic of all God's action? How can it be explicated? To set forth its quintessence we must put it over against sin, man's defiant misuse of his finite freedom which has estranged him from God and now renders him liable to divine judgment. Sin, man's defiant misuse of his finite freedom, has negated any claim which as a creature he might have levied on the Creator's blessing. Grace, therefore, stands in antithesis to sin. It is God's utterly inscrutable attitude of mercy and kindness which motivates His self-sacrifice in Jesus Christ, a redemptive action for which no reason can be assigned. Contradicting and nullifying all norms of logic and justice, grace offers forgiveness and reconciliation where wrath and exile are properly merited. Notice a text like Rom. 3:23, "For all have sinned, and come short of the glory of God." Notice also a text like Rom. 4:4, "Now to him that worketh is the reward not reckoned of grace, but of debt." Notice once more a text like Eph. 2:8-9, "For by grace are ye saved through faith; and that not of yourselves: it is the gift of God: not of works, lest any man should boast." Grace, then, viewed negatively, baffles reason totally and completely. Viewed positively, however, it is the omnipotent help which God in His freedom chooses to give through Jesus Christ and by his Spirit, liberating man from his self-incurred bondage and misery, reestablishing a right relationship with himself. "The first and primary meaning of grace," says Mikolaski,

is the generous love of God, His goodwill, lovingkindness, or favor, by which His blessings are bestowed on mankind and a new era opened. *God's grace is His unmerited favor by which He saves an unworthy world.*[5]

Grace, consequently, must not be regarded as if it were some impersonal entity, akin to a force of a fluid, operating apart from God. Rather, grace is God redemptively in action through Jesus Christ and by His Holy Spirit. Personal through and through, grace, let it be repeated, is God acting. John 1:14 stresses the Christocentric personalism of grace: "And the Word was made flesh, and dwelt among us, (and we beheld his glory, the glory as of the only begotten of the Father,) full of grace and truth." Acts 15:11 carries the same stress, "But we believe that through the grace of the Lord Jesus Christ we shall be saved, even as they." And this stress on Christocentric personalism is repeated in 2 Cor. 8:9, "For ye know the grace of our Lord Jesus Christ, that, though he was rich, yet for your sakes he became poor, that ye through his poverty might be rich." Karl Rahner is therefore correct when he affirms that

> Grace is God himself, his communication, in which he gives himself to us as the divinizing loving kindness which is himself. Here his work is really *himself*, as the one communicated. From the very first this grace cannot be conceived as separable from God's personal love and man's answer to it. This grace must not be thought of "materialistically"; it is only put "at man's disposal" by letting itself be used as is the way with the freest grace of all, the miracle of love.[6]

Grace, which is God freely and lovingly and savingly at work in the lives of fallen and self-frustrated human beings, has existential effects which cannot be psychologically analyzed: God working through Jesus Christ and by his Holy Spirit enables a man to be and do what otherwise tantalizes him as merely an impossible possibility. Paul, for example, bears this witness in 1 Cor. 15:10, "By the grace of God I am what I am: and his grace which was bestowed upon me was not in vain: but I laboured more abundantly than they all: yet not I but the grace of God which was with me." In Eph. 3:8 the same apostle disclaims any credit for the success of his ministry, attributing his effectiveness entirely to grace: "Unto me, who am less than the least of all saints, is this grace given, that I should preach among the Gentiles the unsearchable riches of Christ." So Paul would no doubt have endorsed the comment made by W. H. Griffith-Thomas: "Grace is, first, a quality of graciousness in the Giver, and then, a quality of gratitude in the recipient, which in turn makes him gracious to those around." [7]

Concerning the nature of grace, then, there is a fairly broad consensus among Christians of all theological alignments. But when its outworking and outreach are under discussion, heated disagreement flares up. Theologians who align themselves with John Calvin, proudly naming fourth century Saint Augustine and twentieth century Benjamin B. Warfield as representative spokesmen, contend that divine grace, though unlimited in its sufficiency, is nevertheless limited in its efficiency—and limited by God himself. According to this major tradition in Christian thought, grace does not universally and indiscriminately provide every human being with an opportunity for a redemptive relationship to God that includes the forgiveness of sin and the promise of eternal beatitude. Instead, as Calvinistically interpreted, grace in its effective outworking and outreach avails only for elect individuals, those human beings whom in his sovereignty God has predestinated from all eternity to be the recipients of his mercy. Whatever linguistic and logical *legerdemain* is employed to mitigate the inescapable corollaries of this position, it maintains that nonelect individuals are outside the orbit of God's effective grace. Extreme in his statement of the Calvinist position, Herman Hoeksema, until his death the foremost theologian of the Protestant Reformed Churches, uncompromisingly developed the implications of the Canons of Dort (such at least was his self-appraisal):

> God loves the elect because they are righteous in Christ; he hates the reprobate because they are sinners. The elect alone are the object of grace; for them alone the gospel is good news. For the reprobate God has no blessing at all, but only an eternal hatred. Rain and sunshine, the hearing of the gospel, the sacrament of baptism (if administered to a person as an infant)—all are curses heaped on the reprobate.[8]

Other theologians of what Daane calls the decretal school, adhering as they do to some formulation of an alleged *gestalt* of destiny-determining divine decrees, urge

> that God is the ultimate cause and the primary source of sin, that the function of the proclamation of the gospel is to make some men ripe for judgment; that God created sin...; that God takes pleasure in the death of sinners; that preaching is *per se* a curse for the reprobate; that everything that occurs is a divine wish-fulfillment, for if anything were to occur contrary to what God wills, God would not be sovereign but a godling who had created more world than he can take care of....[9]

Daane, who is himself a Calvinist, has so justly excoriated this position that he deserves to be heard at length:

> How pervasively this view has penetrated and shaped Reformed theology! Here is the theological bottomland from which has arisen what is often regarded as the correct Reformed un-

derstanding of God's immutability and of sovereignty. Here is the source of the assertion that God is the cause and source of sin, yet not responsible for it. Here is the root of an unconditional theology that not only rightly rejects Arminian theology (although with wrongly formulated reasons) but which also insists that God is so imperturbable that he is not free to be moved with compassion for the plight of man. Here is the origin of the position that reprobation is ultimately not an act of divine justice *in response* to sin, but something that has its ground in God himself. Here arises Reformed theology's tendency to cast a threatening shadow over all reality.[10]

Despite the wide acceptance of this position, especially among contemporary evangelicals, it quite flatly contradicts the overwhelming testimony of Scripture to the universality of God's salvific grace. A mere *catena* of passages discloses the fact, for fact it is, that the divine purpose in Jesus Christ embraces not a segment of the human family but the race *en toto*:

> Behold the Lamb of God, which taketh away the sin of the world. (John 1:29)
> For God so loved the world, that he gave his only begotten Son, that whosoever believeth in him should not perish, but have everlasting life. (John 3:16)
> For if by one man's offence death reigned by one; much more they which receive abundance of grace and of the gift of righteousness shall reign in life by one, Jesus Christ. Therefore, as by the offence of one judgment came upon all men to condemnation; even so by the righteousness of one the free gift came upon all men unto justification of life. For as by one man's disobedience many were made sinners, so by the obedience of one shall many be made righteous. Moreover the law entered, that the offence might abound. But where sin abounded, grace did much more abound: That as sin hath reigned unto death, even so might grace reign through righteousness unto eternal life by Jesus Christ our Lord. (Rom. 5:17-21)

(Note the repetition of the phrase "much more" which asymmetrically outbalances the ruin of humanity in Adam by the race's redemption in Christ. Since all humanity came under judgment in Adam, all humanity must come into at least the possibility of eternal life through Christ.)

> For God hath concluded them all in unbelief, that he might have mercy upon all. (Rom. 11:32)
> Who gave himself a ransom for all, to be testified in due time. (1 Tim. 2:6)
> But we see Jesus, who was made a little lower than the

angels for the suffering of death, crowned with glory and honour; that he by the grace of God should taste death for every man. (Heb. 2:9)

The Lord is not slack concerning his promise, as some men count slackness; but is longsuffering to us-ward, not willing that any should perish, but that all should come to repentance. (2 Pet. 3:9)

And he is the propitiation for our sins: and not for ours only, but also for the sins of the whole world. (1 John 2:2)

It takes an exegetical ingenuity which is something other than a learned virtuosity to evacuate these texts of their obvious meaning: it takes an exegetical ingenuity verging on sophistry to deny their explicit universality.

A Protestant may—no, must!—criticize Karl Rahner sharply for many of the views which he ingeniously espouses. But a Protestant—in other words, a Biblicist—can applaud Rahner's insistence on the all-inclusiveness of grace. So one finds himself wishing that decretal theologians might catch a glimpse of the vision which enthralls Rahner and which ought, eliminating Rahner's dogmatic mirages, likewise enthrall every Biblicist:

If we wish to be Christians, we must profess belief in the universal and serious salvific purpose of God towards all men which is true even within the post-paradisean phase of salvation dominated by original sin. We know, to be sure, that this proposition of faith does not say anything certain about the *individual* salvation of man understood as something which has in fact been reached. But God desires the salvation of everyone. And this salvation willed by God is the salvation won by Christ, the salvation of supernatural grace which divinizes man, the salvation of the beatific vision. It is a salvation really intended for all those millions upon millions of men who lived perhaps a million years before Christ—and also for those who have lived after Christ—in nations, cultures and epochs of a very wide range which were still completely shut off from the viewpoint of those living in the light of the New Testament.[11]

And if redemptive particularism be argued against redemptive universalism, the argument loses its cogency in the light of a principle which runs throughout Scripture: redemptive particularism subserves the ends of redemptive universalism. Thus E. Y. Mullins, discussing God's loving purpose for the race, rightly maintains that Abraham's election and through him Israel's election were not individual or national but racial in their ultimate design. God, Mullins writes,

had in view not one family or nation, but the whole of mankind. There were chosen families and a chosen nation. But these were not only ends in themselves, they were also means toward a larger end. At one crisis in the world's history Noah and his family were chosen as the channel of God's blessing to mankind. Later God chose Abraham, whose descendants became the nation of Israel. God's promise to Abraham was the disclosure of his purpose toward mankind: "I will make of thee a great nation, and I will bless thee and make thy name great; and be thou a blessing; and I will bless them that bless thee, and him that curseth thee will I curse; and in thee shall all the families of the earth be blessed" (Gen. 12:2, 3). This promise was repeated to Abraham many times in substantially the same form. We do not rightly understand the calling of Abraham unless we see in him the manifestation of God's world-wide purpose of grace.[12]

The universality of grace, it must be made clear, does not mean universalism! It means merely that God is at work in Jesus Christ and by his Holy Spirit sovereignly and sincerely —yes, and seriously, as Rahner points out—providing the potential of salvation for every human being. But that potential depends for its actualization on a believing response. Kenneth J. Foreman, a Presbyterian and thus a Calvinist, has said emphatically what needs to be said:

On God's side, all barriers were down. There was nothing else that even God could do to restore the broken bond. Nothing else? One thing only: to force man's will, compel his assent, reconcile him against his will. One thing—but God would not do it. He would not treat man like a tree trunk or a rock. Not a single writer in the New Testament, not a converted person depicted on its pages, thinks of his conversion as of a tidal wave that washed him ashore without his choice or against his will. Paul, in whose case the hand of God was clearly in evidence, said years later to King Agrippa: "I was not disobedient to the heavenly vision." The vision was a bolt from the blue; it had the effect of an attack with a deadly weapon. Yet in retrospect, Paul can speak of it as something to which he could have been disobedient. Peter's sermon at Pentecost addresses persons whom he later describes as "born anew" (1 Peter 1:3), but he does not address them there in Jerusalem as logs and rocks. The very fact that the Christians used the words *kerygma, kerusso, euangelion*, to describe their missionary efforts, suggests that the news could be understood, the heralding heeded. But it was more than an announcement, it was a summons. "God . . . commands all men everywhere to repent" (Acts 17:30) . . . If it be objected that this leaves too much to man's decision, we can only say that to control man as one would a log or a rock is to treat him as something less than a man, and this God does not do. God deals personally with personal beings, as Dr. Oman laid it out so beautifully years ago. Grace that left no option whatever would not be grace, it would be something else. We should have to say, By force were ye saved, and not of yourselves.[13]

The the truth of universal grace—"all of grace and grace for all"—is shot through with mystery, we unhesitatingly confess. It needs to be safeguarded against the dangers of semi-Pelagianism and the hazards of an Arminianism that John Wesley would repudiate; it needs to be safeguarded as well against the enticements of the universalism to which Karl Barth nearly succumbs. It needs, moreover, to be rethought and resystematized if it is to function as a corrective of the sub-biblical decretalism which largely dominates evangelicalism today. The truth of God's universal grace needs to be proclaimed with adoring fervor, a grace that springs from a love which cannot be limited temporally (Matt. 28:20), geographically (Mark 16:15), racially, religiously, economically, sexually (Gal. 3:28), or culturally (Rom. 1:16), a love which has no limits except the limits which unbelief imposes. It is this universal salvific grace, that, if preached in the Spirit's power, may bring in our time another evangelical awakening like that which had John Wesley as its herald. And if and as it does, Charles Wesley's hymn "Free Grace" will once more express the praise of a church set free by grace from any view of grace that would make grace less inclusive than God's all-inclusive love.

Come let us join our friends above,
The God of our salvation praise,
The God of everlasting love,
The God of universal grace.

'Tis not by works that we have done;
'Twas grace alone His heart inclined.
'Twas grace that give His only Son
To taste of death for all mankind.

For every man He tasted death;
And hence we in His sight appear,
Not lifting up our eyes beneath,
But publishing His mercy here.

By grace we draw our every breath;
By grace we live, and move, and are;
By grace we 'scape the second death,
By grace we now Thy grace declare.

From the first feeble thought of good
To when the perfect grace is given,
'Tis all of grace; by grace renew'd
From hell we pass through earth to heaven.

We need no reprobates to prove
That grace, free grace, is truly free;
Who cannot see that God is love,
Open your eyes and look on me;

On us, whom Jesus hath call'd forth
To assert that all His grace may have,
To vindicate His passion's worth
Enough ten thousand world's to save.[14]

NOTES

1. Samuel J. Mikolaski, *The Grace of God* (Grand Rapids, Mich.: William B. Eerdmans Publishing Company, 1966), p. 96.

2. James Daane, *The Freedom of God* (Grand Rapids, Mich.: William B. Eerdmans Publishing Company, 1973), p. 171.

3. *Ibid.*, p. 171.

4. Karl Rahner, *The Christian of the Future* (London: Burns and Oates, 1967), p. 96.

5. Mikolaski, *op. cit.*, p. 49.

6. Karl Rahner, *Nature and Grace* (New York: Sheed and Ward, 1964), p. 128.

7. Quoted by Mikolaski, *op. cit.*, p. 42.

8. Quoted by Daane, *op. cit.*, p. 24.

9. Daane, *op. cit.*, p. 79.

10. *Ibid.*, p. 160.

11. Karl Rahner, *Theological Investigations Volume V, Later Writings* (London: Darton, Longman and Todd, Ltd., 1966), pp. 122-123.

12. Edgar Mullins, *The Christian Religion in Its Doctrinal Expression* (Philadelphia, Pa.: The Judson Press, 1917), pp. 340-341.

13. Kenneth Foreman, *Identification: Human and Divine* (Richmond, Va.: John Knox Press, 1963), pp. 116-117.

14. Mildred Wynkoop, *A Theology of Love* (Kansas City, Mo.: Beacon Hill Press of Kansas City, 1972), p. 93.

2

He Died for All:
The Universal Dimensions of the Atonement

DONALD M. LAKE

My little children, I am writing this to you so that you may not sin; but if any one does sin, we have an advocate with the Father, Jesus Christ the righteous; and he is the expiation for our sins, and not for ours only but also for the sins of the whole world. —1 John 2:1-2

Recent converts and not a few laymen are puzzled when they hear that there are some theologians who argue that the atoning work of Jesus Christ is limited in its efficacy, i.e., the atonement of Christ belongs only to the elect and not to the entire world of humanity! To the casual reader of the New Testament, the universal significance of Christ's death and resurrection as well as his present priestly ministry seems too obvious even to question. Digging a little deeper into the theological basis for such discussions, one finds more theological rationalization than scriptural support.

The purpose of this chapter is to explore the basis and implications for a universal application of the atoning work of Christ. It is not the purpose of this chapter to analyze the various theories of the atonement, except as these theories have a bearing upon the extent of the atonement's application. The history of theology abounds with theories as to how and why the life, death, resurrection and ascension of Jesus Christ makes salvation possible for mankind, but it is a *fact that these redemptive events in the life of Jesus provided a salvation so extensive, so broad as to potentially include the whole of humanity past, present and future!*

I. Christ the Second Adam

The atonement, generally speaking, refers to the sum total

of Christ's person and work. What he did to provide salvation for mankind cannot be separated from who he was. It is in this light that the Pauline interpretation of Christ's person as the *Second Adam* receives its fullest understanding. In Romans 5, Paul contrasts the evil and condemnation brought into the world through the first man, Adam, and the grace and salvation brought through Jesus Christ as the Second Adam.

> But the free gift is not like the trespass. For if many died through one man's trespass, much more have the grace of God and the free gift in the grace of that one man Jesus Christ abounded for many. And the free gift is not like the effect of that one man's sin. For the judgment following one trespass brought condemnation, but the free gift following many trespasses brings justification. If, because of one man's trespass, death reigned through that one man, much more will those who receive the abundance of grace and the free gift of righteousness reign in life through the one man Jesus Christ.
>
> Then as one man's trespass led to condemnation for all men, so one man's act of righteousness leads to acquittal and life for all men. For as by one man's disobedience many were made sinners, so by one man's obedience many will be made righteous. Law came in, to increase the trespass; but where sin increased, grace abounded all the more, so that, as sin reigned in death, grace also might reign through righteousness to eternal life through Jesus Christ our Lord. (Rom. 5:15-21)

Orthodox theology has never denied the causal relationship between Adam's sin and the universality of human depravity. Without endorsing any particular theory of imputation, it is difficult to deny humanity's fallen condition without a historical Adam, or in some way, giving God the blame for an imperfect creation. No man stands outside of Adam's sinful posterity; all humanity reflects his primal disobedience in every man's own rebellion against God. It is this fact that makes verse 18 of Romans 5 even more potent: *Then as one man's trespass led to condemnation for all men, so one man's act of righteousness leads to acquittal and life for all men.*

> Paul learnt from his Jewish faith the close tie-up between events at the beginning of the world and a setting right of earth's wrongs at the end of the age. This principle (known as *restitutio in integrum*) permitted him to teach that as the old creation had been ruined by Adam's Fall and paradise lost, so Christ's obedience and vindication by God would lead to a new order of harmony and reconciliation, with paradise regained. But he does not say simply, "The second Adam restores what the first Adam lost", although that is included. By his use of the "much more" contrast (vv. 17, 20) he goes on to demonstrate

that the ultimate Adam gains for His people far more than ever
their connection with the old order could have meant.[1]

There is to be noticed in this passage a shifting between
"all" and "many," but C. K. Barrett's observation seems accurate when he says: "By 'many' he can hardly mean anything different from the 'all men' of v. 12 (cf. also 1 Cor.
xv. 22). This inclusive use of 'many' is Hebraistic; in Old
Testament usuage 'many' often means not 'many contrasted
with all' but 'many contrasted with one or some.' " [2] But
if the "all" here is indeed an all-inclusive *all*, does that mean
that all men are actually to be saved? Before I turn to a
more direct answer to that question, I want to look at John
Calvin's treatment of this passage.

In the first place, Calvin discusses this passage most frequently in Book II of the *Institutes* where he is dealing with
Christ as Redeemer. His main emphasis is upon Christ's work
of redemption and its surpassing worth when compared with
the damage done by Adam to mankind. But it is to be observed
that Calvin's atonement passages do not deal with this text
at all! What is important, however, is the fact that the issue
of *limited atonement* does not appear in Calvin, but belongs
to second generation Calvinists. Yet, it must be emphasized
that Calvin himself lays little stress, if any, upon the universal
significance of the atonement. Where the subject does come
to light in his *Institutes* is in Book III where he responds
to criticisms about his view of God's sovereignty.[3] But it
must be emphasized that the question of the extent of Christ's
redemptive grace had received no real examination by Calvin.
For him the question is rather: does God will to save all
men? That is a question of election, not of the atonement.
This fact is all the more surprising, since Calvin is one of
the church's greatest exegetical theologians.

If later Calvinism failed to deal with the universalism implied in this fifth chapter of Romans, 20th century Calvinists
have not failed to do so. In Karl Barth's doctrine of reconciliation and election, we find a contemporary reformed
theologian wrestling with this inherent universalism. In analyz-
ing Jesus' final prayer before the cross, Barth remarks:

> Was He not even then representing God and therefore the world
> and sinful men? In the light of it, what else does His "Thy
> will be done" mean but that this first word of His was and re-
> mained His final word? So, then, in this prayer we can see the
> essence of the positive content of the suffering and dying of Je-
> sus—the act of righteousness ($\delta\iota\kappa\alpha\acute{\iota}\omega\mu\alpha$) and obedience ($\acute{\upsilon}\pi\sigma\tau\alpha\gamma\acute{\eta}$)
> of the one man, in the power of which the vindication of all
> men was accomplished as the promise of life ($\delta\iota\kappa\alpha\acute{\iota}\omega\sigma\iota\varsigma$ $\epsilon\acute{\iota}\varsigma$ $\zeta\omega\acute{\eta}\nu$),
> in which in the last judgment many will be represented righ-

teous (δίκαιον) in the sight of God and His angels and the whole world. (Rom. 5:18f.) [4]

Later in part 1, volume IV of Barth's *Church Dogmatics*, he turns again to the question of Adam and Christ.

> This Pauline argument is usually called the parallel between Adam and Christ. But at the very least we ought to speak of the parallel between Christ and Adam. For there can be no doubt that for Paul Jesus Christ takes the first place as the original, and Adam the second. . . . It is not autonomously that the line of Adam and the many who are concluded with him in disobedience runs close to that of Jesus Christ in whose obedience God has willed to have and has had mercy on many and indeed on all. . . . It is in relation to the last Adam that this first Adam, the unknown of the Genesis story, has for Paul existence and consistence, and that in what is said of him he hears what is true and necessarily true of himself and all men. It is beyond the threshold which Jesus Christ has crossed, and every man in Him, that he hears in Him the sentence on himself and all men as a Word of God and not of man—a sentence against which there can be no appeal passed on the man of sin, who was every man, but who no longer exists now that God has had mercy on all with the same universality with which He once concluded all in disobedience.[5]

Commenting upon Barth's doctrine of grace, G. C. Berkouwer calls attention to the universal dimensions of our faith. "Scripture itself," says Berkouwer, "speaks of the grace that *reigns* through righteousness to eternal life through Jesus Christ our Lord (Rom. 5:21)." [6]

Now what can be said about the universalism implied in the Romans 5 passage? The analogy and connection between Adam and Christ, Adam's sin and human fallenness as well as Christ's redemptive work and the triumph of grace provide a clue to their relationship. Augustine erred in his interpretation of Rom. 5:12 because he took his theology from a poor Latin text of this passage rather than the Greek. In his Latin translation, he read *in quo* for the ἐφ' ᾧ (*eph' ho*) meaning that we sinned *in Adam*, rather than that we sinned because of Adam. Here theologically a distinction needs to be made between *original sin* and *original guilt*. The text of Rom. 5:12-14 clearly argues that man's solidarity with Adam has led to man's receiving from him a sinful tendency toward evil, but the text does not support the conception that we are guilty for Adam's sin. Indeed the text goes so far as to argue that guilt is possible only where a known law exists. And without any violation of a known law, there cannot be any consciousness of guilt. "Sin is not counted where there is no law" (v.

13). C. K. Barrett states that this "putting to the count" is "a commercial term—'put in the ledger.'"[7] Consequently the effect of Adam's sin is universal, but its personal significance depends upon the individual. Here we have an affirmation that the concept of corporate solidarity does not preclude nor exclude the concept of personal responsibility. The human race is one, and the effects both of Adam's sin as well as Christ's redemption or atonement affects the whole of humanity. The total impact of the Christian faith upon culture—all cultures, but particularly Western culture—is a logical by-product of this solidarity. Yet, Adam's sin did not, in a technical sense, make mankind sinners. As Reinhold Niebuhr has aptly said: "Man sins inevitably but not necessarily!"[8] In the same sense, the redemptive work of Christ is *there* as a universal given: man is forgiven, reconciled, redeemed and restored in the finished work of Christ. But its efficacy is not automatic. No more than man's sinfulness is an inherited fact as a by-product of Adam's disobedience.

But it must ever be reaffirmed that Christ's redemptive work has far greater effect than Adam's sinfulness. This fact is sadly neglected in the Calvinistic supralapsarian theologies, in which election is separated from the decrees of creation and fall. Election can only have significance where it has Christ's redemptive work as a background, but the assumption of New Testament theology is that Christ's redemptive work takes its significance from man's plight. We cannot, therefore, allow the decree of election and reprobation to rob us of the surpassing abundance of God's grace in Jesus Christ! Furthermore, Paul clearly indicates that Christ's atonement is related to "those who receive the abundance of grace and the free gift of righteousness" (v. 17). Toward the end of this chapter, I want to explore the practical and psychological consequences that a true, legitimate and genuine universalism has for mankind and modern culture, but this much is clear: man's fall began with Adam, his restoration and recovery are here in Christ!

II. The Drawing Power of the Cross

According to John's interpretation of Jesus' redemptive word, "God so loved the world that he gave his only Son, that whoever believes in him should not perish but have eternal life. For God sent the Son into the world, not to condemn the world, but that the world might be saved through him" (3:16-17). Yet, this apparent universalism is challenged or modified by a particularism that appears later in John's account of the discourse on the bread of life. In chapter six, Jesus says:

> I am the bread of life; he who comes to me shall not hunger, and he who believes in me shall never thirst. But I said to you that you have seen me and yet do not believe. All that the Father gives me will come to me; and him who comes to me I will not cast out. For I have come down from heaven, not to do my own will, but the will of him who sent me; and this is the will of him who sent me, that I should lose nothing of all that he has given me, but raise it up at the last day. For this is the will of my Father, that every one who sees the Son and believes in him should have eternal life; and I will raise him at the last day. . . . Do not murmur among yourselves. No one can come to me unless the Father who sent me draws him; and I will raise him up at the last day. (vv. 35-40, 43-44)

How can we reconcile these two rather distinct emphases in the Johannine Gospel? It may be helpful to see how Calvin deals with this problem.

In his commentary on John's Gospel, he lays primary stress upon love as the motivation for God's redemptive work in Christ. He attacks any interpretation that finds the origin or source of God's redeeming activity in man; only God's love motivates God to provide salvation in Christ. Calvin does not deal with the word *world* until he comes to the phrase "That whoever believes in him should not perish." Here he states that God "has used a general term, both to invite indiscriminately all to share in life and to cut off every excuse from unbelievers. Such is also the significance of the term 'world' which He had used before. . . . He is favourable to the whole world when He calls all without exception to the faith of Christ, which is indeed an entry into life." [9] But he is quick to point out that such a universal appeal is conditional by God's elective decree:

> Moreover, let us remember that although life is promised generally to all who believe in Christ, faith is not common to all, but God opens the eyes only of the elect that they may seek Him by faith.[10]

It is obvious that in all of Calvin's theology, one of his major problems is how to explain the origin of faith without violating the biblical doctrine of grace. The doctrinal intention behind his double predestination is also to be understood in this light. Even if faith is understood as trust, Calvin saw no way to allow man that single responsibility without becoming somewhat synergistic. As a result the universal dimension of John 3:16 becomes lost in a theological subtlety. What can an offer of grace mean if the one to whom the offer is made is incapable of receiving it?

Calvin's position on John 3 is, of course, reenforced by Christ's statements in John 6:35-44. On the other hand, the words of Jesus about his impending death would seem to challenge Calvin's interpretation of the two previous passages. What does he do with John 12:32?

> Jesus answered, "This voice has come for your sake, not for mine. Now is the judgment of this world, now shall the ruler of this world be cast out; and I, when I am lifted up from the earth, will draw all men to myself." He said this to show by what death he was to die. (John 12:30-33)

Calvin comments:

> When He says *all* it must be referred to the children of God, who are His flock. Yet I agree with Chrysostom, who says that Christ used the universal word because the Church was to be gathered from Gentiles and Jews alike, according to the saying, "There shall be one shepherd and one sheepfold." (John 10:16) [11]

Perhaps I have devoted too much space to Calvin's views, but it is important, I think, to hear the perspective of one outstanding exegete who has interpreted these passages in a manner consistent with a higher view of predestination than is represented by the writers of these essays. The critical judgment remains: has Calvin been consistent with the text and its most obvious meaning? Personally, I cannot help but give a negative answer to this question. If we allow the passages to stand themselves without bringing a theological perspective from outside the text, we may be able to harmonize John's apparent intentions in a manner that does justice both to his universalism as well as his particularism. Leon Morris' approach appears to do more justice to the text:

> Because it is God who is working out His purpose in the events associated with Calvary, and because there is but one God, the salvation there wrought out is effective for all mankind. Thus Christ is spoken of not in terms of any restricted group, but of all mankind. The Samaritan believers refer to Him as "indeed the Saviour of the world" (Jn. 4:42). John tells us explicitly that "God sent not the Son into the world to judge the world; but that the world should be saved through him" (Jn. 3:17). Christ's "flesh" is given (undoubtedly a reference to Calvary) "for the life of the world" (Jn. 6:51). Universality is implied moreover in the reference to the "other sheep" which are "not of this fold" (Jn. 10:15f.). At the very least this extends the mission of Jesus beyond the Jewish nation, and once started on the Gentiles who is to say where it will end? ... Nothing less is implied by Jesus' statement, "I, if I be lifted up from the earth, will draw all men unto myself" (Jn. 12:32). This is not the propagation of a doctrine of universalism, but it does mean that there are many who are to be drawn to the Christ.

We draw a similar conclusion from the reference to giving "eternal life" to as many as God has given Him in the same breath as the assurance that He has been given "authority over all flesh" (Jn. 17:2). These words mean that Jesus will give life to men of all nations, and the preceding statement, "the hour is come" links this with the cross. And this is implied surely in the "whosoever" of passages like John 3:16, "whosoever believeth on him should not perish, but have eternal life". "Whosoever" is wide enough to include anyone at all, not only the members of one nation.[12]

Paul's own commentary upon the cross is reflected in 1 Cor. 1:18ff.: "For the word [preaching] of the cross is folly to those who are perishing, but to us who are being saved it is the power of God." This fact also helps to explain Paul's self-limitation both as to style as well as content in his preaching: "For I decided to know nothing among you except Jesus Christ and him crucified" (1 Cor. 2:2; see also Gal. 6:14). The universality of Christ's redeeming work is matched by the concept of "cosmic redemption" which also finds expression in Paul's Christology as well as his ecclesiology. In his letter to the church at Colosse, Paul writes:

> He is the head of the body, the church; he is the beginning, the first-born from the dead, that in everything he might be pre-eminent. For *in him all the fullness of God was pleased to dwell, and through him to reconcile to himself all things, whether on earth or in heaven, making peace by the blood of his cross.* (Col. 1:18-20)

Looking once again at the three basic passages in John's Gospel (3:16-17; 6:35-44; 12:30-33), we can clearly trace the lines of grace and particularly the universalism of that grace. God's redemptive work is initiated by the sole motivation of the divine *agape*, but mankind has loved darkness rather than the light of God's redeeming love. Consequently, God must not only take the initiative to make salvation possible, but he must also initiate the means by which men come to know that grace and love: God must and will woo men to himself. It is to be noted that God "commends his love" not *commands* it. (See Romans 5:8.) We can see the element of truth in the *moral influence theories* of the atonement: God's grace and love overwhelms us, rather than overpowering us, i.e., irresistible grace! In the history of the church, it is not accidental, therefore, that the cross more than any other event of Christian history has become the focal point of Christian art. In contrast to the Buddha who forsook his wife and child to discover the way of enlightenment, we present men with a selfless

Christ whose substitutionary sacrifice on the cross, whose pure love for mankind overwhelms us:

> Greater love has no man than this, that a man lay down his life for his friends. (John 15:13)

Here I think, we see a rather clear distinction between those theologies that major upon divine decrees, divine sovereignty and whose interpretation of grace is something close to power. Perhaps Luther saw this perspective better than Calvin. For Luther, God's grace was nothing less than his love. Even a casual glance at the sermons in the earliest apostolic history will confirm these interpretations. It was with the gathering in Jerusalem on that first Pentecost heard that they had crucified the *Jahweh* of Judaism as well as the long-expected Messiah that the hearers were "cut to the heart"! (Acts 2:36ff.). Let us never fail to center our theology on the cross and let us never fail to make clear that that cross is open to all men!

> Therefore remember that at one time you Gentiles in the flesh, called the uncircumcision by what is called the circumcision, which is made in the flesh by hands—remember that you were at that time separated from Christ, alienated from the commonwealth of Israel, and strangers to the covenants of promise, having no hope and without God in the world. But now in Christ Jesus you who once were far off have been brought near in the blood of Christ. For he is our peace, who has made us both one, and has broken down the dividing wall of hostility. (Eph. 2:11-14)

III. "Not for Our Sins Only"

Few biblical texts are stronger in their stress upon the universal potentiality of Christ's atonement than 1 John 2:1-2! Calvin never recognizes the universal dimension in his references to this text in his *Institutes*; however, in his commentary on this text, Calvin states his position and interpretation clearly:

> He added this for the sake of amplifying, in order that the faithful might be assured that the expiation made by Christ, extends to all who by faith embrace the gospel.
> Here a question may be raised, how have the sins of the whole world been expiated? I pass by the dotages of the fanatics, who under this pretense extend salvation to all the reprobate, and therefore to Satan himself. Such a monstrous thing deserves no refutation. They who seek to avoid this absurdity, have said that Christ suffered sufficiently for the whole world, but efficiently only for the elect. This solution has commonly pre-

vailed in the schools. Though then I allow that what has been said is true, yet I deny that it is suitable to this passage; for the design of John was no other than to make this benefit common to the whole Church. Then under the word *all* or whole, he does not include the reprobate, but designates those who should believe as well as those who were then scattered through various parts of the world. For then is really made evident, as it is meet, the grace of Christ, when it is declared to be the only true salvation of the world.[13]

Calvin's point is to deny the universality of the atonement by making the word *all* refer to the worldwide distribution of the church, rather than the universally potential redemptive work of Christ. Is such an interpretation of the text legitimate and natural?

There are actually two theological problems with this important text: first, does the Greek word ἱλασμός (*hilasmos*) mean *expiate* or *propitiate*? And second, does the word or phrase περὶ ὅλου τοῦ κόσμου (*peri holou tou kosmou*) "for the whole world" geographically or in the sense of humanity? The former question is not of real interest for our purposes, but the second problem is basic to our understanding of the text. I cannot find an older or more recent commentator who follows Calvin in this rather peculiar interpretation of the phrase "for the whole world." J. P. Lange, an older commentator remarks appropriately:

> The Apostle's design was manifestly to show the universality of the propitiation, in the most emphatic manner, and without any exception. This renders any and every limitation inadmissible. We must not except with Calvin the *reprobos*, because of predestination; it is rather the double *decretum absolutum* which is here excluded. Neither is it admissible to take κόσμος as *ecclesia electorum per totum mundum dispersa*.[14]

A more recent exegetical source claims that

> ...*for the sins of the whole world.* "The Gospel 'speaks to our condition,'" says C. H. Dodd, "when it assures us, not only that God loves the world and is ready to forgive our sin, but that His love has been expressed concretely and objectively in history to provide a means of sterilizing human wickedness and effecting a forgiveness which is not merely an amnesty or indulgence but a radical removal of the taint" (*The Johannine Epistles* [New York: Harper & Bros.; London: Hodder & Stoughton, 1946; "Moffatt New Testament Commentary"], pp. 28-29).[15]

Here is what Karl Barth calls a "biblical universalism" that is grounded in the work of Christ rather than some easy conception of divine goodness and human worth.[16] There is no way to soften the force of this text. It stands as an eternal witness to God's saving work in Christ, a work wrought for the whole of mankind, not simply Jew nor Gentile exclusively, and not certainly only for those numbered among the elect. To limit the efficacy of Christ's redemptive work and mission by the claim that it would waste God's grace through human rejection is to lower God's love to the level of man's rebellion and rejection!

1 John 2:1-2 does not stand alone in John's universalism. In chapter 4, verses 14 and 15, this same theme reoccurs:

> We have seen and testify that the Father has sent his Son as the Savior of the world. Whoever confesses that Jesus is the Son of God, God abides in him, and he in God.

Paul W. Hoon's observations on this last text are well worth noting:

> The redemptive aspect of the Incarnation is distinctively stressed here (as in 2:1-2), together with the universality of the claim that Christ's saviorhood exerts on all men: *Savior of the world*. The church has no more sacred task than to announce this claim, and finds here the dynamic of its missionary endeavor.... Missionary concern, observe, is not something tacked on to the gospel, nor something to be artificially aroused; on the contrary, it inheres in the very purpose and act of God himself—*the Father . . . sent his Son as the Savior of the world*—and in what we have found and declare Christ's saviorhood to be in our own experience—*we have seen and testify*. We proclaim Jesus as Savior to all men because we have known God to save us in him. Nothing less than this can really inspire and sustain the missionary endeavor of the church.[17]

IV. World Reconciliation: Universalism, Election and Christian Missions

How can we distinguish and defend a truly biblical universalism from the perversions of the Alexandrian universalism of an Origen or from the contemporary distortions of the cults such as the Jehovah's Witnesses? In the case of Origen (c. 105-c. 254) as well as his predecessor Clement (c. 150-c. 215), both theologians of the school of Alexandria, their doctrine was called *Apocatastasis*, and they argued that in the end hell would be emptied and all would be saved—even the devil and his demonic followers.[18] Like Calvin, we say: "Such a monstrous thing deserves no refutation." But the rejection of the perversion still leaves unsolved our basic problem.

Throughout the history of theology, it has been customary to make the distinction between a potential universalism and an actual universalism. Christ's work on the cross was sufficient to redeem all mankind, but its application depends upon man's response of faith, by which he lays hold of Christ and shares in the fulness of Christ's atoning work. The Baptist theologian A. H. Strong, whose views on election are as high as those of Calvin, argues for this distinction.

> The Scriptures represent the atonement as having been made for all men and as sufficient for the salvation of all. Not the *atonement* therefore is limited, but the *application* of the atonement through the work of the Holy Spirit.[19]

As far as I am concerned this is a perfectly understandable distinction, and I am willing to accept it. It is analogous to the discovery of a chemical solution to the problem of cancer. The discovery may be valid and the drug itself most effective, but it will promote the health only of those who take it! So it is with the question of an all-sufficient atonement. Its application is no more automatic than the administration of a life-giving drug.

There is, however, another approach to this problem. Calvin himself, and later Calvinism, was almost forced into a limited atonement theology by means of his interpretation of the doctrine of election and predestination. Even in the above quotation from A. H. Strong there is a hint of this elective restriction: *the Holy Spirit applies the atonement only to those who are elect, and since the basis of election is God's arbitrary decree, we have only pushed the problem one step back.* The universal significance of the atonement will never be seen unless we free the atonement itself from the restrictive idea of an arbitrary decree of election. If we, as Calvin and all later Calvinism does, deny the possibility of faith as a condition for election, we rob the atonement of any significant universal dimension. A drug that cures cancer for everyone is a poor drug if its application is limited by the doctor's decision to allow only whites to take it! We must, therefore, turn our attention to the relationship of atonement and the issue of election. And when we have done this, we will discover that a proper understanding of election will also serve to illuminate one of the great problems of Christian missions: *what about those who died without ever hearing of Christ and his atonement?*

The *ordo salutis* of Rom. 8:29-30 as well as 1 Pet. 1:2 (the translation of the King James is better in this passage) distinguishes between *foreknowledge* and *predestination.* Jacobus Arminius and later Arminians interpreted this distinction to mean that God's decision to apply the atonement was based upon his knowledge and awareness of those who would, when rightly confronted with the claims of the gospel, believe. Faith was never understood as a meritorious work—something qualifying man for salvation, but simply the morally neutral means by which the grace of Christ was received. The man who is brought into a court of law accused, confesses, is condemned and then accepts the judge's offer of pardon can hardly claim afterwards either that he was innocent of the charges or that he was acquitted on the basis of some meritorious worth of his person. This same man could, hypothetically, reject the offer of pardon. Both at the human level as well as at the divine, neither human judge nor God himself can force men to accept the pardon offered in Jesus Christ, and to accept the pardon is nothing less than an admission of guilt and condemnation. The acceptance of the pardon certainly does not imply some meritorious work on the part of the believer, making him deserving of salvation. Calvin and later Calvinists never seem to be able to see this fundamental distinction unfortunately!

What does this mean with reference to the atonement and particularly our responsibility to share the good news of the gospel with all men in every generation? Calvinists have been missionary minded, and have argued that God has ordained the means as well as the end. The doctrine of election has served to solve the problem of those who died without ever hearing the gospel: if they were part of the elect, they were saved without hearing; if not numbered among the elect, their not-hearing was of no consequence. When the atonement, however, is understood as having potential significance for all mankind, this radically changes the perspective. A valid offer of grace has been made to mankind, but its application is limited by man's response rather than God's arbitrary selection. God knows who would, under ideal circumstances, believe the gospel, and on the basis of his foreknowledge, applies that gospel even if the person never hears the gospel during his lifetime.

The task of evangelism and missions is to bring the *knowledge of salvation*, not the salvation itself. That salvation has already been brought in the all-sufficient work of atonement through Jesus Christ. The point is: *a universal atonement truly honors God's grace and frees God from the charge that he is responsible, through election, for excluding some from his kingdom.* Exclusion from the kingdom is a responsibility that belongs to man, and a truly biblical universalism demands that we interpret our doctrine of election in a manner consistent with this theological perspective. W. M. Sinclair's comments are supportive of this interpretation of the relationship of the atonement and election. In commenting upon 1 John 2, he says:

> *And not for ours only, but also for the sins of the whole
> world.*—This statement must not be limited. Its scope is that
> Christ's redemption was offered for the whole of mankind,
> from Adam to the last man. Who lay hold of the redemption,
> must be determined on other considerations. (Com. chap. iv. 14;
> John i. 29; iv. 42.) Multitudes may be saved through this re-
> demption who never heard of Christ (Acts x. 34, 35; Rom. ii.
> 14, 15). St. John's objection in introducing this truth here is to
> rebuke the arrogance of those Christians who looked down on
> the non-Christian world as outside the Fatherhood and mercies
> of God.[20]

We must obey the Great Commission to go into all the
world to preach the gospel to every creature (Matt. 28:18-20).
We must understand, however, that not all will believe, but
the offer is valid and the means of grace are extensive enough
to include the sins of all men—the debt of sin for every man
has already been paid—and every man ought to be invited
to share in the universality of Christ's atonement. Man limits
the efficacy of that atonement, not God!

There is, however, a pertinent psychological element in
the atonement that needs to be examined before moving to
a final point in our discussion. Don S. Browning has sought
to apply the insights of psychotherapy to the atonement, but
his dependence upon a process theology and his defense of
a *Christus Victor* theory of the atonement limits his perspective
somewhat.[21] From the psychological perspective, we can
understand the inherent insecurity of the Puritans whose theology combined a high view of predestination with an almost
morbid sense of introspection. The Puritan diaries reveal a
constant searching for signs of confirmation that they were
numbered among the elect. When we understand the truly
universal significance of the atonement, such introspection
becomes unnecessary.

Paul Tillich's restatement of the doctrine of justification
by faith touches at the heart of this problem: *justification
by faith means the acceptance of our acceptance.*[22] The
atonement as a work of God in Christ for all men reaffirms
Paul's great pronouncement: *God is for us!* (Rom. 8:28-39).
God has accepted us! Indeed he has not even spared his own
Son. As one who has spent many hours in the calling of
pastoral counseling, I know how few Christians fully appreciate
the fact that God has accepted them. It isn't only Martin
Luther who has thought of God as a condemning Judge rather
than gracious Father, but the atonement demonstrates this
theological affirmation. When we, in any way, limit the potential of Christ's redeeming work, we make room for a
dangerous uncertainty in the redeeming love of God. The Puri-

tan's willingness to be damned for "the glory of God" reflects a distorted understanding of what God was doing in Christ. We must not and we need not ever question our acceptance: *the cross is for all men and it continues to draw all men!*

V. Limited Atonement

The purpose of the essays composing this volume is not to be polemical. None of the writers desires to revive the old and tragic controversies of Calvinism and Arminianism, and where I have referred to Calvin, my purpose has been to let him speak, to allow him to set forth his own interpretation of the Word of God. He is a thorough and capable exegete, and no student of Scripture should be without his counsel! It is equally appropriate to include in this chapter a brief account of those who interpret the Scriptures to teach a limited view of the atonement. I have selected Louis Berkhof's *Systematic Theology* as representative of this general position, although many worthy exegetes have defended this position.

Berkhof first seeks to define the exact point at issue. He says:

> The question with which we are concerned at this point is not (a) whether the satisfaction rendered by Christ was in itself sufficient for the salvation of all men, since this is admitted by all; (b) whether the saving benefits are actually applied to every man, for the great majority of those who teach a universal atonement do not believe that all are actually saved; (c) whether the *bona fide* offer of salvation is made to all that hear the gospel, on the condition of repentance and faith, since the Reformed Church does not call this in question; nor (d) whether any of the fruits of the death of Christ accrue to the benefit of the non-elect in virtue of their close association with the people of God, since this is explicitly taught by many Reformed scholars. On the other hand, the question does relate to the design of the atonement. Did the Father in sending Christ, and did Christ in coming into the world, to make atonement for sin, *do this with the design or for the purpose of saving only the elect or all men?* That is the question, and that only is the question.[23]

The point, I think, is clear, but many misrepresent the Calvinistic or Reformed view by making it appear as if they do not recognize a universally potential view of the atonement. Berkhof's way of stating the issue also indicates why I earlier raised the question of election. We can see more clearly now why the issue of the atonement cannot be separated from the larger framework of the issue of election. "The Reformed position," explains Berkhof, "is that Christ died for the purpose of actually and certainly saving the elect, and the elect only."[24]

So far Berkhof's position seems clear enough, but it is when he moves to a defense of these views that one discovers the foundations upon which he argues. His reasoning is grounded less in the exegesis of Scripture than it is in *a priori* theological reasons. Without any intention of distorting the logical and biblical nature of his argument, I want to limit myself to two of his major points. (The reader should read the entire section for himself, if possible.)

> a. It may be laid down, first of all, as a general principle, that the designs of God are always surely efficacious and cannot be frustrated by the actions of man. This applies also to the purpose of saving men through the death of our Lord Jesus Christ. If it had been His intention to save all men, this purpose could not have been frustrated by the unbelief of man. It is admitted on all hands that only a limited number is saved. Consequently, they are the only ones whom God has determined to save.

> . . . .

> d. It should also be noted that the doctrine that Christ died for the purpose of saving all men, logically leads to absolute universalism, that is, to the doctrine that all men are actually saved. It is impossible that they for whom Christ paid the price, whose guilt He removed, should be lost on account of that guilt. The Arminians cannot stop at their half-way station, but must go all the way.

> e. If it be said, as some do say, that the atonement was universal, but that the application of it is particular; that He made salvation possible for all, but actually saves only a limited number,—it should be pointed out that there is an inseparable connection between the purchase and the actual bestowal of salvation. The Bible clearly teaches that the design and effect of the atoning work of Christ is not merely to make salvation possible, but to reconcile God and man, and to put men in actual possession of eternal salvation, a salvation which many fail to obtain, Matt. 18:11; Rom. 5:10; II Cor. 5:21; Gal. 1:4; 3:13; Eph. 1:7.[25]

Berkhof is not without his biblical texts, and the section lists approximately fifteen central texts; however, the argument turns not upon biblical proof texts but rather upon the nature of his logic. Point "a" points to a divine determinism that makes history unintelligible and God the cause of evil. Point "d" misses the most fundamental point of all biblical revelation, but I pass it by here since I intend to conclude the chapter with it. Point "e" seems to deny what he has previously admitted when he says that the question is not "whether the satisfaction rendered by Christ was in itself sufficient for the salvation of all men, since this is admitted by all." How can this claim be consistent with this latter point?

What has obviously escaped Berkhof's analysis is that the atonement is indeed a universally valid offer of redeeming grace. More importantly since Christ has finished his work of redemption upon the cross, the ground of our salvation has completely shifted. What is it that condemns a man? Is it his sins, large or small, numerous or few, that condemns a man and sends him into a Christless eternity? The answer of the New Testament is an absolute *"No!"* The critical examination of the works of the sheep and goats in the parable of Matt. 25:1-46 really turns upon the phrase: "Truly, I say to you, as you did it not to one of the least of these, you did it not to me" (v. 45). More importantly is the text from John's Gospel where Christ says:

> For God so loved the world that he gave his only Son, that whoever believes in him should not perish but have eternal life. For God sent the Son into the world, not to condemn the world, but that the world might be saved through him. *He who believes in him is not condemned; he who does not believe is condemned already, because he has not believed in the name of the only Son of God.* (3:16-18)

What condemns a man is not sins. Why? Because Christ's redemptive and atoning work is complete and satisfying. Even man's rejection cannot frustrate the purposes of God. Berkhof is right, but he has missed the point. The atonement is indeed a universal fact: the issue of every man's salvation turns not upon his sins, but rather upon his relationship to the Son! This explains both the nature of the unforgivable sin as well as the nature of the Holy Spirit's ministry through the church. We are told by Christ that the work of the Holy Spirit is to convict men of sin, not *sins*. Why the singular? Because there is only one sin God cannot forgive, and that is the rejection of the Lord Jesus Christ as one's Savior. Frankly, I am convinced that this is the proper basis for interpreting Heb. 10:25f. as well as Heb. 6:4-6. In John 16:7-11, Jesus outlines the convicting work of the Holy Spirit. He will convict or convince men of sin *"because they do not believe in me.*

Christ's intercessory work at the "right hand of the Father" is a constant reminder that the work of redemption is finished, the atonement has been paid. We are told in the book of Revelation, that Satan accuses the brethren day and night (Rev. 12:7-12). Christ's presence in God's presence answers Satan's accusations. Those whose faith is in Jesus Christ have acknowledged his atoning sufficiency, and it is only they whom Satan accuses. The rest of mankind has rejected Christ's substitutionary work of reconciliation. The atonement is indeed a complex and profound reality, none of the theories fully exhausts its meaning; but those theories which center upon the love of God and focus attention upon man's rejection or acceptance of Christ's work as over against those theories that stress sin as a basis are, at least, partially correct. Sin may have made the cross necessary, but the cross has now made sin irrelevant as far as man's relationship to God is concerned. This is, perhaps, a little too strong, but the fact is, that man's problem now is not so much sin or sins, but his reaction to what God has done in Christ. Has he accepted that finished work or rejected it? If he rejects it, there "no longer remains a sacrifice for sins" (Heb. 10:26).

> Therefore, if any one is in Christ, he is a new creation; the old has passed away, behold, the new has come. All this is from God, who through Christ reconciled us to himself and gave us the ministry of reconciliation; *that is, God was in Christ reconciling the world to himself, not counting their trespasses against them,* and entrusting to us the message of reconciliation. So we are ambassadors for Christ, God making his appeal through us. We beseech you on behalf of Christ, be reconciled to God. For our sake he made him to be sin who knew no sin, so that in him we might become the righteousness of God. (2 Cor. 5:17-21)
>
> To those who hold the position of unlimited atonement—that Christ died for all, but that only those who respond in faith are saved—the issue centers around the love of God, the scriptural teachings that Christ died for all, the sincerity of the invitation of salvation which goes out to all, and the freedom of man. How can God be said to love the world, as John 3:16 states that he does, if he sent his Son to die only for the elect? Or in what sense could it be said that God is not willing that any should perish, but that all should come to repentance (II Pet. 3:9), if Christ did not die for all? Are we to suppose that the elect are the only ones who labor and are heavy laden and that they are thus the only ones to whom the invitation of Jesus is issued (Matt. 11:28) or that the elect are the only ones who are invited to take the water of life without price (Rev. 22:17)? Do not these very invitations presuppose that the free response of man, though not meriting salvation, is nevertheless the condition upon which the benefits of the atonement are dispensed? Moreover, there are clear assertions in Scripture that Christ died for all (II Cor. 5:14), that he gave himself a ransom for all (I Tim. 2:6), that he is the expiation of the sins of the whole world (I John 2:2; cf. also I Tim. 4:10; Tit. 2:11), and that he tasted death for every man (Heb. 2:9).[26]

NOTES

1. Leon Morris, "I John" in *The New Bible Commentary: Revised*, edited by D. Guthrie, J. A. Motyer, A. M. Stibbs and D. J. Wiseman (Grand Rapids, Mich.: Wm. B. Eerdmans Publishing Co., 1970), pp. 1025-1026.

2. C. K. Barrett, *Harper's New Testament Commentaries: The Epistle to the Romans* (New York: Harper & Row, 1957), p. 114; see also *The Interpreter's Bible*, Vol. 9, p. 466.

3. Karl Barth, *Church Dogmatics*. Volume IV, Part 1 (Edinburgh: T. & T. Clark), 1956, pp. 272-273.

4. John Calvin, *The Institutes of the Christian Religion*, Book III, chapter 24, sections 15 and 16.

5. Barth, *Ibid.*, pp. 512-513.

6. G. C. Berkouwer, *The Triumph of Grace in the Theology of Karl Barth* (Grand Rapids, Mich.: Wm. B. Eerdmans Publishing Co., 1956), p. 364.

7. Barrett, *op. cit.*, p. 112.

8. Reinhold Niebuhr, *The Nature and Destiny of Man: A Christian Interpretation* (New York: Charles Scribner's Sons, 1949), pp. 178-264; 241f.

9. J. Calvin, *Calvin's New Testament Commentaries: St. John Part One 1-10* (Grand Rapids, Mich.: Wm. B. Eerdmans Publishing Co., 1959), p. 74.

10. *Ibid.*, p. 75.

11. J. Calvin, *Calvin's New Testament Commentaries: St. John Part Two 11-21 and I John* (Grand Rapids, Mich.: Wm. B. Eerdmans Publishing Co., 1961), p. 43.

12. Leon Morris, *The Cross in the New Testament* (Grand Rapids, Mich.: Wm. B. Eerdmans Publishing Co., 1965), pp. 159-160.

13. J. Calvin, *Calvin's Commentaries: Catholic Epistles* (Grand Rapids, Mich.: Wm. B. Eerdmans Publishing Co., 1948), pp. 172-173. Some have suggested that Calvin changed his views later in life, but I cannot find any evidence to confirm these suggestions.

14. John Peter Lange, *Lange's Commentary on the Holy Scriptures*. 12 volumes (Grand Rapids, Mich.: Zondervan Publishing House, n.d.), Vol. 12, *in loc.*, p. 45.

15. Amos N. Wilder, "The First, Second and Third Epistles of John: Introduction and Exegesis," *The Interpreter's Bible*, Vol. 12, pp. 228-229.

16. Barth, *Ibid.*, Vol. IV, Part 3, p. 487f.

17. Paul W. Hoon, "The First, Second and Third Epistles of John: Exposition," *The Interpreter's Bible*, Vol. 12, p. 283.

18. James Atkinson, "Universalism," in *A Dictionary of Theology* edited by Alan Richardson (Philadelphia, Pa.: The Westminster Press, 1969), p. 352.

19. A. H. Strong, *Systematic Theology* (Philadelphia, Pa.: The Judson Press, 1907), p. 771.

20. W. M. Sinclair, "The Epistles of John," in *Ellicott's Commentary on the Whole Bible* edited by Charles John Ellicott in 8 volumes. (Grand Rapids, Mich.: Zondervan Publishing House, n.d.), Vol. 8, pp. 476-477.

21. Don S. Browning, *Atonement and Psychotherapy* (Philadelphia, Pa.: The Westminster Press, 1966). A similar study could be done for sociology and economics.

22. *See Paul Tillich's works generally*, but specifically his *The Courage To Be* (New Haven, Conn.: Yale University Press, 1952).

50

23. L. Berkhof, *Systematic Theology* (Grand Rapids, Mich.: Wm. B. Eerdmans Publishing Co., 1939), pp. 393-394.

24. *Ibid.*, p. 394.

25. *Ibid.*, pp. 394-395.

26. Robert H. Culpepper, *Interpreting the Atonement* (Grand Rapids, Mich.: Wm. B. Eerdmans Publishing Co., 1966), p. 125.

3

Conditional Election

JACK W. COTTRELL

Since the Reformation era no biblical doctrine has been more misrepresented and more maligned than the doctrine of soteriological predestination (or election). Many people do not consider the idea of predestination to be biblical at all. This is because they have equated it in their minds with a particular interpretation of predestination, namely, the one developed by Augustine and made popular through the influence of John Calvin. Recognizing Calvinistic predestination to be alien to the Bible, they dismiss it or explain it away altogether.

This is extremely unfortunate, since the doctrine of predestination is definitely scriptural; and when rightly understood it is one of the most significant and rewarding teachings of the Bible. It enhances the majesty, wisdom, love and faithfulness of God; and it strengthens the heart of the believer. The whole counsel of God is not proclaimed when this doctrine is ignored.

The main concern of this chapter is to present the positive biblical teaching about election or predestination. This will require, however, some consideration of false or inadequate ideas of predestination, especially those which arise from the Calvinistic tradition.

I. The Biblical Doctrine of Election

The New Testament terms that are especially relevant are the words *prooöridzo*, meaning "to predestine, to predetermine, to decide beforehand"; and *eklogomai*, meaning "to elect, to choose, to select." Related terms are the adjective *eklektos*, meaning "elect" or "chosen"; and the noun *eklogē*, meaning "the election."

In the context of the doctrine of election there is no significant theological distinction between the words *predestine* and *elect*.[1] The word *predestine* includes a time element by means of its prefix, and it may be a more general term;[2] but no doctrinal point can be made by drawing a sharp distinction here.

In this chapter the word *elect* will ordinarily be used, since it is the more common, versatile and convenient of the two.

A. *The Structure of Election*

It is very important to see that the biblical doctrine of election is much broader in scope than election to eternal glory. Its broadest context is the total redemptive purpose of God. In choosing the cast for the grand drama of redemption, the sovereign God selected certain people to fill certain roles or to accomplish specific limited tasks.

1. THE ELECTION OF JESUS

The primary character in the drama is the Redeemer himself, the one who must do what is necessary in order to set humanity free from sin's guilt and bondage. The one chosen for this role is Jesus of Nazareth, son of a humble Jewish maiden. He alone is qualified to accomplish this task, because he alone, by God's plan, is the incarnate Son of God.

This election of Jesus is the central and primary act of election. All other aspects of election are subordinate to it and dependent upon it. It is the very heart of the redemptive plan.

Through Isaiah the prophet the Lord speaks of Jesus as the elect one: "Behold, My Servant, whom I uphold; my chosen one in whom my soul delights"[3] (Isa. 42:1). Matt. 12:18 quotes this passage and refers it to Jesus. At the transfiguration God spoke directly from heaven and announced the election of Jesus in these words: "This is My Son, My Chosen One; listen to Him!" (Luke 9:35). As Peter says, Jesus is the elect cornerstone (1 Pet. 2:4, 6).

The election of Jesus was part of the divine plan even in eternity, before the worlds were created. Foreknowing both the obedience of the Redeemer and the disobedience of his enemies, God predetermined the accomplishment of redemption through Jesus of Nazareth (Acts 2:23; 1 Pet. 1:20). Jesus was predestined or foreordained to die for the sins of the world (Acts 4:28).

2. THE ELECTION OF ISRAEL

Although Jesus has the leading role in the drama of redemption, there is a large cast of supporting characters. These are necessary in order to prepare the way for Christ's appearance upon the stage of history.

The primary element of God's preparatory plan was the election of Israel as the people who would produce the Christ. Deut. 7:6 says, "For you are a holy people to the LORD your God; the LORD your God has chosen you to be a people for His own possession out of all the peoples who are on the face of the earth." (See Deut. 14:2.) The Israelites were God's "chosen ones" (1 Chron. 16:13). Paul begins his sermon in the synagogue at Antioch by reminding his fellow Jews that "the God of this people Israel chose our fathers, and made the people great during their stay in the land of Egypt" (Acts 13:17).

Several significant points about the election of Israel must be noted. In the first place, it was an election to service and not to salvation. Being chosen as the people from whom the Christ would come carried with it some of the highest privileges known to man (Rom. 9:4, 5), but salvation was not necessarily among them. Whether an Israelite was saved or not did not depend simply on his membership in the chosen people. The nation could serve its purpose of preparing for the Christ even if the majority of individuals belonging to it were lost.

This leads to a second point, namely, that the election of Israel was the election of a group or a corporate body, not the election of individuals. As Daane says, "Divine election in its basic Old Testament form is collective, corporate, national. It encompasses a community of which the individual Israelite is an integral part." [4] Berkouwer grants that even Romans 9 must refer to the nation of Israel and not to the eternal destiny of individuals.[5] In other words, God's purpose of preparing for the Messiah was served through the nation as such, not necessarily through the individual members of the nation.

In the third place, however, it must be noted that at times certain individuals connected with Israel were chosen for special roles in order to facilitate the purpose of the nation as a whole. In order to create Israel, God chose Abraham, Isaac and Jacob (see Neh. 9:7; Rom. 9:7, 13). He chose Moses (Ps. 106:23) and David (Ps. 78:70), among others; he even chose certain Gentile rulers to help carry out his purpose for Israel (e.g., Pharaoh: Rom. 9:17; Cyrus: Isa. 45:1).

The fact that God elected these individuals for specific service in the history of salvation does not, however, mean that they were elected to personal salvation (or condemnation, as the case may be).

Since Israel was chosen specifically to prepare the way for the Messiah's appearance, her purpose was accomplished and her destiny fulfilled in the incarnation, death and resurrection of Jesus Christ (Acts 13:32, 33).[6]

3. THE ELECTION OF THE CHURCH

The drama of redemption is not complete, of course, when Israel has finished her role. Neither is it complete even when Christ has accomplished his saving work in history. Christ was chosen in order to redeem sinners and to bring them back into fellowship with God. Thus the drama is not complete until his redemptive work has borne its fruit, until there is a body of redeemed persons. These, too, are included in the historical enactment of the drama.

God had already decided to create on this side of the cross a new nation, a new Israel. Her role differs from that of Old Testament Israel. Her purpose is not the preparation for the coming of Christ, but rather participation in his saving work and the proclamation of it. This new elect body is the church.

As was the case with Old Testament Israel, the election of the church is a corporate or collective election. The church as a body is now God's elect people, chosen to complete God's purpose of redemption. This corporate election of the church is reflected in Peter's reference to the "chosen race" (1 Pet. 2:9) and in John's description of local congregations as the "chosen lady" and her "chosen sister" (2 John 1, 13).

As with Old Testament Israel, the election of the church is an election to service. The church is God's vehicle for the proclamation of the good news of redemption in Christ. When Peter describes the church as a "chosen race," he adds this purpose for the choosing: "that you may proclaim the excellencies of Him who has called you out of darkness into His marvelous light" (1 Pet. 2:9).

Just as God chose certain individuals for special service in relation to Israel, so did he select a group of individuals who would be his instruments in establishing the church. From among his disciples Jesus "chose twelve of them, whom He also named as apostles" (Luke 6:13). Later he asked them, "Did I Myself not choose you, the twelve...?" (John 6:70) Christ is speaking to the apostles when he says, "You did not choose Me, but I chose you, and appointed you, that you should go and bear fruit... " (John 15:16; see 13:18; 15:19). Likewise was the Apostle Paul chosen for special service (Gal. 1:15, 16).

In many ways, then, Old Testament Israel and the New Testament church are parallel with respect to God's electing purpose. The election of each is a corporate election; each is elected to service (Israel for preparation, the church for proclamation); and certain individuals are chosen for special roles in connection with each.

B. *The Election of Individuals to Salvation*

In addition to these similarities, however, there is one important difference. With the establishment of the church a new dimension is added to the purpose of election; for now it is not only election to service; but also election to salvation. The church is elected not only for the proclamation of, but also for participation in, the saving work of Christ. The church is the very object of Christ's love and redemptive sacrifice (Acts 20:28; Eph. 5:25). We are chosen unto salvation (2 Thess. 2:13).

This raises the most controversial question associated with the whole subject of election, namely, what is the relationship of individuals to the process of election to salvation? Are individuals elected or predestined to salvation? If so, in what way? These important questions will now be discussed in detail.

1. THE UNCONDITIONAL ELECTION OF INDIVIDUALS

Probably the best-known view of individual election is the one associated with Calvinistic theology.[7] Calvinism teaches that certain individuals are unconditionally elected or predestined to become believers in Jesus Christ and thus be saved. From among the total mass of sinful humanity, even before it has been created, God chooses which individuals he wants to respond to the gospel call. When the call is issued, those who have been chosen are irresistibly enabled to answer it. These are saved, while the rest of mankind is condemned to hell forever.

On what basis does God choose the ones whom he saves? This is known only to God himself, and he has determined not to reveal it. God has his own reasons for the decisions which he makes, but they cannot be known by men.[8] Thus from the standpoint of human knowledge, the election is totally unconditional. There are no established conditions which one may meet in order to qualify for being chosen.

This view was taught by John Calvin. In the *Institutes* he says:

> As Scripture, then, clearly shows, we say that God once established by his eternal and unchangeable plan those whom he long before determined once for all to receive into salvation, and those whom, on the other hand, he would devote to destruction. We assert that, with respect to the elect, this plan

> was founded upon his freely given mercy, without regard to human worth; but by his just and irreprehensible but incomprehensible judgment he has barred the door of life to those whom he has given over to damnation. . . . [9]

Also to the point is Calvin's statement that "God was moved by no external cause—by no cause out of Himself—in the choice of us; but that He Himself, in Himself, was the cause and the author of choosing His people." [10]

The Westminster Confession of Faith explains it thus:

> Those of mankind that are predestinated unto life, God, before the foundation of the world was laid, according to his eternal and immutable purpose, and the secret counsel and good pleasure of his will, hath chosen in Christ, unto everlasting glory, out of his mere free grace and love, without any foresight of faith or good works, or perseverance in either of them, or any other thing in the creature, as conditions, or causes moving him thereunto; and all to the praise of his glorious grace. (III:5)

According to Calvinism, then, specific individuals are the object of election; and they are chosen unconditionally.

2. THE CONDITIONAL ELECTION OF A CLASS OF INDIVIDUALS

A major part of Christendom has never been able to accept the concept of the unconditional election of individuals as biblical. They declare that Scripture just does not teach such an idea, which appears to be unjust and arbitrary on God's part and seems to lead to pessimism and quietism on man's part. Many who oppose this concept assert instead that election is based on certain conditions which anyone may meet; and it is the election of a certain class or group, not the election of specific individuals.

This view is held by many Arminians and is sometimes thought to be *the* Arminian view on the subject. Emphasizing the corporate character of election, Dr. H. Orton Wiley, the eminent Nazarene theologian, has stated, "I hold, of course, to *class* predestination." [11] He finds it objectionable to say that "God has determined beforehand whether some should be saved or not, applied to individuals." [12]

Another Nazarene theologian, Mildred B. Wynkoop, states that theories about predestination are the watershed between Calvinism and Wesleyan Arminianism.[13] She traces the origin of the idea of personal, particular, individual predestination to Augustine.[14] Arminius' theory of predestination, she says, is just the opposite: "Individual persons are not chosen to salvation, but it is Christ who has been appointed as the only

Saviour of men. *The way of salvation is predestined.*" [15]

Robert Shank, in his recent book, *Elect in the Son*, presents a similar view. Election, he says, is primarily corporate and only secondarily particular.[16] Individuals become elect only when they identify with or associate themselves with the elect body.[17] He summarizes his view of election as "potentially universal, corporate rather than particular, and conditional rather than unconditional." [18]

3. THE CONDITIONAL ELECTION OF INDIVIDUALS

The view just discussed is a deliberate attempt to present a biblical alternative to the Calvinistic doctrine of unconditional, particular election. Such an alternative is necessary, for the Calvinistic view as a whole is definitely contrary to Scripture. It is likely, however, that the pendulum has swung too far in the opposite direction. Biblical election to salvation is indeed conditional, but it is also individual or personal. The distinctive element in Calvinistic election is its unconditional nature, not its particularity. Only the former must be rejected; to reject the latter also is an overreaction and a distortion of the Bible's own teaching.

What is the biblical doctrine of election? As understood here, it is the idea that God predestines to salvation those individuals who meet the gracious conditions which he has set forth. In other words, election to salvation is conditional and particular.[19]

a. *Individual election.* A popular belief among non-Calvinists is that "God predestined the plan, not the man." The Scriptures, however, show that it is always *persons* who are predestined and not just some abstract, impersonal plan.[20] This is so obvious that it hardly seems necessary to mention it. In Rom. 8:29, 30 Paul is speaking of *persons.* The same persons who are predestined are also called, justified and glorified. In 2 Thess. 2:13 he says that "God has chosen you," the Christian people of Thessalonica, "for salvation." Eph. 1:4, 5, 11 speaks of God's predestination in relation to his plan, but it is specifically stated that God predestined *us* (*persons*) to adoption as sons *in accordance with* his purpose and plan.

Election, then, is not limited to an impersonal plan but applies to persons as well. But does it apply to *particular* persons? Are specific individuals predestined to salvation? The answer is yes. No other view can do justice to biblical teaching in several respects.

First it should be noted that the Bible often speaks of predestination in terms that specify particular individuals. Many passages do refer to the elect in general, but other references focus upon specific persons. In Rom. 16:13 Rufus is identified as an elect person. In 1 Pet. 1:1, 2 the apostle greets the elect Christians in certain specific geographical locations. A very clear statement of the predestination of individuals to salvation is 2 Thess. 2:13. Here Paul says to the Thessalonian brethren that "God has chosen you from the beginning for salvation." This statement cannot be generalized and depersonalized.

Another point that should be noted is that Rev. 17:8 speaks of those "whose name has not been written in the book of life from the foundation of the world." This is a negative statement; but it would be meaningless to say that some persons' names have *not* been written in the book of life since the beginning unless there are others whose names *have* been written there from the beginning.

There is some question as to whether names can be blotted out of the book of life (see Ex. 32:32, 33; Ps. 69:28; Rev. 3:5). If so, these would not be the names written there from the foundation of the world, but those having the status, perhaps, of the seeds which sprouted in rocky or weedy soil (Matt. 13:20-22). Those who overcome are specifically promised that their names will not be blotted out (Rev. 3:5), and these are in all probability the ones written from the foundation of the world.

In any case, there are certain individuals whose names have been in the book of life since the foundation of the world, and whose names will not be blotted out. Who can these be except those whom God has predestined individually to salvation? And the point here is that their very *names* have been known to God from the beginning. What can this be but individual predestination? "Rejoice that your names are recorded in heaven"! (Luke 10:20)

How is it possible that God could determine even before the creation which individuals will be saved, and could even write their names in the book of life? The answer is found in the fact and nature of God's foreknowledge. The Bible explicitly relates predestination to God's foreknowledge, and a correct understanding of this relationship is the key to the whole question of election to salvation.

Rom. 8:29 says, "For whom He foreknew, He also predestined to becomes conformed to the image of His Son, that He might be the first-born among many brethren." Peter addresses his first epistle to those "who are chosen according to the foreknowledge of God the Father" (1 Pet. 1:1, 2). In other words, God's foreknowledge is the means by which he has determined which individuals shall be conformed to the image of his Son (in his glorified resurrection body).

To say that God has foreknowledge means that he has real knowledge or cognition of something before it actually happens or exists in history. This is the irreducible core of the concept, which must be neither eliminated nor attenuated. Nothing else is consistent with the nature of God.[21]

One of the basic truths of Scripture is that God is eternal. This means two things. One, it means that when time is considered as a linear succession of moments with a *before* and a *now* and an *after*, God is infinite in both directions. He has existed before now into infinite past time (i.e., eternity) without ever having begun, and he will exist after now into infinite future time (again, eternity) without ever ending. "Even from everlasting to everlasting, Thou art God" (Ps. 90:2).

But to say that God is eternal means more than this. God's eternity is not just a quantitative distinction between him and his creation. Eternity is also qualitatively different from time. That God is eternal means that he is not bound by the restrictions of time; he is above time. At any given moment, what is both past and future to a finite creature is present to God's knowledge. It is all *now* to God, in a kind of panorama of time; he is the great "I AM" (Ex. 3:14).

To get some idea of the majesty of the infinite and eternal Creator, as contrasted with the finiteness of all creatures, one must read the Lord's challenges to the false gods and idols in Isaiah 41-46. The very thing that distinguishes God as God is that he transcends time, and sees it from beginning to end at one and the same moment. God challenges the false gods to recite past history and to foretell the future. They cannot, but he can, because he is God; and his knowledge of past and future *proves* he is God. Here is what he says:

"Present your case," the LORD says.
"Bring forward your strong arguments,"
The King of Jacob says.
Let them bring forth and declare to us what is going to take place;
As for the former events, declare what they were,
That we may consider them, and know their outcome;
Or announce to us what is coming.
Declare the things that are going to come afterward,
That we may know that you are gods;
Indeed, do good or evil, that we may anxiously look about us and fear together.
Behold, you are of no account,
And your work amounts to nothing;
He who chooses you is an abomination. (Isa. 41:21-24)

Who has declared this from the beginning, that we might know?
Or from former times, that we may say, "He is right!"?
Surely there was no one who declared,
Surely there was no one who proclaimed,
Surely there was no one who heard your words. (Isa. 41:26)

"Thus says the LORD, the King of Israel
And his Redeemer, the LORD of hosts:
'I am the first and I am the last,
And there is no God besides Me.
And who is like Me? Let him proclaim and declare it;
Yes, let him recount it to Me in order,
From the time that I established the ancient nation.
And let them declare to them the things that are coming
And the events that are going to take place.
Do not tremble and do not be afraid;
Have I not long since announced it to you and declared it?
And you are My witnesses.
Is there any God besides Me,
Or is there any other Rock?
I know of none.' " (Isa. 44:6-8)

"Remember the former things long past,
For I am God, and there is no other;
I am God, and there is no one like Me,
Declaring the end from the beginning
And from ancient times things which have not been done,
Saying, 'My purpose will be established,
And I will accomplish all My good pleasure';
Calling a bird of prey from the east,
The man of My purpose from a far country.
Truly I have spoken; truly I will bring it to pass.
I have planned it, surely I will do it." (Isa. 46:9-11)

In light of the biblical teaching concerning God's eternity and foreknowledge, and the relation between this foreknowledge and predestination, it should be evident that predestination must be of individuals. Surely God foreknows everything about the life of every individual. He cannot help but foreknow, just because he is God. He sees the entire scope of every individual's destiny—even before the foundation of the world.[22]

b. *Conditional election.* Many Arminians affirm God's foreknowledge while at the same time denying individual predestination. Some just ignore the inconsistency involved, while others dismiss it with a kind of embarrassed mumbling.[23] The reason why they are so determined to reject individual election is that they believe it to be inseparable from the Calvinistic doctrine of election. This is not the case, however, Calvinism does teach individual predestination, but this is not what makes it Calvinism. The essence of the Calvinistic doctrine, as noted earlier, is that election is unconditional. The watershed is not between particular and general, but between conditional and unconditional election. The Calvinistic error is avoided by affirming *conditional* election.

The foreknowledge of God has been emphasized. God elects individuals according to his foreknowledge. But the question may well be asked, foreknowledge of what? The answer is that he foreknows whether an individual will meet the *conditions* for salvation which he has sovereignly imposed. What are these conditions? The basic and all-encompassing condition is whether a person is *in Christ*, namely, whether one has entered into a saving union with Christ by means of which he shares in all the benefits of Christ's redeeming work. Whom God foreknew to be in Christ ("until death"—Rev. 2:10), he predestined to be glorified like Jesus himself.

This is the import of Eph. 1:4, which says that "He chose us in Him"—in Christ—"before the foundation of the world." The elect are chosen *in* (ἐν) Christ, that is, because they are in Christ; they are not chosen *into* (εἰς) Christ, that is, in order that they may be in Christ. They are in Christ before the foundation of the world not in reality but in the foreknowledge of God.

That the basic condition for election is our being *in Christ* preserves the Christocentric character of predestination, which seems to be a major concern for many.[24] It must not be forgotten that Jesus Christ is *the* elect one, and that all other redemptive election is in him. Thus even though election is conditional, it all depends upon Christ and the gracious benefits of his saving work.

Of course, there are also conditions which one must meet in order to *be* in Christ, i.e., in order to enter into saving union with Him and to remain in this union. The basic condition, of course, is faith (Gal. 3:26; Eph. 3:17; Col. 2:12). Other related conditions are repentance and baptism (Acts 2:38; Gal. 3:27; Col. 2:12). These conditions are in no way to be interpreted as meritorious on man's part, since they are graciously and sovereignly imposed by God himself. Thus having set forth these conditions for being in Christ, God foreknows from the beginning who will and who will not meet them. Those whom he foresees as meeting them are predestined to salvation.

How, then, is biblical predestination to be described? The Calvinist says, "God unconditionally selects certain *sinners* and predestines them to become *believers*." This is contrary to the teaching of Scripture, however, which instead says, in effect, that God selects all *believers* and predestines them to become his *children* in glory.[25]

In other words, it is important to see exactly what it is to which individuals are elected. They are predestined to salvation itself, not to the means of salvation. They are not predestined to become believers; they are not predestined to faith. Their choice of Jesus Christ is not predestined; the choice is foreknown, and the subsequent blessings of salvation are then predestined.[26]

The Bible is quite clear about this. Rom. 8:29 says that those whom he foreknew were predestined by God "to become conformed to the image of His Son, that He might be the first-born among many brethren." The reference to Christ's being the "first-born" is a reference to his resurrection from the dead into a glorified state (Col. 1:18; Rev. 1:5). Our being conformed to his image here refers to our glorification (Rom. 8:30), when we will receive a resurrection body like his own (Phil. 3:21). Thus we are chosen to become God's glorified children, Christ being the first-born among many brethren. (Similar to this is Eph. 1:5, which states that we are predestined unto adoption as children.)

Believers are predestined not just to receive future glory, but also to enjoy the present benefits of Christ's saving work. As 2 Thess. 2:13 says, "God has chosen you from the beginning for salvation ($\epsilon i\varsigma$ $\sigma\omega\tau\eta\rho i\alpha\nu$)." In 1 Pet. 1:2 this salvation is seen to include a life of good works and justification by the blood of Christ ("chosen . . . that you may obey Jesus Christ and be sprinkled with His blood").

The biblical doctrine of election, then, definitely includes the conditional election of individuals to salvation. Through his foreknowledge God sees who will believe upon Christ Jesus as Savior and Lord, and become united with him in Christian baptism; then even before the creation of the world he predestines these believers to share the glory of the risen Christ.

II. Election and Related Doctrines

It is now proposed to show that the doctrine of election outlined above is consistent with biblical teaching as a whole. Attention will be focused on two related doctrines in connection with which objections are often raised, namely, the doctrine of God and the doctrine of man. It will be shown that conditional, individual election is most consistent with these two doctrines.

A. *The Nature of God*

The strongest objection to this understanding of election is that it violates the biblical teaching concerning the nature of God. This objection, which is raised most often by Calvinists, must be taken very seriously. We shall see, however, that it is without basis, since conditional, individual election is perfectly consistent with the sovereignty, grace and justice of God.

1. THE SOVEREIGNTY OF GOD

No doctrine is more important than the sovereignty of God. M. B. Wynkoop has rightly said: [27]

... God's total sovereignty is the basis of the whole of Christian theology. No philosophical theory which permits the slightest break in that sovereignty can be permitted. Every Christian doctrine hangs on this doctrine. ... A less than sovereign God cannot support Christian faith.

One of the most common objections to conditional election is that it necessarily violates God's sovereignty. Berkouwer sums up the objection thus: "In such a notion God's decision is made dependent on man's decision." [28] It is clear, he says, that predestination according to foreknowledge "casts shadows on the sovereignty of God's election and is a flagrant contradiction of the nature of Christian faith." [29] This is why it was rejected by both John Calvin[30] and the Synod of Dort.[31] Calvin's rejection of foreseen faith, as summarized by Berkouwer, is as follows:[32]

... He sees in it an attack against God's greatness. It supposes a waiting God whose judgment and final act depend on and follow upon man's acceptance and decision, so that the final and principal decision falls with man; it teaches self-destination instead of divine destination. (*Inst.* I, xviii, 1)

This is basically the same objection voiced by Roger Nicole: [33]

I find it objectionable that in the Arminian position the ultimate issues seem to depend upon the choice of man rather than upon the choice of God. And it seems to me that both the Scriptures and a proper understanding of divine sovereignty demand that the choice be left with God rather than with man. ...

Herman Hoeksema's idea of divine sovereignty, according to James Daane, is that "nothing God does is a *response* to what man has done. God is never conditioned by man. Man's actions cannot become conditions for God's responses." [34] Thus divine sovereignty must rule out conditional election.

In response to such an objection, it is freely admitted that conditional election does mean that in some sense God reacts to a decision made by man. But it must be insisted that this in no way violates the sovereignty of God.[35] This is supported by two considerations.

In the first place, an arrangement under which God reacts to man's choices would violate his sovereignty *only* if God were forced into such an arrangement, only if it were a necessity imposed upon God from without. But this is not the case. It was God's sovereign choice to bring into existence a universe inhabited by free-willed creatures whose decisions would to some extent determine the total picture.[36] When God established the system of conditional election, it was God alone who sovereignly imposed the conditions.[37] God's freedom to decree whatever he pleases is the proof and essence of his absolute sovereignty. Samuel Fisk points out that God's free and voluntary decision to allow man a measure of self-determination "is something which only a great and omnipotent God would do."[38] Rather than detract from his sovereignty, it actually enhances it and glorifies it more.

In the second place, to deny conditional election in principle because it presents God as reacting to man's action ignores the fact that God has reacted and does react to human decisions in even more basic ways than this.

Of primary importance is the fact that man's decision to sin is a contingent factor to which God has reacted. This is the very essence of Christianity: because man has sinned, God has provided redemption. Virtually every action of God recorded in the Bible after Gen. 3:1 is a *response* to human sin. The Abrahamic covenant, the establishment of Israel, the incarnation of Jesus Christ, the death and resurrection of Christ, the establishment of the church, the Bible itself— all are part of the divine reaction to man's sin. As C. S. Lewis has pointed out, God would not forgive sins if man had committed none. "In that sense the Divine action is consequent upon, conditioned by, elicited by, our behaviour."[39]

Likewise, God's judgment on unrepentant sinners is a reaction to human sin. It is very interesting that Berkouwer himself argues for this point,[40] even though in so doing he undermines his whole case against conditional election. His inconsistency here is the result of his inability to accept an unconditional reprobation that is symmetrical to unconditional election. Thus he says that "Scripture repeatedly speaks of God's rejection as a divine answer in history, as a reaction to man's sin and disobedience, not as its cause." God's rejection of sinners "is clearly His holy reaction against sin."[41] It is "a reactive deed, a holy, divine answer to the sin of man."[42]

In light of such affirmations as this, how can Berkouwer or any Calvinist continue to argue that conditional election is a violation of the sovereignty of God? If God can maintain his sovereignty while reacting to man's sin, he surely can do so while reacting to man's (foreseen) faith.

Another area in which God reacts to human decisions is prayer. C. S. Lewis argues in his *Letters to Malcolm* that if God can react to sin, he certainly can react to prayer.[42]

We may press this question further and ask, if God can react to sin and prayer without compromising his sovereignty, why can he not so react to foreseen faith? The answer, of course, is that he can and does. To say that this makes God dependent on man or that man is thereby *causing* God to do something is an unfounded caricature. The whole idea that unconditional election is the *sine qua non* of the sovereignty of God is, as Shank says, "theological humbug" and "one of the great fallacies of Calvinism."[44]

2. THE GRACE OF GOD

Another equally strong objection to conditional election is that it violates the grace of God. That is, if God elects by means of his foreknowledge of faith, this would make man to some extent the cause or source of his own salvation. Where, then, is grace?[45]

Both Augustine and Calvin rejected conditional election as inconsistent with grace and as implying justification by works.[46] This was due in part to the fact that many people whom they opposed still taught some kind of salvation by merit, and therefore they taught predestination on the basis of foreseen *merit*. Ambrose, for instance, commenting on Rom. 8:29, says that God "did not predestinate before he foreknew, but to those whose merit he foreknew, he predestinated the rewards of merit."[47] One of Calvin's main opponents, Pighius, was, as Wendel says, "the inheritor of a long tradition which had endeavoured to make predestination dependent upon foreknowledge of merits."[48] This certainly prejudiced Calvin's formulation of the problem, as shown in the following statement:[49]

> ... But it is a piece of futile cunning to lay hold on the term foreknowledge, and so to use that as to pin the eternal *election* of God upon the *merits* of men, which election the apostle everywhere ascribes to the alone purpose of God. ...

It is quite proper to reject foreseen merit as incompatible with grace. But the Calvinist does not stop here. Even when one rejects all notions of merit and insists on foreseen *faith*, not works, the Calvinist still cries that grace is vitiated. This is because he cannot see the biblical distinction between faith and works. Berkouwer asserts that "election does not find its basis in man's works and *therefore* not in his foreseen faith." [50] Whether it be merit or faith that is foreseen, "God's decision is made dependent on man's decision. The initiative and the majesty of God's grace is overshadowed." [51] Grace is thus "limited and obscured." [52]

This kind of objection to conditional election overlooks one of the most basic principles in the system of grace, namely, that faith and works are qualitatively different. Grace is consistent with *faith* as a condition, but not with *works* as a condition (Rom. 4:4, 5, 16; 11:6). "For by grace you have been saved through faith," *but* "not as a result of works" (Eph. 2:8, 9). In these passages Paul clearly shows that faith is not in the category of works. They are qualitatively distinct.

Thus we must agree that foreseen works, merit, or holiness as a condition for election would be contrary to grace. But must we say the same about foreseen faith? Of course not. Faith by its very nature is consistent with grace, whether foreseen or not. If God can *give* salvation on the condition of faith *post facto*, then he can predestine a believer to salvation as the result of his foreknowledge of that faith.[53] Thus to say that election is of grace does not mean that it is unconditional; it simply means that it is not conditioned on works.

One of the basic problems here and with the Calvinistic system in general is the notion of *sovereign grace*. Berkouwer's thesis is that election according to foreseen faith is simply synergism and is just another way of opposing "the sovereignty of God's grace." [54] He speaks of the "*skandalon* of sovereign grace." [55]

The idea of sovereign grace indeed is a *skandalon*, but it is one that was created by man when the concepts of God's sovereignty and God's grace were fused and confused together. Surely God is sovereign in all things, but his sovereignty does not absorb and cancel out his other attributes. His wisdom, his love, and his grace are not just synonyms for his sovereignty. God's sovereignty expresses itself in terms of absolute power, the power of sheer might and strength, the power to create and to destroy. But grace is expressed in a totally different kind of power, namely, the drawing power of love and compassion and self-sacrifice (see John 12:32).

In the concept of sovereign grace, sovereignty dominates and overwhelms grace, so that grace is not allowed to be grace. The shepherd is dressed unnaturally in the garb of the warrior.

We must let grace come to us on its own terms. Grace does not want to force its way. Like Christ, it stands at the door and knocks (Rev. 3:20). The Bible teaches very plainly that the gifts of grace are appropriated by faith. If by works, then grace is no longer grace. On this all agree. But likewise, if it is by sovereign imposition, then grace is also no longer grace.

Conditional election, then, is quite consistent with grace; it opposes only the false hybrid of *sovereign* grace.

3. THE JUSTICE OF GOD

Finally it should be noted that the conditional election of individuals is consistent with the justice of God. God's justice leads him to treat all persons alike, and to bestow no special favors with respect to salvation.

This is the point of the Bible's teaching that God is no respecter of persons. (See Acts 10:34; Rom. 2:11; Eph. 6:9; Col. 3:25; 1 Pet. 1:17.) The Calvinist often quotes this biblical teaching to prove unconditional election. This is done by taking it to mean that God does not take account of anything in the person himself (i.e., no certain conditions) when selecting him to receive the gift of faith and salvation. The principle is given in Scripture, however, to show exactly the opposite, namely, that God *does* reward and punish *only* on the basis of what he finds in the person himself. The contexts in which the principle is asserted establish this. It is meant to teach God's justice and fairness in judgment.

The very thing that would violate this principle of justice would be deciding on an individual's eternal destiny without taking account of anything in him. But this is exactly what the doctrine of unconditional election asserts. Only the doctrine of conditional election, where God elects to salvation those who comply with his graciously given and announced terms of pardon, can preserve the justice and the impartiality of God.[56]

B. The Nature of Man

Since conditional election is seen to be consistent with the biblical doctrine of God, does it follow that there is now no reason to reject it? No, because the nature of man is also at issue here. In fact, the basic reason for Augustinianism's rejection of conditional election and affirmation of unconditional election lies in this area. Thus it remains to be shown that conditional election is consistent with the biblical doctrine of man.

1. TOTAL DEPRAVITY

Why does the Calvinist continue to insist on unconditional predestination, even when sovereignty and grace are not at stake? What is the imperative which necessitates it? The answer is the doctrine of total depravity, which in its essence means that all persons as the result of Adam's sin are from birth unable to respond in any positive way to the gospel call. There is a total inability to come to the decision to put one's trust in Christ. This point is truly the keystone in the Calvinistic system. This is what makes unconditional election logically and doctrinally necessary.

This is shown in the frequent objection that foreseen faith solves nothing, since God gives the faith to whomever he chooses.[57] Why must *God* choose the ones to whom he will give faith? Not in order to preserve his sovereignty, but because no one in the sinful mass of mankind is able to respond when the gospel is preached. Therefore if any at all are going to respond, God must decide which ones to make able to believe:

The situation is like that of a doctor who has perfected a technique that will restore sanity to the most mentally deranged persons. For some reason he cannot use it on all such persons, so some must be selected and others rejected. Since the individuals in question are too insane even to know what is going on, the doctor himself simply views the patients and decides on the basis of reasons wholly unknown to them which ones shall be made sane again.

The fact is, however, that the Bible does not picture man as totally depraved. Man as a sinner is truly depraved and corrupted (Jer. 17:9), even to the point of being dead in his trespasses and sins (Eph. 2:1, 5; Col. 2:13). This does not mean, however, that he is unable to respond to the gospel call. The parallel between Eph. 2:1-10 and Col. 2:11-13 shows that even the person who is dead in his sins is regenerated *through his faith* in Christ, i.e., he believes before he is regenerated. His regeneration or his coming to life depends upon his faith. This is seen in Col. 2:12, which says that in baptism a person is risen with Christ (i.e., made alive, regenerated) through faith in the working of God.

Thus a person cannot come to faith without the gospel (Rom. 10:17), but he *is* able to respond to the gospel in faith. God foreknows who will make such a response, and these he predestines to salvation.

2. HUMAN RESPONSIBILITY

Conditional election alone preserves the integrity of free

will and thus of human responsibility, without which a moral system is impossible. God does not force man to sin; man chooses to sin of his own free will. Thus the individual is responsible for his sin and for his rejection of grace, and he justly suffers the punishment for it. Just as God does not force a person to sin, neither does he force anyone to accept grace. A person chooses to accept grace when he decides to meet the conditions which God has established for receiving it. Of course, there is no merit in making the decision, for the condition is one of grace and not of works. Nevertheless a person is responsible for making the decision himself. If he does not make it, he has only himself to blame.

One other point must be emphasized, namely, that the authentic, free-will character of an individual's decision is not nullified by God's foreknowledge of it. Some Arminians object to individual predestination on such a basis. How can human choices be truly free, they say, if God knows them in advance? In order to preserve human freedom, they are compelled to diminish the majesty of God's foreknowledge. Some argue that God has voluntarily limited his own foreknowledge.[58] The idea is that God, by his own choice, does not know in advance who will accept Christ; he must wait until the actual decision is made.

This view, however, ignores the biblical teaching concerning God's eternity. The idea that God has voluntarily limited his knowledge has no biblical basis, and it is simply unthinkable in view of the majestic portrait of the eternal God discussed earlier. But to think that God would *have* to limit his foreknowledge in order to preserve human freedom is precluded likewise by the eternity of God. For after all, even the free-will decisions of men are made within the framework of time. They are truly free decisions, but they are the decisions of time-bound creatures. But God is eternal, above time, knowing the end from the beginning. To say that God could not foreknow truly free human decisions is either to exalt man too highly or to reduce God to a creaturely status.

A similar objection is this: if human decisions are foreknown, then they are certain to occur. But if they are certain, how can they be free and contingent? This again ignores the distinction between time and eternity, and overlooks the reality of history. True, every decision is certain as far as God's foreknowledge is concerned, but foreknowledge is not foredetermination. Every decision must be made in the arena of history. It is not *real* until produced by a human will in history. The fact that God foreknows what that choice will be does not mean he caused it. He simply knew in advance what would be freely decided. He can do this because he is God, not man.

Only the conditional predestination of individuals, then, can preserve the majesty of the eternal God and the integrity of free will and human responsibility.

Conclusion

In summary the doctrine of predestination with regard to salvation and damnation may be described thus: (1) There *is* an absolute, unconditional predestination, made without reference to foreknowledge. This is general or group predestination, corporate predestination, the predestination of the plan or of classes of men. By absolute sovereign decree God determined to save whoever responds to his free offer of salvation and to damn whoever rejects it. (2) There is also a conditional predestination, made by means of God's foreknowledge. This is particular predestination, the election of individuals to salvation or the reprobation of individuals to damnation. Because God foreknows each person's decisions, he predetermines each person's destiny.

This is the doctrine of predestination as taught by Arminius himself. Bangs summarizes one of Arminius' statements thus:[59]

> By an absolute predestination God wills to save those who believe and to damn those who persevere in disobedience; by a conditional predestination God wills to save those individuals whom he foresees as believing and persevering and to damn those whom he foresees as not believing.

But it is only incidental that Arminius taught this view of predestination. Of infinitely greater importance is the fact that the Bible teaches it.

NOTES

1. Robert Shank attempts to distinguish them thus: "Both election and predestination are acts of determination, but the election is God's choice of men *per se*, whereas the predestination looks beyond the fact of election itself to the *purposes and objectives* comprehended in election." Also, he says, "Election is the act whereby God chose men for Himself, whereas predestination is His act determining the *destination* of the elect whom He has chosen." (*Elect in the Son* [Springfield, Mo.: Westcott Publishers, 1970], p. 156.) This distinction, however, is neither inherent in the terms nor warranted by the various contexts. The word *proöridzo* as such does not contain the idea of destination; nor is the use of the middle voice for *eklegomai* theologically conclusive (as Shank claims), since this is the common form of the word whenever used. That both terms are used with reference to the purposes, objectives and circumstances of election is evident from a

comparison of Rom. 8:29, 30 and 1 Pet. 1:2. (See also 2 Thess. 2:13, where *haireomai*, a synonym for *eklegomai*, is used.)

2. It refers to events as well as to persons. See Acts 4:28.

3. All Scripture quotations are from the New American Standard Bible.

4. James Daane, *The Freedom of God: A Study of Election and Pulpit* (Grand Rapids, Mich.: Eerdmans, 1973), p. 104.

5. G. C. Berkouwer, *Divine Election*, trans. Hugo Bekker (Grand Rapids, Mich.: Eerdmans, 1960), pp. 210ff. His main concern is to avoid the conclusion of individual reprobation as a symmetrical counterpart of individual election.

6. "God's election of Jesus does fulfil the purpose of Israel's election . . ." (Danne, *op. cit.*, p. 107.)

7. The Calvinistic system of theology did not actually originate with John Calvin, but rather with Augustine.

8. Berkouwer, *op. cit.*, p. 60.

9. John Calvin, *Institutes of the Christian Religion*, III. xxi. 7, trans. Ford Lewis Battles (vol. XXI in *The Library of Christian Classics*, ed. John T. McNeill. Philadelphia: Westminster, 1960), II, 931.

10. Calvin, "A Treatise on the Eternal Predestination of God," in *Calvin's Calvinism*, trans. Henry Cole (Grand Rapids, Mich.: Eerdmans, 1956), p. 46.

11. H. Orton Wiley and others, "The Debate Over Divine Election," *Christianity Today*, IV (October 12, 1959), p. 3.

12. *Ibid.*, p. 5.

13. Mildred Bangs Wynkoop, *Foundations of Wesleyan-Arminian Theology* (Kansas City, Mo.: Beacon Hill Press, 1967), p. 14.

14. *Ibid.*, pp. 30, 31.

15. *Ibid.*, p. 53.

16. Shank, *op. cit.*, p. 45.

17. *Ibid.*, pp. 50, 55.

18. *Ibid.*, p. 122.

19. See Jack Cottrell, "Conditional Election," *The Seminary Review*, XII (Summer 1966), 57-63; also, Cottrell, "The Predestination of Individuals," *Christian Standard*, CV (October 4, 1970), 13-14.

20. The plan, of course, is predetermined by God. This applies both to the redemptive work of Christ (Acts 4:28) and to the establishment of the church. But this is not the point of predestination to salvation.

21. Most Calvinists try to avoid the clear implications of God's foreknowledge by changing the meaning of it from "foreknow" to "forelove" or something similar. The idea of cognition is made subordinate to some other concept. For instance, Roger Nicole says, "The passages dealing with foreknowledge are not at all difficult to integrate, inasmuch as the term foreknowledge in Scripture does not have merely the connotation of advance information (which the term commonly has in nontheological language), but indicates God's special choice coupled with affection" (H. Orton Wiley and others, op. cit., p. 10). This is an arbitrary definition, however, and is not consistent with the use of the term in Acts 2:23, where it can mean no more than prescience. See Samuel Fisk, *Divine Sovereignty and Human Freedom* (Neptune, N.J.: Loizeaux Brothers, 1974), pp. 73-75, 106-7.

22. Calvin acknowledged that this was the view of the early church fathers, and even of Augustine for a time. But he suggests that we "imagine that these fathers are silent" (*Institutes*, III. xxii. 8; *op. cit.*, pp. 941-2). Berkouwer notes that "Bavinck goes so far as to call this solution 'general,' for it is accepted by the Greek Orthodox, Roman Catholic, Lutheran, Remonstrant, Anabaptist, and Methodist churches" (Berkouwer, *op. cit.*, p. 37).

23. For instance, Wiley objects to applying predestination to individuals, yet grants that God has foreknowledge of who will believe in Christ (Wiley and others, *op. cit.*, pp. 5, 15). Shank's treatment of foreknowledge is puzzling:

"Thus it is evident that the passages positing foreknowledge and predestination must be understood as having as a frame of reference *primarily* the corporate body of the Israel of God and *secondarily* individuals, not unconditionally, but only in association and identification with the elect body . . ." (Shank, *op. cit.*, p. 154). It is as if corporate election were the opposite of unconditional election. Further, Shank says that "whether God has actively foreknown each individual—both the elect and the reprobate—may remain a moot question. The Biblical doctrine of election does not require such efficient particular foreknowledge, for the election is primarily corporate and objective and only secondarily particular. The passages positing foreknowledge and predestination of the elect may be understood quite as well one way as the other" (*Ibid.*, p. 155).

24. See Shank, *op. cit.*, pp. 27ff.; Berkouwer, *op. cit.*, pp. 132ff.

25. The Calvinistic mind sees election as bringing about the transition from unbelief to belief, hence making unbelievers the object of election. The Arminian says that this transition is made by a free act of will; election then is an act of God directed toward the believer after the transition has been made. Ignoring this important distinction, Daane criticizes the Arminian view of election as being unpreachable in that "it turns God's election into a human act." It makes election to be merely "a description of the possibilities of human freedom." Thus "Arminianism cannot preach election because it does not regard election as an act of God and, therefore, as an action of his Word; election is merely a possible response the sinner may make to the Word" (Daane, *op. cit.*, pp. 15-18). His criticism misses the mark, however, since election is not something directed toward unbelievers but toward believers. True, the transition from unbelief to belief is not an act of God, but it is not the result of election either. See Fisk, *op. cit.*, pp. 37-40.

26. The supralapsarian-infralapsarian controversy is misplaced. It argues whether God's decree to elect is prior to or subsequent to his decree regarding the Fall. But the focal point of election is not man's decision to sin, but rather his decision with regard to God's offer of grace. The crucial question is whether God's decree to elect is prior to man's decision to accept Christ or whether it follows it. The latter is the biblical view.

27. Wynkoop, *op. cit.*, pp. 87-88.

28. Berkouwer, *op. cit.*, p. 42.

29. *Ibid.*, p. 35.

30. *Ibid.*, p. 36.

31. *Ibid.*, p. 26.

32. *Ibid.*, p. 36.

33. Wiley and others, *op. cit.*, p. 5.

34. Daane, *op. cit.*, p. 25.

35. For a fuller discussion see Jack Cottrell, "Sovereignty and Free Will," *The Seminary Review*, IX (Spring 1963), 39-51.

36. See C. S. Lewis, *Letters to Malcolm: Chiefly on Prayer* (London: Geoffrey Bles, 1964), p. 72. He says, "Yet, for us rational creatures, to be created also means 'to be made agents'. We have nothing that we have not received; but part of what we have received is the power of being something more than receptacles."

37. James Daane presents an irresponsible and totally false caricature of conditional election when he says, "Reformed theology rejects Arminianism because it makes God comply with *human* conditions. It rejects the notions that God is not free to operate except within conditions laid down by man and that God cannot save man unless man first decides to believe and choose God" (Daane, *op. cit.*, p. 127). He then refers to "the Arminian's imposition of restrictions on God" (*Ibid*).

38. Fisk, *op. cit.*, pp. 51-52.

39. Lewis, *loc. cit.*

40. Berkouwer, *op. cit.*, pp. 183ff.

41. *Ibid.*, p. 183.

42. *Ibid.*, p. 184.

43. Lewis, *loc. cit.*

44. Shank, *op. cit.*, pp. 143-4.

45. Daane says that "Arminians held that God decreed to elect all men and then, in response to the unbelief of many men, decreed to elect only those who believe. Reformed thought found this unacceptable, for it surrenders the truth of man's salvation by grace alone" (Daane, *op. cit.* p. 54).

46. Berkouwer, *op. cit.*, p. 36. See Wynkoop, *op. cit.*, p. 56.

47. Ambrose, *De Fide*, lib. V. n. 83, cited by Harry Buis, *Historic Protestantism and Predestination* (Philadelphia, Pa.: Presbyterian and Reformed, 1958), p. 9.

48. Francois Wendel, *Calvin: The Origins and Development of His Religious Thought*, trans. Philip Mairet (New York: Harper and Row, 1963), p. 271.

49. Calvin, "The Eternal Predestination of God," p. 48; cf. p. 64. See also the *Institutes,* III. xxii. 3, where Calvin speaks of the foresight of holiness and good works.

50. Berkouwer, *op. cit.*, p. 42; italics supplied.

51. *Ibid.*

52. *Ibid.*, p. 43.

53. See Fisk, *op. cit.*, pp. 77-78; and Shank, *op. cit.,* pp. 125, 144-5.

54. Berkouwer, *op. cit.*, p. 47.

55. *Ibid.*, p. 8.

56. See Fisk, *op. cit.*, p. 47. Wiley makes an unfortunate statement when he says that "it impugns God's justice, for him to decide—regardless of whether a man believes or not—whether he can, whether he will be saved" (Wiley and others, *op. cit.*, p. 5). Dr. Wiley means this as a criticism of unconditional, individual predestination; but it does not accurately represent that position nor anyone else's.

57. See Carl Bangs, *Arminius: A Study in the Dutch Reformation* (Nashville, Tn.: Abingdon Press, 1971), p. 219.

58. For instance, T. W. Brents, *The Gospel Plan of Salvation* (reprint, Nashville, Tn.: Gospel Advocate, 1966), pp. 92ff.

59. Bangs, *op. cit.*, p. 221.

4

". . . The Spirit of Grace" (Heb. 10:29)

WILLIAM G. MacDONALD

The most complicating factor for system building in theology is the personhood of God. Non-Christian theistic philosophers routinely reject the truth that God is personal, and thereby they simplify their theological constructs. A force, idea, or principle is far more consistent and controllable in thought than a living personality, so they fabricate philosophical systems unencumbered by the vagaries of will, sensitivity, responsiveness and the various other features of dynamic personhood. When something impersonal or something less than a complete personality is centralized as the universal "God," the resultant theology inevitably collides with the Christian faith.

Christian theology that is true to the whole revelation of God includes not only the personal vision of God, but it also guards the doctrine of God from every deadly impersonal determinism. As for evangelical theology, while it contends objectively for "the faith once and for all time delivered to the saints," it is sure that the object of that faith is none other than the *living* God. His "living" depicts not only inexhaustible vitality but his anthropomorphic accommodation of himself to temporal and even spatial (the "Most High") relatedness to mankind. It means that the "life" of him who is perfect in himself is over against mankind in such a way as evincing a measure of *undeterminedness*, that is, as having contingency in matters of decision, and having flexibility, compensatory adjustment, and real openness to meaningful prayer in the reciprocity of "I-Thou" relationships with man.

The concept, "person," in the normal modern sense of that word is found nowhere in the Bible under that terminology. The Bible nevertheless uses the term "spirit" to disclose God's inner self. God *is* spirit, and man *has* a spirit. Both man and God have common ground of being, inasmuch as man—unlike the animals—was given a spirit that "imaged" God. To think of God as spirit is to view him as personal, that is, as a self, and in this case as one corresponding on a colossal scale to man's personal selfhood. In saying this, we are not thereby constructing God in man's image, but merely consenting to the biblical revelation that teaches the eternal nature of God's Spirit and the derived character of man's spirit, fashioned in God's image.

A deterministic principle (e.g., evolutionary process, behaviorism, dialectical materialism, historical fate) may be conceptualized by the god-makers as "god," or as the ground under some more popular image of the deity, but it must never be thought to be identical with the God whose revelation came in full in Christ and is preserved for us in the biblical writings.

Moving in closer to the situation in Christian theology, we must caveat against the construction of any theological system, however well-meaning, the culmination of which would remain unchanged had God—to speak hypothetically and foolishly—"died" before, at, or just after the creation, leaving the world to run down determinatively through time according to his "first-and-last will and testament." If everything that is or ever shall be, and all that will ever happen, is predetermined from the beginning, the world's fate is sealed, and man, having no decisive say in his destiny, is deprived of his individual significance except in relationship to other human beings. Such a teaching jeopardizes both the personhood of God and of man.

Since men would rather not expose themselves to intimate contact with the self-revealing God, they consequently are prone to retreat into determinisms that shield them from direct dealings with God, and the awesome responsibilities of such encounters. In the non-Christian religious world Islam (lit., "surrender") is a most pronounced exemplification of deterministic theology. Islamic theology makes the supreme Will of Allah the all-important determinant of the affairs of men, and the Spirit of God seems at best aloof and remote. Christians should be alerted by this to the fact that a transbiblical view of the will of God can be propounded at the expense of the love of God, that making sovereignty the center and circumference of a theological system is no guarantee in itself that the system will be biblical and reveal the God who rules in love, as opposed to a god who merely loves to rule. In the Bible we read that "God is spirit," "God is love," "God is good." Never do we read "God is will" (though God certainly "wills"), nor "God is power" (though God has all-sufficient might), nor "God is mystery" (although his ways are past finding out by human means alone).

Now we know that the Spirit of God is his complete self, extending from the depths of God to every place he chooses to touch or reside. We are not to understand the Spirit as some kind of tritheistic "third God," in the same manner Justin Martyr denominated the Logos as a "second God," but the Spirit is God himself in his invisible holy reality presenting himself. In the living God, therefore, there are analogical components we recognize in ourselves. God knows, God wills, and God feels (apart from physical sensation). Excepting physical sensibilities and sin, God is all that we are metaphysically—and even more so! (The personhood of man was not lost in the Fall; only the holiness of his personhood was surrendered.) Evangelical theology is confined happily to thinking of the metaphysical personhood of God in anthropomorphic categories legitimatized by God's creating man in his own image.

Paul Tillich, the most celebrated philosophical theologian in the USA in the fifties and sixties, sought to move beyond the personal concept of God—while including it dialectically as a symbol—by postulating a transpersonal or suprapersonal God, "being itself," above the traditionally conceived "God," [1] to whom one would not pray or speak as if he were a Being. In so doing Tillich ultimately broke the essential point of correspondence between God and man-in-his-image. If God is ultimately "the transpersonal One," the lines of correspondence and communication between God and man become inoperable, whatever games the unenlightened may play in prayer, using the personal symbol. But in biblical theology man is presented as a miniature "god" with faculties of communication appropriate to use "in spirit" when truth is appropriated for worship of God. This holds true for sinning Samaritans (John 4:23-24) or anyone else who will respond to the divine call.

I. The Doctrine of Grace as the Heart of Biblical Revelation

The concept of the grace of God is grounded in the doctrine of God's holy Self, his personhood, his metaphysical "spirituality." This personal understanding of grace is exemplified preeminently in the incarnate Lord. And since "grace" is at the center of God's activities in the world as the superlative statement of his intimate Self, we cannot expect to fathom the depths of that grace except as the Spirit leads us there, to an ever-deepening experience of God's engulfing us in his expressed love.

Let the writer call the reader to a task at this point and

inquire for his working definition of grace. And what do you have? My guess is that the first concept that came to your mind was the well-worn catechetical phrase, "unmerited favor." This cliché of ours is deficient precisely where all the determinisms are unacceptable. The personal "involvement" of God is not required. That definition of grace stresses something good that comes to man and the undeserved character of that good. But nothing in the definition demands that the giver give any of himself in or with his gift or "favor." The rain falling on the farmland of the selfish, build-a-bigger-barn farmer, the welfare check left regularly in the alcoholic's mailbox, the "wheel of fortune"'s selection of a monetary winner are all forms of "favor"—some would say "fate"—that were not merited. In light of the New Testament we cannot settle, however, for a concept of grace that would be capable of being handled through a computer without personal interaction. "Unmerited favor" may well be a serviceable term for explicating the factitious term, "common grace," but it falls short of the glory of "the grace of God . . . for . . . salvation."

To proceed in the manner of defining grace as is often done in terms of its minimal essence divisible into two kinds—"common" grace and "special" grace—rigs a jig on the theological worktable that is bound to distort either the one or the other kind. It is not merely a matter of classifying one as impersonal and the other personal. For it is possible to attach God's name to "unmerited favor," to give it a personal handle. To declare that the agency of grace is personal, i.e., an agent, the personal God, still leaves too much unsaid, because the whole term, "God's unmerited favor," under such conditions must be equally as applicable to common grace as to special grace, but not antithetical in terms of what makes one common and the other uncommon. My point is this: The difference between the *action* of God in so-called common grace and that in special grace is so deep-seated as to make inappropriate the quest for a least common denominator of grace that is compatible with the theological classifications of "common" and "special."

A major thesis propounded in this chapter can be stated in a few words: The grace of God flowers into expression in the New Testament and is uniquely spiritual. But the explication of this statement about grace must be delayed momentarily, while consideration is made of the phenomena that reveal God's providential goodness in stocking the world with good things for man's benefit and giving man potentials for making the most of life in the world. All that God has given man in nature and in the constitution of his own being—the structures of the old creation—are to be attributed to the good-ness/kindness/love of God for his creatures. The theological term "beneficence of God" as providentially expressed in the mul-tiplexity of the harmonious systems of creation and in sus-taining man as the crown of creation is a useful term for this in that it preserves the biblical idea without compromising the uniqueness of grace. Or, to put the cause for the effect, one does well to use the biblical term "the goodness of God" to categorize the outpouring of God's loving care on all men, sending sunshine and rain on good and bad men alike, giving man food and enjoyment, and supplying him with the various life-fuels needed to sustain his journey through time as a nat-ural man.

When John the Baptist was queried as to the relative merits of John's and Jesus' ministries, he replied with a generaliza-tion that is apropos to this discussion of the goodness of God to all men. The prophet said, "No one can receive anything except what is given him from heaven" (John 3:27). All the resources God placed in nature, the vitality God gave man, the position he gave man as co-regent with him in ruling the created world, and all the potentials and possibilities for a good life can be described as certainly having a "gift" charac-ter. But this goodness of God as expressed in impersonal gifts should not be doubled in terminology with the word that is central in the New Testament for God's giving us himself in his Son and Spirit. Even though the basic words "gift" and "grace" are paronymous in the original (*charisma* and *charis*), and even if we attach the somewhat pejorative quali-fier "common" to the word "grace," we flatten out the majesty of that most central salvific word in the New Testament by making it commensurate with another concept.

Invariably, the gifts of creation are something (food, re-sources, places to live, etc.) or someone (parents, friends, companions, etc.) or some specific of permuted circumstances, but in no such gifts or good times does God give *himself!* God's goodness can be extended to man without God's inclusion of himself in the package, that is, *without God's giving the Spirit.* God supplies man with consumables and possibilities and "new mercies" every day, but under this old-creation shower of blessings depicted in the Old Testament and New Testament, he does not admit man to the tree of life; he does not share with him the sacred stuff of which eternal life is made—his own spiritual life!

As stated above there is no single salvific word, other than a proper name, that sums up the New Testament so well as "grace." It is used in such a way that it is distinguishable from love. Love can be one-directional and unrequited even as *agape*. Grace in the New Testament means love given and getting through to its object by being received. Specifically, it means love's giving oneself to one who welcomes the giver as "gift." *God's* grace, then, is God's giving us himself in Jesus Christ (objectively), and (subjectively) it is the Holy Spirit received as the Spirit of Jesus Christ. This conception of grace does not set up a polarity between love and grace. On the contrary, there is a continuity between them in that grace is the fulfillment of love. "God is [as to his nature] love," and God is, in the expression of his love to believers-receivers, "the God of all grace" (1 Pet. 5:10). As the presence of God's love in man, the Spirit is "the Spirit of grace" (Heb. 10:29). Jesus himself incarnated the grace of God in an immensurable *pleroma* (John 1:14, 16), so that in a programmatic sense it can be said that "grace and truth came through Jesus Christ" (John 1:17).

Whatever secrets God may have kept to himself under the administration of Moses and the law (Deut. 29:29), the new administration of grace is one of open disclosure of God's love for mankind and of his will to relate to man on the basis of grace: "For the grace of God *has appeared* for the salvation of all men" (Titus 2:11). God has revealed his whole heart; *he loves man*—all men, everywhere, all nations, everyone! God the Savior "desires all men to be saved" (1 Tim. 2:4), "not wishing that any should perish, but that all should reach repentance" (2 Pet. 3:9), and he made it possible to "have mercy upon all" (Rom. 11:32). Indeed, "the mystery of his will" (Eph. 1:9) concerning "the riches of his grace" (Eph. 1:7) "he *has made known* to us" (Eph. 1:9).

Paul spoke of a past day when the Colossians "*heard and understood* the grace of God in truth" (Col. 1:6). The carryover mystery that had to wait until the New Testament to be divulged was this: God would unite by his grace the Jews and nationals from every segment of world society together in one body in Christ (Eph. 1:4-3:20). That mystery of God's universal love and plan was fully disclosed in the gospel. That which in the middle sixties of the first century was totally obscure in the Pharisaic synagogues of Jerusalem was basic knowledge to the Gentile believers far away in Colosse and in many other places as well.

When scripture says God "accomplishes all things according to the counsel of his will" (Eph. 1:11), it means that he has no one but himself to consult in matters of decision and is responsible only to himself for what he does. It does not mean that all operation of "will" in the universe is nothing less than the expression of one *absolute* Will. That would destroy the concept of "person," since generically there would be only *one* Will at work in the universe, absorbing all others into itself. God's will is limited by two factors: (1) his holy, loving nature that determines his will; (2) his granting of miniature sovereignty within the limits of finitude to man. A theology built on the "decrees" of God, that has to be interpolated between the lines of scripture, instead of clarifying God's plan, ultimately wraps up the will of God in inscrutability. Such unintelligibility of the will of God results in grace being clouded over too. No one can be sure that God indeed loves *him*, if God has willed by eternal decision to love some and reject others according to an undisclosed schema.

Jesus, on the other hand, expressed God's gracious will to *everyone* who wanted, that is, "willed" to follow God's gracious plan (John 7:17). Moreover, he was candid as to whom God's grace would be hidden and unavailing, viz., to the self-righteous, the stingy rich, the unforgiving, and the self-satisfied. These groups of people exclude themselves from God, not vice versa.

The will of God is this: that where sin reigns grace will reign instead. The will of God for man, therefore, is *grace*. His will is gracious, but grace is not another name for will, much less irresistible will. Grace, having personal dimensions of comity, flows from God's whole personality to man's whole personality without violating man's right by creation to choose his destiny.

II. The Meeting of Spirit and Spirit, of Grace and Faith

Will can be imposed on others less powerful than oneself without the concurrence of their will. But grace is never imposed. Grace can only be received. Grace is a *spiritual* transaction and a continuing relationship. Justification came in the Old Testament in the name of God and took the external form of a promise. Justification comes in the New Testament "in the name of the Lord Jesus Christ *and in the Spirit of our God*" (1 Cor. 6:11), and fulfilled God's gracious promise (Gal. 3:14).

God has freedom to love man precisely because he is love, and not raw power. He is almighty in respect to his creation, but he is not absolute power. He cannot commit deicide; he is immortal. He cannot deny himself; he is faithful. He cannot lie; he is the truth. He cannot be unfair; he is just. His being the Almighty is not to be pressed to the absurd asseveration that God can do absolutely anything. God's sovereignty, therefore, is his administrative *role* or *work* to which his nature is perfectly suited. His sovereignty is his *rightful relationship* to his creation. It is derived from his nature as the One best suited to rule as well as the One whose sole right it is to rule by virtue of being Creator.

If one insists that sovereignty is of the very essence of God, an attribute of his nature without which he could not be God, then his very deity itself is imperilled. For such a position requires someone other than God from eternity for him to rule. Creation, then, would have been necessary to his very existence or being, and would not have been the gratuitous overflow of his love and glory. We would be compelled to posit always something other than God, ancillary to him. He would no longer be the first and last, the eternal, but a co-eternal with "governees."

God is free, therefore, to be the sovereign Lord; he is not free to lie. This means that he can delegate—surrender if you please—part of his sovereignty *without ceasing to be God.* On the other hand, God cannot surrender, relinquish, give up, or otherwise divest himself of his truth for any moment of time, for truth is eternal, or else it is not true. Hence, God was free to hand over to the first man the role of ruler over all creation below him in the created order, viz., his children, the earth, sea (fish), and sky (birds) (Gen. 1:28). For this task God became Adam's counselor, and until sin entered, they conferred regularly each day. Adam had "dominion" and God supported him in this delegated rulership.

Now when we ask the question of the nature of man's freedom, we must look first at the first man. To him God gave the right to make himself independent as well as the privilege of staying with God and living forever. If the opening chapters of Genesis mean anything, they mean that God actually— not speciously—gave Adam the freedom to determine his own destiny. *If* it were true that God made eternal decrees by which he decided the destiny of every individual he would create, decreeing eternal life for some and foreordaining by decree eternal damnation for the others,[2] then we would have to accept the following ineluctable implications:

(1) God is the only one who is real; men are God's toys.

(2) God is Will.

(3) God is impassible [and some would say "impossible," too!], and the tears of Jesus over the unbelieving chosen people at Jerusalem were either: (a) hypocritical, or (b) Jesus was not identical with the God of the all-embracing decrees, or (c) Jesus was sinning by not rejoicing in the Will of God for those for whom he wept.

(4) God is dark—inscrutable.

(5) God is hatred, not only because he has hated more people than anyone else, but because his hatred persists from the eternal past.

One must look elsewhere than the Bible to find such a view of predestination as that stated above, from which we have shown in the implications how irreconcilable such a conjecture is with the doctrine that God is love, the standard for all justice, and the would-be friend of his crowning creation—mankind.

John Greenleaf Whittier in his poem, "The Minister's Daughter," relates a scene on Sunday afternoon as a minister, who had just that morning been guided in his sermon by the decretal theology, strolled with his young daughter in a garden "through the apple-blossoms of May":

> Then up spoke the little maiden,
> Treading on snow and pink:
> "O father! these pretty blossoms
> Are very wicked, I think.

> "Had there been no Garden of Eden
> There never had been a fall;
> And if never a tree had blossomed
> God would have loved us all."

> "Hush, child!" the father answered,
> "By his decree man fell;
> His ways are in clouds and darkness,
> But he doeth all things well.

> "And whether by His ordaining
> To us cometh good or ill,
> Joy or pain, or light or shadow,
> We must fear and love him still."

> "O, I fear Him!" said the daughter,
> "And I try to love him, too;
> But I wish He was good and gentle,
> Kind and loving as you." [3]

Let us return to the biblically revealed God whose "fulness" is love (Eph. 3:17-19). This God out of his love for man endowed him with the option to return his love or spurn it. On the one hand, God can command man as his creature; on the other hand, he risks leveling himself with man in the mutuality of spirits, the reciprocity of selves that occurs *whenever* love is given, received, and returned again—even in the unequal parent-child occasions of love. This freedom of God for man was expressed in his giving to man the option to accept and return his love and thereby to share his life, or to reject his love and go on through life using up his vitality in independent existence, enjoying only God's "goodness to all" regardless of their responsiveness.

If God is love, why did he hate (Mal. 1:3; Rom. 9:13) Esau without a cause? In a point of fact, God did not hate Esau, the man, as we use the word "hate." The Hebraism "to love one and hate the other" means in contemporary English to give priority or preference to one over the other. It does not imply animosity and malicious will against the one given second place. This use of "hate" in the words of Jesus on occasion bears out the special sense in which "hate" when used _in the presence of alternatives always has a different meaning than when used with one object alone. For instance, the true disciple must love and follow the Lord and "hate" his father, mother, and wife (Matt. 6:24); or the man who has two bosses must inevitably "hate" one of them (Matt. 16:13).

The honored line of the Messiah could not descend through the twins, Esau and Jacob, so God chose the least promising of the two (as is his custom—1 Cor. 1:27-28) in order to magnify his grace. Esau in first esteeming his birthright as valueless was "immoral" in so doing, and his tears later over this decision could not change the choice that would be lifelong in effect (Heb. 12:16-17). But, God did have a lesser but real "blessing" for Esau imparted to him by his father, Issac, and as far as the biblical record goes he lived out his life in peace after the incident of his being wronged by his brother's pretending to be he.

Among other wives Esau married Abraham's granddaughter (Ishmael's daughter), and the chronicling of his descendants is considered of sufficient importance to occupy the entire thirty-sixth chapter of Genesis. What is more, when Jacob sought his forgiveness and moved in on the same turf with him, he turned from his old hatred to forgiveness, and they lived together, attended their father's funeral as reconciled brothers, and only split when the blessings of God upon them *both* had become so great that the land of south Canaan was not of sufficient space to accommodate their combined holdings.

If that is how God treats a man whom he "hates," there are many men who would like for God to so hate them too! It is not the same story of blessing when one considers all of Esau's descendants in Edom over the next millennium. Esau's own role in life was limited, indeed, by God's choice of his brother as a messianic progenitor, but Esau's *destiny* is another matter. Esau forgave the first time his forgiveness was asked. Esau did not retaliate though he had rights. Esau made room for his fraternal twin, and he finally "took the walk" to carve out of the red sandstone of Edom a new homeland, letting his brother, having been crippled by God's angel, remain unmoved except to absorb his old territories. In his mature years Esau did not receive a new name as did his brother, but he did act with the ethical integrity that well befits the grandson of Abraham. "God knows those that are his," and maybe—just maybe—one of the surprises when "the sons of God are manifested" in eternity will be some locks of immortal red hair visible in a crowd of Old Testament redeemed and belonging to that one and only man that scripture says God "hated."

When God and man meet in the proclamation of the gospel on the plains of decision, both the Word and Spirit come into focus at God's end of the field and sin and spirit at man's end. God's messenger unsheathes the sword of the Spirit, the Word of God. In short, by that word man is slain, and by the Spirit he is created anew. God's call to him is a *summons* to repentance (Acts 17:30), but on the other hand, it is an *invitation* to receive grace (John 3:16; Rev. 22:17). As Creator God rightfully commands man to confess his infidelity in sin. As Savior God graciously appeals to man to look to him and be saved. The former is judgment; the latter is grace.

Assuming the man here considered accepts in faith God's invitation and thereby receives God's grace, what is the order of the implementation of that grace in his experience? Some theologians would insist that the discernment of an order of operation in speaking of regeneration is as difficult as determining which spoke moves first when a wheel turns on its axle. With that verdict I would agree on the practical level of pastoral theology, but when it comes to matters of sequence of initiative in exposing this love affair between God and man, more can be said than merely to assert simultaneity. The initiative belongs exclusively to God. God calls man by "the word of his grace" (Acts 14:3).

The gospel, then, as objective grace, must have priority (Acts 18:27). The poor-in-spirit man turns from himself (as did the Prodigal) and believes God. His faith is the focused action of his whole spiritual being. That is, his cognitive, volitional, and emotional self actively renounces sin before God and positively holds to "the word of God's grace" extended to him. His repentance and faith is entirely shaped, then, by the word on which it is based. But he does his own repenting before God and believing. In response to faith—trusting commitment to God—he receives the Spirit as the guarantee of abiding grace. The whole experience may be depicted thus with man's response surrounded by God's Word and Spirit:

[Word (repentance, faith) Spirit]

God initiates and consummates the experience. He calls faith forth and graciously answers faith with the Spirit delivered within.

This coming of the Spirit in *regeneration* is what is really new in the "new" covenant made in Christ's blood. God, of course, in all his dealings with man by his "word" is also "spirit." As Jesus said, his words were "spirit and life." Thus we would not say that the Spirit is not involved at the outset of man's encounter with God. He is. But the Spirit, while using the Word of God to convict man of sin and to offer grace to remove it, deals with the soul as Subject to subject, not as irresistible Will to soulless object. It is an encounter, a meeting, a hearing of evidence against the man and his plea, an offer of divine pardon and life, but it is not yet a "new birth" until man grasps the gift of grace in faith, permitting the Spirit to enter the core of his being.

Can we, then, speak of "prevenient" grace, using a theological term that has seen lots of wear? In one sense, that is, *objectively*, it must be said that all grace is prevenient. Here we are using grace as a synonym of the gospel. While we were still in sin, the Apostle Paul wrote (and we could add, while the rest of us were unborn), Christ died for the ungodly. Since "the Spirit of life in Christ Jesus" (Rom. 8:2) was not given to anyone as Christ-in-you until Jesus was raised from the dead (John 7:37-39; 20:22), it can be further stated that grace abounding over mankind's sins at the cross was all "prevenient" *historically* to anyone's acceptance and experience of it.

To go further and inquire if grace is *subjectively* "prevenient" involves either a redefinition of grace or a restatement of the objective sense in which grace "comes before." Yes, the Spirit "convicts," the Father "draws," and the Son "calls," and all these synchronous acts are merciful and loving, indeed. But as soon as God becomes operative *within* the life, we must drop all "pres" and speak now of *grace* having come and abounding in spiritual presence. Grace is the first light of day in the "new creation." It is the first breath of life in the "new man." It is the first "new land" that appears rising out of the chaotic welter of the old creation and is the *terra firma* on which we now stand (Rom. 5:2) in justification.

On the lighter side we note that grace was "prevenient" in Paul's letters, "intravenient," and "postvenient," too. He began his letters with a pronounced blessing of grace, referred to grace repeatedly throughout most of his letters (except Philemon where grace is never more forcefully implied) and he closed them with a benediction of grace. Other apostles do almost as much. To be in Christ is to be surrounded in grace (John 1:16—*charin anti charitos*).

The work of grace in man, that is, the coming of the Spirit as the new life in regeneration is unique to the New Testament. Many leaders in the Old Testament era had dynamic operations of the Spirit working through them, but none—not even John the Baptist, the greatest of them all as per the word of Jesus— had what makes a man a new creation, i.e., Christ in you by the Spirit. Case in point: When Jesus' own twelve, endowed by him with spiritual *dynamis* and *exousia* to share his ministry (Luke 9:1), became separated from him in death, they had no basis for any communion with him. After his resurrection, however, they never lost spiritual contact with the ascended Lord throughout the *Acts*.

God cannot—and to say the same thing—*will not* regenerate a heart that will not admit him. God respects the sovereignty-within-limitations with which he endowed man at creation. God will confirm Pharaoh in the hardheartedness he has manifested toward God. He will not renew such a heart. Jesus will deliver men everywhere from the demonic spirits that bind them, but never will he "cast out" unbelief or more sinister disbelief from anyone's heart. He will speak truly, "very truly," to the Pharisee Nicodemus, but he will wait for him indefinitely to make his decision about a "new birth." It must also be remembered that the dramatic conversion of the "chief of sinners" on the road to Damascus was not the overpowering of a God-hater, but the enlightenment of a badly mistaken man who up to that time had thought he was serving God and was doing so "in all good conscience"!

In the Old Testament faith preceded justification. In the New Testament faith also precedes justification. Additionally, in the New Testament with justification comes regeneration— "the spirit of life"—and sanctification—"the spirit of holiness." It does violence to the clear tenor of Scripture to reverse the order in the interest of a theological system and demand that regeneration precede faith rather than follow. That order makes faith virtually meaningless. It also would mean that justification and sanctification are separable states from regeneration. But if they all be considered simultaneous, then "faith" seems at best redundant. Does God even believe for us?

It is beautiful and true to say that salvation from sin is all of God. But it is untrue to deny the necessity for man to respond in personal faith to God, or to say that because man is "dead in trespasses and sins" that he cannot respond in faith, or in any way—absolutely. Therefore it is said:

Awake, O sleeper, and arise from the dead, and Christ shall give you light. (Eph. 5:14)

One without God sleeps in the death of his sins, but when God's call awakens him, he can respond in faith, or he can resist the Spirit and go back to sleep in death.

Man, even in his sins and rebellion against God, is constantly putting his faith somewhere. It is his nature to be a believer. Not the possibility of faith, but the object of his faith, then, becomes the important consideration. Believing permits the Holy Spirit to work and grace to be received.

One of the most common misunderstandings about faith is that initial faith in God is "a gift of God" or "a gift of the Spirit." One would never conclude this from the great "faith" chapter of the New Testament that says:

> And without faith it is impossible to please him. For whoever would draw near to God must believe that he exists and that he rewards those who seek him. (Heb. 11:6)

There are five passages in the New Testament that are construed by some to teach that individual faith is the immediate work of God in us, a phenomenon over which we have no control. The most well known of these and easiest to dispose of is the classic passage on soteriology in Eph. 2:8-9. The text says:

> For by *grace* [Gr. a feminine noun] you have been saved through *faith* [another feminine noun]; and this is not your own doing, *it* [a neuter pronoun] is the gift of God.

The "gift" is *salvation* as the resultant state of grace accepted through faith. The grammar will not permit "faith" to be the antecedent of "it."

The "fruit of the Spirit" is love amplified, whose varieties are listed in Gal. 5:22. Virtually all the modern translations understand *pistis* there as "faithfulness," and not "faith" (as in the KJV). By the same meaning, "faithfulness," we should understand *pistis* in Rom. 12:3, where the context and text itself see the individual in relationship with the whole body of believers. Faith concerns one's own relationship to God, whereas faithfulness is a whole life-style in the ecclesial "body" of believers. God is to be credited for all faithfulness or dependability in man, but just as man has to do his own dying, and choose his own *destiny* whatever his alotted *role* in life may be, so, too, it is his significance-giving responsibility to begin and continue to believe God all the days of his life: "As the outcome of your faith," Peter wrote, "you obtain the salvation of your souls" (1 Pet. 1:9).

In Mark 11:22 we hear the exhortation of Jesus to the disciples saying (literally): "*Ei* (if) *echete* (you have) *pistin* (faith) *theou* (of God)." A woodenly literal translation can be made out to say, "If you have God's faith," but it is far more accurate to follow those translators who interpret *theou* as an objective genitive and translate as with the RSV, "Have faith in God." The Bible never speaks of "God's faith," per se, unless this be the one exception. God has aseity, and faith for him would be somewhat superfluous. Since God is always presented as the proper object of faith, it would ambiguous to speak of him as a "believer" as well. But God does trust his people to return his love.

One passage remains to be examined and this time *pistis* is clearly a *charisma* of the Spirit (1 Cor. 12:9), being one of nine "gifts" listed there. Two observations are crucial: (1) The context would indicate that the faith spoken of here is not given to make one a believer, but it is given to a believer to benefit the entire church in some manner. (2) The context also would suggest that this—to use a Latin term—is *fides miraculosa*, for doing exploits for God, and not the *fiducia* (faith as trust and commitment) that determines one's destiny in God. (3) In the exercise of this *charisma* God gives some specific experience of assurance that enables the sharer to *see* the action or effect as a *fait accompli*. In some sense God opens for him preternatural sensibilities that are not amenable to psychological assessment and articulation.

Changing the figure, it can be said that the receiver hears in the Spirit a divine word limited to the local, temporal situation for performing "signs and wonders" in the worldly community or for meeting some need in the Community of the Spirit, and he participates in some way in its fulfillment. Kathryn Kuhlman, in whose ministry this kind of faith has been manifested multiplied thousands of times over decades, confesses on her telecasts and in her books that she cannot explain how this faith works and that she, claiming not to be a healer, is held in awe of this work of God as much as anyone.

Furthermore, we conclude that: (1) Ordinary faith (*fiducia*) is made a possibility for man on the basis of the first creation, and need not await the new creation; Abraham and the Old Testament "believers" corroborate this observation. (2) The Christian faith (*fides*), the content of the gospel, may rightfully be considered a gift from God and the result of the new creation that began with Jesus' resurrection. (3) It is proper to consider objective faith, that is, the Christian faith (*fides*), as a gift from God; and it is improper to consider subjective faith, that is, personal reception and retention of the gospel, as "a gift from God." It does not glorify the grace of God to predicate to it more than the biblical revelation itself claims. Such ambiguity ultimately undermines the whole divine-human encounter. To treat subjective faith (*fiducia*) as "a gift of God" demands the explication that God *"believed"* for you, as if your soul were nonexistent, and you were totally insignificant, over and beyond all your sinfulness.

Let us be clear about this matter. What is "the gift of God"? Answer: "Jesus" as the *object* of faith historically given, and the "Spirit" as the *result* of faith internally given. We can speak generally, then, of the gospel of Jesus Christ, as the gift, of the grace of God as the gift, of the life of the Spirit as the gift, of the fruit of the Spirit as the gift, but we must respect the preposition that sets "faith" off as personal response (*dia pisteos*). We do not magnify God if we say that God gives a gift that only he can receive, that he extends his gift from one position and then turns 180° to receive it from man also, because—so the reasoning goes—man, being "dead in sins," is *absolutely* dead, metaphysically as well as morally. Neither scripture, nor history, nor experience warrant the notion that the mortal state of sin means the metaphysical impossibility of faith. It is not a question of whether the sinner can choose the good, or remake his life, or act at the level of his highest aspirations. It is the question of whether he can receive a gift for which he cannot take credit, a question whether he exists as a sinful *man* or merely exists as a sinful abstraction.

He who comes to God must come believingly, diligently, and ready to receive the promised "Spirit of grace." "In spirit" he receives "the Spirit"; through (*dia*) faith he receives the grace of God. The giving is totally God's to do, and the receiving in faith is the wisest, most commendable, and most integrative (of one's whole psyche) act that man ever does. At this point I can hear someone crying, "foul," by saying, "You are making faith into a meritorious work." Never. It is a response *to God*, not something done *before God*; a "work" must be independent if it is to provide grounds for a man's own boasting. But the remarkable thing about faith is that while it is no basis for man's boasting before God, it is *the basis for God's boasting in men*! Case in point: the hall of faith in Hebrews eleven, including such suffering men of faith of whom "the world was not worthy." God is pleased by faith and honors it—even though it is only a *response* to him. The faith-response is not passive, as though we were only spectators. John glimpsed a beautiful scene in the revelation of Jesus and inquired as to the identity of the white-robed people who surrounded and served the Lamb on the throne of God. The answer underscores the *active* character of faith: "These are they who . . . have washed their robes and made them white in the blood of the Lamb." *They* washed them!

III. The Holiness and Vulnerability of "the Spirit of Grace"

The contact of Holy Spirit and human spirit must be taken into consideration with all seriousness. There is no place for the wicked man to hide from God except in his own evil heart. God is not to be accused of spiritual assault or breaking and entering. God respects man's identity as a person, even if men do not always respect each other as such. The entrance of the divine Spirit into one's life is a stupendous and unforgettable event deemed worthy of celestial celebration—a party given by the angels—and is as traumatic as being born! Moreover it is a holy experience for the man, for the Spirit is holy and sanctification is the predictable result of the Spirit's presence in one's life.

The theology of decrees claims that the entry of the Spirit in man is not extraordinary but a form of grace common to all, especially the reprobates. It views man as totally depraved, which is defined by its advocates variously all the way from total moral turpitude to total inability to respond to God. But then how does one account for man as you find him in Scripture or in experience? If man is a moral zero—or more precisely worse than nothing as a negative quantity, a despicable evil on the face of the earth—how then does one explain all that contradicts this view, for instance, in the many Gentiles who "do by nature what the law requires"? How does one explain any good thing that any man does? The answer according to decretal theology is fashioned by giving the Spirit another—and this time a nonredemptive—triple task: (1) to restrain the evil in man from full expression; (2) to encourage and enable man to do whatever good he does; (3) to impart the skills and good taste to man to perform cultural tasks. This tremendous task of "common grace" is called one of "the least recognized, but one of the most far-reaching activities of the Holy Spirit." [4] This kind of theology ultimately levels the New Testament with the Old Testament and makes John 7:37-39 inconsequential. On its own merits it depersonalizes man—if one so "totaled" can be any further depersonalized—because it robs him of all privacy. While natural revelation teaches us that all people "live and move . . . in God," we cannot construct the corollary that God "lives and moves in all men," as the theology alluded to demands, and liberal Quakerism dogmatizes.

The "image of God" remains in fallen man (Gen. 9:6) and as a micro-mini "god" (Ps. 82:6), he can do good—morally, socially, and culturally—even if he is lost and cannot find his way back to God. He can still copy God in certain remembered ways, even though he cannot commune with the *holy* God, toward whom he is "dead" in his sins. Holiness is the personal presence of God being what he is. That is a circular definition, and it only points to the indefinable grandeur of the presence that can be known only when experienced within one's life. To predicate to the Spirit daily and ceaseless operations within man, however, while denying the "holy" character of the Spirit's presence, belittles the Spirit beyond biblical recognition. The more accurate word than "belittles" is "depersonalizes," for the Spirit of God is thereby reduced to a function, a *deus ex machina*, needed to enforce decrees and explain that which runs counter to a system of supposed divine totalitarianism.

God *has* set a moral censor in man to restrain the evil and encourage the good, but the biblical term for this guard of morality is "conscience" and not the Holy Spirit. God has given man as man the capacity to create culture, to produce that which will outlast his temporal mortality. He has the potential of being a creator and only he among the creatures of earth has this ability. It is his not by a special infusion of the Holy Spirit, but by virtue of the fact that his life was originally shaped "in the image of God," the Creator.

We must return to the thesis, therefore, that whenever the Spirit of God enters a person's life it means:

(1) that God comes as the holy One, whose holiness purifies the heart to which he comes and that God the Spirit cannot divest himself of his pervading holiness when he comes in.

(2) that God does not invade a person's privacy, but enters only where he is welcomed.

(3) that such entries of the Spirit of Jesus Christ into individuals is missing in the Old Testament (though a miniscule number of chosen individuals were "charismatized" to perform feats and services for Israel in the power of God's Holy Spirit. John the Baptist was the greatest of the prophets, yet the least person in the kingdom of God has the Spirit of grace in a manner John did not have.

(4) that such an entry of the Spirit into one's inner man is the identifying characteristic of the post-resurrection-of-Jesus faith of the New Testament, and that ontologically, a New Testament new creature is one who has received the Spirit of Christ.

(5) that the one New Testament word that best describes the New Testament coming of the Spirit into a life is "grace," and that to speak of any activity of God as "grace" that does not include the overcoming of sin by the life of the Spirit within is to obfuscate "grace" beyond biblical recognition.

God is so great in his moral excellence, so absolute in his goodness, so full in his love, that he can expose himself to the agony of rejected love without bitterness or change. He can compress his grandeur into a One-to-one meeting with man with all the risks for him that such an encounter involves. He does not have to play it safe and meet a man reduced to zero in a One-to-it (a 'dead' abstraction) relationship. On the contrary, in Jesus, where all God's nature was gloriously displayed, we see him loving his own until the end of his mortal life (John 13:1), and we see him forgiving without their intercession those who were attempting to rob him of his life by nailing him to a cross. He gave his life, making it impossible for him to be robbed of it.

The doctrine of the deity of Christ will not let us think of "God" as being expressed elsewhere than in Jesus as to his corporeality. Scripture teaches that he is the image of the invisible God (Col. 1:15; Heb. 1:3). We are only, then, paraphrasing scripture when we say that man has slapped and punched God in his mortal face, that man has spit upon the deity—and that Jesus did not spit back! It is heartbreaking to hold that scene even momentarily in mental view. But it was true. God is like that. He can be hurt by his creatures, and we must conclude from biblical history as well as all history up to the present that we are not speaking of an isolated *modus operandi* of God in the first century. God has always been secure in himself, yet relationally vulnerable.

This relational vulnerability, this *personal* openness to frustration—to use the theological term—this *passibility of God* over against his creation is the enormous cost he is willing to bear that his grace may be freely offered and freely received. God's grace, to use a tautology, is no more and no less resistible than God himself. To treat God's grace as if it were irresistible will asserting itself robs grace of all its glory. The glory of "predestination" is its Christocentricity. Grace is glorious as God's supreme expression of himself in man precisely because it is uncompelled. It is as magnificent and tender as Jesus was in his dealings with people. It is grounded in God's love ("God so loved the world...") and calls man to return God's love ("My son, give me your heart"). Grounding grace in intransigent will and hidden decrees would caricature God as a monolithic monster, would make grace as faceless as law (but see 2 Cor. 4:6), and would exchange the openness of the future under the living God for fatalism. What is even worse, as the most elementary logic would demand, we would have to insist that God alone was culpable for having opened the polluted watergate of sin in the world. But biblical revelation says: "...sin came into the world through one man..." (Rom. 5:12).

Culpability in God would be lethal for theology. Vulnerability in God, on the other hand, is not offensive to a true theology. God's vulnerability is not grounded in finitude but in the personal shape and perfection of God's being. It is his glory to reveal himself under the conditions of vulnerability. If we deny this, then we have no grounds upon which to accept the fact of the incarnation. In a sense Jesus may have suffered as much or more when the rich and legally righteous young ruler came to him as he suffered in Pilate's hall. Jesus "loved" (*agapao*—Mark 10:21) that upright leader of men who retreated from him and went away despondently. I wonder if Jesus may have mused: "Alas, we put him on the enemies list by eternal decree; I must bring my emotions into line with divine will." Never! His love was not a masked hate; that would have been out of character for Jesus. His love was real and the tragedy of that man's momentous decision is matched in pathos by the Lord's own vulnerability on that occasion.

Having dealt at length with the nature of "the Spirit of grace" (Heb. 10:29) and the vulnerability of that Spirit in the concourse of God-man relationships, it becomes unnecessary here to explicate in detail all the ways in which man rejects God to his own detriment and damnation. The Spirit can be slandered—that is, blasphemed (Matt. 12:32; Mark 3:28-29)—resisted resolutely (Acts 7:51), insulted by apostasy (Heb. 6:4-6; 10:26-31), put out like fire (1 Thess. 5:19), refused (Heb. 12:25), and grieved (Eph. 4:30). Grace can be frustrated (Gal. 2:21), emptied of effect (2 Cor. 6:1), and no longer the ground under one who turns to another means of justification (Gal. 5:4). To turn to the positive possibility, we see men of faith interacting with God and being taken seriously by God. Moses, for instance, pled with God for mercy for the rebellious Israelites after the golden calf incident, and "The Lord," he said, "hearkened to me that time also" (Deut. 9:19).

When we move to the New Testament scene man stands in faith, not before relentless. Will, nor inscrutable decrees fixed forever beyond him, but he stands before "the throne of grace" (Heb. 4:16). It is God's willingness to give that makes his throne (i.e., rulership or decisive administration) such a wonderful place. What God gives there, whatever its full extent, always includes himself in the gift. God's Spirit is given and that experience is properly called grace, because the primary transaction at "the throne of grace" is to dispense Jesus' fullness (John 1:17) by "the Spirit of grace."

When all this age is past and time has run out for all who would construct their lives without God, there will be, nevertheless, myriads of grace-made people. When the elements disappear under them and the sky dissolves over them, they will stand secure in grace under the rainbow of love, as the spectacle of the new creation unfolds before them. God will have a people who joyously return his love. They will radiate forever the love of Christ, a love the limitless dimensions of which, wrote the Apostle Paul, are truly *inscrutable* (Eph. 3:19).

NOTES

1. Paul Tillich, *Systematic Theology*, Vol. 2. (Chicago, Ill.: University of Chicago Press, 1957), pp. 11-12; *Biblical Religion and the Search for Ultimate Reality* (same publisher, Phoenix edition, 1964), pp. 25-34; *Christianity and the World Religions* (New York: Columbia University Press, 1963), p. 88; *The Courage to Be* (New Haven: Yale University Press, 1952), pp. 186-190.

2. Whether this position be called hyper-Calvinism or not, it was the plain and clear teaching of John Calvin in his most influential theological work: *Institutes of the Christian Religion*, Book III, chapter 21, section 5.

3. John Greenleaf Whittier, *The Complete Poetical Works of John Greenleaf Whittier* (Boston, Mass.: Houghton Mifflin Co., 1848, 1894), pp. 459-60.

4. Edwin H. Palmer, *The Holy Spirit* (Philadelphia, Pa.: Presbyterian and Reformed Publishing Co., 1971), p. 29. See.the entire chapter, "The Holy Spirit and Common Grace," 29-39, in which Palmer insists repeatedly that this intensive and extensive working of the Holy Spirit in the reprobates has no *saving* values for them since they were rejected by decree eternally. Saul in the Old Testament is cited as a probable example.

5

Responsible Freedom and the Flow of Biblical History

CLARK H. PINNOCK

Introduction

One of the deepest of all human intuitions, even in those persons with philosophical, theological, or psychological misgivings, is the sense of freedom to determine what they shall do and what they shall be.[1] Universal man almost without exception talks and feels *as if* he were free. He perceives himself to be a person capable of rising above his situation, of shaping his life and destiny, and of making a significant impact upon history. This fundamental self-perception is, I believe, an important clue as to the nature of reality. For if the world were a completely determined structure on which no decision of man's would have any effect, that basic intuition of man's that he is an *actor* and a free *agent,* would be nonsensical: there would then be no point to his making plans or exerting efforts intended to transform the world. As Gordon D. Kaufman says:

> In such a situation men could at most conceive themselves as spectators of the passing scene, never as actors in or on it. If the human experiences associating with acting—speaking and listening, observing, planning, studying, imagining, deciding, intending, working—are to be rendered intelligible, it is necessary to conceive man himself as an active agent, in some measure free, creative, and self-determining, and the world in which he lives as plastic and open (to some extent) to human intentions and purposes.[2]

Just how deep this intuition lies may be seen in numerous familiar facts: for example in the fact that human freedom is the precondition of moral and intellectual responsibility, or in the fact that the laws of all civilized societies distinguish between actions performed with deliberate intent and those which are involuntary or unintentional. We listen respectfully to one another's opinions because we believe such utterances are not determined by nonrational fancies. We accept praise and blame because we know ourselves to be free moral agents. Of course genetic inheritance and environmental conditioning *affect* our decisions deeply. But that is not to say they wholly *determine* them. Although we cannot change the past, we can reject it, and to some extent choose what we wish to have influence us. Man's radical freedom to take responsibility for his actions has of course received vigorous defense from the existential philosophers for whom authentic human existence consists in commitment and decision, creativity and individuality, courage and resolve.

When faced with a decision, we *know* with a subjective certainty that we can take one of the two or more alternatives before us. For that reason, we often find ourselves disturbed or perplexed in the face of it. If we believed that our decision was predetermined, we would no doubt cease worrying about the problem and permit ourselves to be swept away by the strongest desire, and would eventually fall into deep resignation and black despair at the sheer pointlessness of our living and acting.

What should we take this intuition of freedom to imply for our understanding of human nature? It is, after all, a massive piece of primary evidence on this subject. Surely it requires us to defend the validity of first person "actor" language for describing human decision making. While it may often be fruitful within the "spectator" language of the scientist to assume that every event has a cause and to search constantly for regularity and predictability, it is not enough to look at complex human behavior solely from that angle. Human reality is large enough to require *both* languages to describe it. So when a theory comes along, whether philosophical, theological, or psychological, which endeavors to deny this intuition of freedom, it is up against a basic human self-perception that will eventually overwhelm it.[3]

When we turn to the Bible, this natural conviction about human freedom is confirmed and strengthened. Man is viewed in Scripture as a responsible agent, created in the likeness of God, who must account morally to his Maker for the way in which he acts and for the decisions which he makes. What stands out in the biblical narrative is not what we might term a "blueprint" model of the universe in which everything is already decided, so that individual enterprises are smothered underneath an exhaustive divine decree (cf. Westminster Confession IV). What stands out rather is the strongly *personal* character of God and his dealings with mankind. The blueprint model of history is mechanistic and sub-personal. It thinks of history as frozen and God as the master manipulator. This is simply not the manner in which the Bible speaks of these things. History, according to the biblical understanding, is a two-sided affair, in which man plays a very significant role, and not at all a frozen situation. In the Old Testament, by way of a preliminary illustration, we find Moses, speaking in the name of the Lord and exhorting the people to *choose* life rather than death, a decision which they could and ought to make (Deut. 30:19). In the New Testament, to take another example, in the parable of the wedding feast, it is assumed that all those who were invited to come could either accept the invitation or refuse it. When some did in fact refuse it, Jesus did not ascribe as a reason for their decision any action or intervention of the king who desired them to come, but attributed the refusal simply to the *will* of those who declined to come ("They would not come," Matt. 22:3). As Jesus on another occasion said to his critics, "You refuse to come to me that you may have life" (John 5:40).

God's dealings with his human creation are dynamic and personal and the responses that we make to him have far-reaching consequences. "He who sows to his own flesh will from the flesh reap corruption; but he who sows to the Spirit will from the Spirit reap eternal life" (Gal. 6:8). An effective exercise by which to have this truth borne home to us in a fresh way is to retell the biblical story and allow it to create its own impression on us. When we do that, all dark thoughts of determinism, fatalism, and "blueprint-predestination" fall away, and we become impressed with the clear biblical witness to significant human freedom.[4]

In seeking to establish the full reality of man's freedom, we are not motivated by any desire to rob God of the glory which is due him as ruler over all. We wish merely to observe that the rule of God according to the Bible does not reduce men to *automata*, nor make the conflict between their sinful desires and God's loving purposes an illusion or a charade. We honor God truly when we characterize his sovereignty in a biblical manner, that is, in a personal rather than a mechanistic way, and when we interpret our human nature as God has actually described it in his Word and written it upon our hearts.[5]

I. The Creation of Man

The doctrine of creation in the Christian system of truth refers to the purposive act of God whereby he has called into existence out of nothing a finite reality alongside himself, in and through which to work out his loving purposes. The doctrine identifies the ultimate origin and source of all finite being, the spatio-temporal context in which all of history unfolds. Although the creation narrative in Genesis should not be ransacked for anticipations of modern science, or for that matter dismissed casually because it does not speak the language of the modern academy, it would be wrong to interpret it simply as a mythical or timeless expression for the relationship of finite being to the infinite, a symbol of a static ontological or structural relationship rather than a mighty act of God at the beginning of time. To do that, empties the concept of creation of its historical meaning in the biblical narrative where creation refers to the initiating activity of God when he established the world, and created the context in which all subsequent history unfolds.

Having called the universe into being, and after creating organic life in plant and animal varieties, God introduced a qualitatively new kind of being—man, a creature who through the exercise of his freedom would be able to shape his own future, a "godlike" creature able to set purposes for himself, to decide and act and achieve, and thus to transform even himself within the historical process. Man is that creature endowed by God with the power to make history and create his future. The account of creation in Genesis 1 portrays God the Creator as a conscious personal will acting purposively by means of his word. For man to be created in the "image of God" can only mean that he has been made to reflect the personhood of God and made capable like him of self-awareness, of self-determination and of responsible conduct. Man is a free agent and not a machine. Because of his nature, man is the visible representative on earth of the invisible Lord, and is meant to exercise his powers in having dominion over the other creatures responsibly as unto his Maker.

The biblical story of the creation of man shows Adam to be living in fellowship with God, and able to choose between loving obedience and rebellious disobedience, enjoying free will in the fullest sense, acting without any coercion. This ability of his to exercise options makes man unique among creatures. Mountains, rivers, plants, even animals, are not able to determine what they will be. The salmon seems to select one stream over another, but it turns out to be the one in which the fish was hatched, the choice being really dictated by instinct. Only man is capable of a free and creative response to his Creator, and able to enter into personal fellowship with him and to take an active part in the shaping of history and his own life.

That is not to say that man creates himself *ex nihilo,* or to deny that the decisions and actions of his fellowman affect him deeply. The free human self develops within *communities* and not off by itself in isolation. All of us are aware of having grown out of the past, of having been shaped by past decisions and actions, both our own and those of others, and also know ourselves to be moving into an open future which will in turn be shaped by the decisions which we are now making.

It has been argued, for example by Antony Flew, that the very idea of creation is incompatible with free will. If God be creator, he contends, he must also be the cause and controller of every thought and action throughout his wholly dependent universe.[7] But this is not so. God can create such beings as he wills, and he has in fact according to the Bible chosen to create some beings with a capacity for free choice. There is nothing philosophically unacceptable in that.[8]

Why did God make man thus? Why did he give to him the gift of freedom which makes sin and evil possible? C. S. Lewis has stated the biblical answer well:

> Because free will, though it makes evil possible, is also the only thing that makes possible any love or goodness or joy worth having. A world of automata—of creatures that worked like machines—would hardly be worth creating. The happiness which God designs for His higher creatures is the happiness of being freely, voluntarily united to Him and to each other in an ecstasy of love and delight compared with which the most rapturous love between a man and a woman on this earth is mere milk and water. And for that they must be free.[9]

This freedom that man was given seems to have been the necessary prerequisite to a deeper knowledge of God. The devotion of a free, rational being is of greater worth and beauty than that of any other creature.

II. The Fall of Man

With the creation of man, we now have God the Creator working out his purposes within the world, and alongside him a race of finite, human creatures able to act and project their intentions. No problem would arise so long as these finite human purposes coincided with the overall divine plan. The course of such a history would continue to express God's will and goals in harmony with man's. However, if by a misuse of their freedom, these creatures should deviate from the divine purpose, an awful tension would begin to show itself within history, and forces at odds with each other and at cross purposes with the divine would begin to transform the previously harmonious situation into a chaotic one, a warfare of purposes. This is what has actually happened in the fall of Adam. Evidently God in his decision to create man placed a higher value on freedom than on sinless conformity to his will. The fall of man into sin convinces us that the course of history is not laid out in advance as a kind of inflexible blueprint. God's plan for mankind does not involve a manipulation of man from behind the scenes. His will consists rather of general purposes or aims for beings who are themselves genuinely free and creative, and who have significant power to shape the course of history.

The fall of Adam was the point in human history when, just as human freedom was becoming a reality, man began to act in a way that was contrary to the will of God and disruptive of the historical process. This is the meaning of the Fall, and the reason why it is so important to uphold its basic historicity. The account is not to be interpreted in terms of a pictorial myth describing the relationship between each sinner and God, even though it also serves that purpose admirably.[10] According to Genesis, and its use by Paul (Rom. 5:12), the Fall is a historical event, antedating all of history and determining its idolatrous character. It denotes the time when man began to work against God's purposes for him, and in a manner actually destructive of his own welfare. In this tragic act of deliberate rebellion, Adam loosed into the world all of those negative historical forces which have not yet been quelled and which in our day threaten to annihilate mankind. To take the Fall to be myth or "saga," and not genuine history, is to shatter the consistency and meaning of the biblical understanding of history and the divine solution to its dilemmas. Let us be clear that when orthodox Christians insist upon the historical character of the Fall, they do not do so out of blind conservatism, but because they see the value of an ancient, but not at all outdated, biblical truth.[11] Gordon D. Kaufman writes:

> Despite the lack of direct historical documentation, however, the fall should be regarded as a genuinely historical event or process; for we cannot understand the continuing historical processes, filled as they are with hatred and disharmony, guilt and mistrust, without presupposing an earlier one through which these came to be what they are.[12]

In a real sense, did the Bible not describe a primeval fall into sin, we would have to postulate one to account for what has ensued.

The fall of man into sin through the misuse of the divinely given freedom constitutes an important clue as to the nature of God's rule. For at this point in history man *vetoed* God's will, deliberately disobeyed his commandments, and willfully rejected his plans. Like the Pharisees and lawyers later on, Adam "rejected the purpose of God" for himself (Luke 7:30). The Fall demonstrates conclusively that God's will is not something that is always done regardless. On the contrary, it is something that can be successfully rejected and contravened. History is the scene of a real struggle between God and the powers of darkness in which man is a combatant, and this conflict is not a fake or a mere appearance, one in which God is directing both sides.[13] God's loving purpose for man can be and has been defied by his human creatures who have chosen to go deliberately against what he had planned. The Fall simply cannot be interpreted deterministically without contradicting the character of the God of the Bible and making him the cause of sin. Boettner's sentiments must be completely repudiated when he writes:

> Even the fall of Adam, and through him the fall of the race, was not by chance or accident, but was so ordained in the secret counsels of God.[14]

Such a position almost makes God into the devil. It arises from an inability to understand the will of God dynamically, as something which is not always and automatically done.

There is a theological theory widely maintained in evangelical circles that Scripture teaches on the one hand that God has divinely decreed all that comes to pass, and on the other that man is a responsible moral agent. Although these two concepts sound like a contradiction, we are told not to object because the Bible teaches them both, and we have no right to protest. The word "antinomy" is used in this connection to describe what appears to be a logical contradiction, and the theory is often dignified by a reference to the physical nature of light whose properties require it to be discussed in terms of both particles and waves even though these two models appear to be contradictory.[15] It seems so neat to be able to say that a given act is both the product of the divine first cause, and also be the product of the human second cause. Could not second causes be completely subordinate to God as first cause, but nevertheless remain genuine and actual causes? After all, what proof is there, Gerstner asks, that if God predestinates something to happen that he has to *force* someone to do it? Surely it is possible for God to predestinate an act to come to pass *by means* of the deliberate choices of individuals.[16]

We do not need to pause over the philosophical merits of this theory as a general cosmological rule (who is to say where God's possibilities end?),[17] because it breaks down so badly on the theological and moral front. Is *sin* also wholly a product of the divine first cause as well as the human second cause? Surely it is not! It is simply blasphemous to maintain, as this theory does, that man's rebellion against God is *in any sense* the product of God's sovereign will or primary causation. The fall of man is an eloquent refutation to the theory that God's will is always done; and helps to disclose to us the true nature of divine predestination. God has overarching purposes for man and for history. He is working (or, "energizing," Eph. 1:11), in all things to bring about reconciliation through Christ. These plans of his will certainly come to fruition. But in working them out he does not have to resort to imposing himself on man in such a way as to violate human freedom, creativity and personality. On the contrary, he works out his plan in the context of human decisions and personality.

Predestination should be seen to refer primarily to the comprehensive purpose of God which is *the structural context* in which history moves and from which it receives its meaningful form and direction. To use an illustration, when my father decided to emigrate to Canada, he "predetermined" me to be a Canadian, and "decreed" that Canada should be the locale in which my own life and freedom should develop. This "predestination" of course did not nullify my own freedom; rather it provided for me *certain prior conditions for its exercise.* In an analogous way, God's will and plan does not conflict with human freedom; it provides the prior condition for it to operate the meaningful historical process which would serve as the context for man's decisions even if those should conflict with God's. And it is perfectly plain from the biblical story that men can and do reject God's will and plan for them.[18]

III. The Cycle of Cumulative Degeneration

Man's history with all its turmoil and strife is rooted in the primeval fall of Adam into sin, the inheritance of which like an avalanche has been rolling down through the centuries with ever-increasing volume. The world that we experience is no longer the world that God made. In his passion for self-glorification, man has cast off the divine rule and authority, and created a situation (yes, man is the creator of something!) in which his own life is threatened with dissolution. As Paul teaches in Romans 1, his turning away from God has resulted in greater and greater degeneration, disobedience, and destructiveness. Instead of history being the context in which genuinely free persons could emerge and develop, and exist within communities of love and trust, the historical process has become increasingly destructive of healthy human life, and genuine community seems only able to be able to exist on a fragmentary and tenuous basis. Kaufman writes:

> Because of his alienation from God and resultant anxiety, man in history became an idolater worshipping a multitude of false gods. In consequence he became enslaved to demonic powers which, as they worked themselves out in history, brought chaos and doom.[19]

The tensions, disharmonies, warfare, and destructiveness with which history is full, those powers that are constantly striving to overcome the forces of love, freedom, and creativity, are to be understood theologically as the direct and inevitable *consequence* of the fall of man. The Fall set into motion a cycle of cumulative degeneration with disastrous historical and human consequences. It has resulted in a situation of man's moral autonomy but also his estrangement from God and anxiety. For individuals it has meant attaching themselves to some finite reality such as money or power or pleasure, and striving to secure one's life by means of them, or else withdrawing from the struggles of existence, retreating from life itself. Cut off from his true orientation in a loving relationship with God, man is obviously lost, and strives to find a substitute god in the finite world at hand.

In the book of Genesis we read the familiar story of the ongoing rebellion of Adam's children. Sin has grown to fuller maturity. Cain rises up to murder his brother Abel, an act which even God cannot talk him out of, and afterward, he neither confesses to it nor accepts punishment for it. In the family of Cain we see the beginnings of civilized life with its potentiality for good and evil, a culture which offers no hope for salvation. The only gleam of hope appears when men began to call upon the name of the Lord (4:26). But despite this, the effects of the Fall are so intense that the writer concludes with an emphatic statement about the wickedness of the human heart.

> The Lord saw that the wickedness of man was great in the earth, and that every imagination of the thoughts of his heart was only evil continually. (6:5)

This rebellion so pained the heart of God, so contrary was it to his own loving purposes for man, that, in a strikingly anthropomorphic expression, the writer says, "And the Lord was sorry that he had made man on the earth, and it grieved him to his heart" (6:6). It is the Old Testament way of saying, in characteristically bold terms, how fundamentally opposite and contrary are the purposes of God and purposes of sinful man as these have been shaped out of the Fall.

After the story of the Flood we read about a tower of Babel, where we see mankind cooperating together to resolve their problems, not by turning in loving obedience to the Lord, but by intensifying their opposition to him. What a perfect picture we have of the ambiguity of man's cultural efforts, so glorious and proud, and yet infected by the poison of sin. How appropriate it is that this story, in which we see sin in full maturity, as we also see it around us in the world today, should stand immediately before the call of Abraham. The Fall has worked itself into history in full measure. The results of man working at cross purposes with God are clearly visible. The tensions, destructive powers, and strife are all present, threatening to annihilate mankind. At such a time, "in the fulness of time," the biblical story changes its key and God moves in, bringing redemption to man, working to reverse the chaotic historical movement man had created by the misuse of his freedom.

It is plain from this biblical account, as well as from our own experience, that all human history is deeply mired in the morass of sin, and that this history is the *context* in which human selves emerge, their communities are shaped, and their ideals are formed. It is not surprising that all of us are corrupted in the process of our formation and that we in turn become further corrupting powers since we are part and parcel of this kind of existence in which human beings are invariably distorted and warped. We are touching here upon the traditional doctrine of original sin. Sin is indeed "inherited," not in a biological sense, as Augustine argued, and certainly not because of a legal imputation of Adam's guilt, as in the federal theology, but *historically*. Man is shaped by the warped social situation into which he is born and in which he grows up to maturity.

Nevertheless, though corrupted by the historical process, and shaped by a twisted past, he cannot escape the realization that he is in a real sense responsible for the present and the future. Although he may wish to escape his responsibility and guilt by arguing that, as a victim of the past he cannot avoid, he ought not to be held responsible, he cannot do so, because he knows it to be otherwise, as Paul argues in Romans 2, and as all history testifies. He is not to blame his parents, as the prophet Ezekiel insists, but to face up to the fact that "the soul that sins shall die" (Ezek. 18:4). The *continuing* misuse of freedom is the basis of our personal responsibility before God. In spite of all extenuating circumstances, the bad conscience which follows a sinful action we perform testifies that we are indeed responsible agents. The Fall has not deprived man of his ability to choose. It rather initiated a historical process in which man uses his freedom in morally perverted ways. It did not nullify the fact of man's freedom; it only altered the moral direction of it. For this reason God continues to confront fallen man with the option of his grace.

> Behold, now is the acceptable time; behold, now is the day of salvation. (2 Cor. 6:2)

IV. The Counteractive Grace of God

History has become the scene where fallen men are working at cross purposes with God, a bleak picture indeed. It is hard to see any way out of the dilemma except by the coming into history of a new redemptive impulse from God's side. There is hope for man only if the power of God's love and reconciliation were to break into this sick history, healing it of its ills. Such a power would not arise immanently from the diseased body itself, but would have to break into the historical order from beyond it, from the God who created all things. This is the basic meaning of the call of Abraham. God is at work within history to turn back the effects of sin and to heal mankind. A man is called, and in him a people is prepared among whom a right relationship with God has been reestablished and through whom redemptive healing can spill over to the entire world. In concentrating upon a single man and a single people, the Old Testament does not mean to imply that God has lost his interest in the affairs of the whole world. As Amos was to remind the people of Israel later, God cares for each and every people within its particular place in history, each having a special role to play (Amos 9:7). In choosing Abraham and ultimately the children of Israel, God was preparing a vehicle of blessing to all the nations of earth (Gen. 12:3, Isa. 49:6). Israel was, to use Barth's terminology, a "provisional representation" of what God desires for all peoples, desiring as he does for all men to be saved and come to a knowledge of the truth (1 Tim. 2:4).

It needs to be said emphatically that the choosing of Abraham has nothing to do with choosing one man to be saved and leaving the rest to perish. God's purpose in calling Abraham is to prepare a people which would serve to bless the whole earth. It is a central aspect of God's strategy to implement his universal saving will. This choice was not for Abraham's benefit alone, but beyond him to Israel and finally to all nations. God does not have a secret plan according to which he only desires to save some. He does not delight in the death of the wicked (Ezek. 18:32). He is not willing that any should perish (2 Pet. 3:9). In Jesus Christ God has declared himself for the salvation of all sinners, and there is no "secret will" of his that has decided otherwise. Jesus

Christ is the revelation of God's "secret plans," and it was for the whole world that he was delivered up.

This is the second point at which the theory of an "antinomy" between blueprint-predestination and human freedom breaks down. If God's sovereignty meant that his will is always done and performed down to the smallest detail, it would mean that his will is also accomplished in the lostness of the lost. But that is not the case. God holds out his hands to those who will not listen to him (Rom. 10:21). He gives his Holy Spirit to those who resist the gift (Acts 7:51). Jesus desired to gather the Jews to himself, but they refused him (Matt. 23:37). Scripture requires us to reject the notion that God's will is always done. There is nothing in Scripture that teaches that God wills that men remain impenitent and perish. People perish because they reject God's plan for them and refuse to do the Father's bidding and for no other reason. It is because, as Isaiah puts it, "when I called, you did not answer, when I spoke, you did not listen, but you did what was evil in my eyes, and chose what I did not delight in" (65:12). It would be difficult in the extreme to try to defend the Christian doctrine of hell if it were true that people ended up there because God secretly willed it.

What was notable about Abraham was his faith, his responsiveness to the divine will. "He *believed* the Lord; and he reckoned it to him as righteousness" (Gen. 15:6). As the writer to the Hebrews put it, "By faith Abraham *obeyed* when he was called to go out to a place which was to receive as an inheritance" (Heb. 11:8). Salvation in the Bible is by the grace of God and is *conditioned* on an obedient response, apart from which it is not actualized. The vast importance of this response is indicated in Hebrews again: "For the good news came to us just as to them; but the message which they heard did not benefit them, because it did not meet with faith in the hearers" (4:2). Abraham is the father of a new people because he was one who heeded the divine call, and although his descendants since then have not always been as responsive as he was to God, nevertheless, within this very community, in its faithful leaders and prophets, in its humble, believing saints, there has always existed a right understanding and response to God which delights his heart. "The friendship of the Lord is for those who fear him, and he makes known to them his covenant" (Ps. 25:14). In the womb of this people, the seed of Abraham, a new possibility for man has emerged, the possibility of entering into a right relationship with God and with fellowman, which is the goal of our being.

Needless to say, this responsiveness on Abraham's part is not a meritorious work of righteousness. Paul makes it clear that salvation is conditioned on faith *so that* it might be based on grace alone (Rom. 4:5, 16). Faith is not working, but trusting in God to save us. It therefore excludes all boasting (Rom. 3:27). To receive the free gift of salvation is not a *work* of any kind. There is no cause in it for any self-congratulation. Abraham was called and used of God, not because he was morally better than others, but because he gladly received God's word and obeyed him.

Even as human history since the Fall has been racing downwards to perdition, God has been working to enter history, with his word of love and healing. Beginning with Abraham, and after a long historical preparation, culminating in Jesus Christ, there has come forth a new human community made up of all the nations, the firstfruits of the community of love and peace which God had intended mankind to be.

Conclusion

It is not necessary to move beyond the book of Genesis to see the basic pattern in the relationship between God and his human creatures. What we detect in this story is not some dark predestinarian decree operating behind the scenes making sure everything works out right. What we do encounter is the freedom of God to respond, positively and negatively to man's freedom. God weaves into his plan for history the significant choices that we make. History is not a computer print-out of programmed decisions set long before by an all-determining Deity. It is much more like a dialogue between the Father and his human respondants. As Rahner put it:

> History is not just a play in which God puts himself on the stage and creatures are merely what is performed; the creature is a real co-performer in this humano-divine drama of history.[20]

God is a person and men are personal, made in his image. Therefore, he deals with man as a person, and allows the creature to be himself. The world is not simply a pure function of the Deity. There is a divinely intended *two-sidedness* in the relationship between God and man. The dialogue is completely real. When God gives his Word, man can either harden his heart or accept it. He can receive the Spirit or resist him. He can obey God's law or refuse to. He can repudiate God's plan of salvation, or accept it. The flow of biblical history shows clearly that God's activity among men is not a kind of *monologue* which God conducts on his own; it is on the contrary a dramatic *dialogue* between God and the creature. History is taken with full seriousness. There is a working together, and also a working against, of God and the created spirits.

We freely grant that the Augustinians, the upholders of a strong doctrine of predestination, do not wish to deny but rather defend the reality of human freedom. They wish to maintain the complete sovereignty of God together with the freedom of man.[21] But they are unable to do so because the Bible does not present an antinomy of this kind. God's will hidden or revealed is not done in the fall and sin of man, nor is it done in the final perdition of the impenitent. These things cannot and must not be ascribed to any all-encompassing decree of his. They occur because God refuses to mechanize man or to force his will upon him. Within the intrinsic limits of finitude, God lets him remain independent and free to create new situations which God himself has not willed. And in that case he does not give man up but rather accepts the new situation, drawing from it such consequences as man certainly does not expect or foresee but which will finally work for the actualizing of his love (Rom. 8:28).

NOTES

1. For a masterful survey in depth of the entire ground, see Mortimer J. Adler, *The Idea of Freedom: A Dialectical Examination of the Conceptions of Freedom*, two vols. (Garden City, N.Y.: Doubleday & Co., 1958, 1961).

2. Gordon D. Kaufman, *God the Problem* (Cambridge, Mass.: Harvard University Press, 1972), p. 104.

3. See Ian G. Barbour, *Issues in Science and Religion* (New York: Harper and Row, 1966), pp. 309-314.

4. We wish to acknowledge at the outset a great indebtedness in our exposition to Gordon D. Kaufman, *Systematic Theology: A Historicist Perspective* (New York: Scribner's Sons, 1968), especially parts 2 and 3.

5. This essay in its own way is a study of the doctrine of predestination, and the reader is referred also to the essays by I. H. Marshall and D. J. A. Clines in this volume which treat this subject in a different manner.

6. See Walther Eichrodt, *Theology of the Old Testament* (Philadelphia, Pa.: Westminster, 1967), II, pp. 122-131: D. J. A. Clines, "The Image of God in Man," *Tyndale Bulletin* 19 (1968), 53-103.

7. A. Flew, *God and Philosophy* (London: Hutchinson, 1966), p. 47.

8. H. P. Owen, *Concepts of Deity* (New York: Herder and Herder, 1971), p. 9.

9. C. S. Lewis, *Mere Christianity* (London: Collins, 1952), p. 49.

10. It was Kierkegaard who attempted to give the Fall an existential interpretation, and his example has been followed by most modern theologians. In reading the narrative it is certainly easy to see oneself in it. That need not imply, however, that it is not also and primarily the story of a *past event*.

11. Francis A. Schaeffer makes it clear how strongly he feels about this matter. "Take away the first three chapters of Genesis, and you cannot maintain a true Christian position nor give Christianity's answers." *The God Who Is There* (London: Hodder and Stoughton, 1968), p. 104.

12. Gordon D. Kaufman, *Systematic Theology: A Historicist Perspective* (New York: Scribner's Sons, 1968), p. 353.

13. This is the theme of an excellent book on this subject by Roger T. Forster and V. Paul Marston, *God's Strategy in Human History* (Wheaton, Ill.: Tyndale House, 1974).

14. Loraine Boettner, *The Reformed Doctrine of Predestination* (Philadelphia, Pa.: Presbyterian and Reformed, 1965), p. 234.

15. See J. I. Packer, *Evangelism and the Sovereignty of God* (London: IVP, 1961), chapter two.

16. John H. Gerstner, *A Predestination Primer* (Grand Rapids, Mich.: Baker, 1963), p. 26.

17. It is surely a *real* contradiction however to assert (1) that God determines all events, and (2) that man is free to accept or reject his will. Fortunately Scripture does not require us to attempt logical gymnastics of this kind. It does not teach that God "determines" all things.

18. At this point we must refer the reader to a very important appendix in Forster and Marston, *God's Strategy in Human History*, pp. 243-296. It is most unfortunate that for many people today Augustine's views on election and predestination are taken to be the biblical ones whereas in fact they are not.

19. Kaufman, *Systematic Theology*, p. 375.

20. Karl Rahner, *Theological Investigations* volume I (Baltimore: Helicon, 1961), p. 111.

21. See, for example, J. W. Wenham, *The Goodness of God* (Chicago, Ill.: IVP, 1974). Compare pp. 51-54 and pp. 186-187.

6

Predestination in the Old Testament

DAVID J. A. CLINES

When we turn to the Bible with our questions about pre-destination, we are running the risk of committing two errors. First, we may fail to see the whole range of the biblical revelation on the subject because *we* have chosen the categories and terms that are going to count as answers to our questions. Secondly, we may mistake the relative importance of the biblical teaching on the subject because *we* are focusing on that subject. Perhaps the Bible does *not* focus on that subject, but only sees it in relationship to something else. But we may give the doctrine, biblical though it is, not its truly biblical significance, but the significance it has come to have for us in our particular stream of theological tradition.

The errors that can be made are, then, errors about the *form* and the *role* of predestinarian thought in the Bible. The best way to minimize such errors is to look at the biblical teaching as a whole. But since that not only is difficult but also affords plentiful opportunities for our own conceptions of what is important to enter in, perhaps the most practical method is to consider the parts of the Bible individually—at least to begin with. Certainly the method to be avoided is to build isolated verses from all parts of the Bible into a logical system, without regard for the larger contexts in which they occur or the overall thrust of the major parts of the Bible.[1]

The method adopted in this essay, therefore, is to examine some books of the Old Testament, from the historical, wisdom, and prophetic literature, with a view to discovering the form and role of predestinarian ideas in them.

I. The Historical Literature

A. *Genesis: The Patriarchal Histories*

Let us begin with the patriarchal histories (Gen. 12-50). The theme of these narratives, most simply stated, is the survival and growth of the family of Abraham. The dramatic unity of the stories, however, lies in the tension between the threats to the survival of the family and the divine promise that they will live and multiply (Gen. 12:2). The threats to survival follow in rapid succession: famine in the land of promise (12:10); Sarai, the wife through whom the promise is to be fulfilled, is taken into the Pharaoh's harem (12:11-20); Abraham's nephew Lot, his male heir, leaves the patriarchal family (ch. 13); Sarai is barren (ch. 16); Sarah falls prey to Abimelech (ch. 20); Ishmael, Abraham's son, is cast out from the family (ch. 21); Isaac, now his only heir, is offered as a sacrifice (ch. 22); Rebekah is barren (25:21); Rebekah and Isaac run the danger of death in Gerar (ch. 26); Esau plots to kill Jacob (27:42); Rachel is barren (30:1); famine drives Jacob and his family out of the promised land and into dangers in Egypt (42:1-4).

Here the *form* that predestination takes is the promise. God has long-term intentions for the Abrahamic family, which he alone will bring about—no word is spoken in Gen. 12:1-3 of conditions Abraham must fulfill.[2] That is surely a predestination. But the specific form that predestination takes is a promise of descendants, a land, divine blessing, and blessing to the Gentiles. That is, the predestining does not point Abraham's attention to immutable decrees established in eternity past, but to a future in which the destiny will progressively be realized. God's predestination is thus not a possession which Abraham and his descendants can count their own, but an announcement of what God will make of the patriarchal family. Abraham's response to the announcement will not be thanksgiving that everything has been settled long ago in the counsels of eternity, but *faith* in God that he will bring that destiny into being.

The promise (predestination) is for the sake of the Abrahamic family *and* of the Gentile nations. The text of Gen. 12:1-3 does not enable us to establish where the emphasis lies: Is it first and foremost on the blessing to Abraham, or climactically on the blessing to the nations? It is not important to decide the priority, but the dual direction of the promise *is* significant. The predestination is not for the sake exclusively of those who are predestined, but for the sake of world blessing;[3] but neither does it relegate them to a secondary role just because they are only part of God's larger intentions. Many traditional studies of predestination have erred in neglecting God's wider intentions that reach beyond his chosen people (Jews or Christians), but it is unnecessary to over-react to this misplaced emphasis with a hesitation to speak of God's predestination of the chosen people.

What now is the *role* of predestination in the patriarchal stories? It might be thought that since the divine promise precedes all that happens, there can be no real crises that call the promise into question but only an outworking of the divine intentions which is recognized by the actors in the story as inevitable. But that is plainly not the mood of the patriarchal narratives. The story is focused, as we have seen earlier, on the hazards which the promise faces just as much as it is on the promise itself. It is from the tension between the promise and the realities of life that the story gains its momentum. So the predestination is not the absolutely determinative factor in what happens. The story is as much about what happens *against* the promise as about how the promise is fulfilled.

That is not to deny that in one way or another everything that happens advances the fulfillment of the promise, or even, perhaps, that in retrospect God's predestination can be seen also in some happenings that were apparently against the promise. Thus Joseph can say that his bondage in Egypt, though plotted by the brothers, was equally intended by God (45:5; 50:20); and perhaps the same thing could be said truly enough of other reverses in the patriarchal fortunes. But that is precisely what these narratives do *not* keep on saying, and it would be wrong to insist that the narrator intends us to extrapolate Joseph's remarks to every detail of the histories. Whether or not it is true that God has planned *everything* in advance, all that the patriarchal stories show is the promise beset by hazards but moving towards fulfillment nevertheless. That is what Genesis 12-50 means by predestination.

B. *Genesis: The Primeval History*

The primeval history (Gen. 1-11) is, unlike the patriarchal history, a history without a promise. It is, in fact, a history in which predestination in general is conspicuous by its absence. We cannot here speak (with one or two exceptions) of the form or role that predestinarian ideas have, but only of what takes their place.

The movement of the primeval history is largely initiated by men; God's action is positive or negative response to the decisions of men. If Adam decides to become an independent being, determining for himself what is good and evil, God's response is to turn him loose from the garden and—make him independent. If Cain defiles the tilled ground with spilled blood, God responds by driving him away from the tilled ground that will no longer yield its strength to him. If man's wickedness spreads so drastically that the earth is "filled with violence" (6:11), God responds by being sorry that he has made man, and by determining to destroy mankind. If the men of Babel say, "Come, let us build a tower with its top in the heavens," God responds, even to the extent of imitating their speech, with: "Come, let us go down and destroy their tower" (11:4, 7). Yet also, when Adam and Eve sense their nakedness before God and prepare makeshift clothes, God responds to this appropriate sense of shame and provides proper clothes for them. When Cain shouts that his punishment, to be driven from the society of men *and* from the presence of Yahweh, is greater than he can bear, God responds even to the murderer and sets a mark on him to protect him from his fellows.

And where is the predestination in all this? To suppose that any of this catches God by surprise, or even that all of these human decisions are merely human decisions which God has to make the best of now that they have happened would doubtless be contrary to the spirit of the Old Testament. But the story does not stop to point to decrees established in the dark counsels of eternity. What is important in the story of mankind, Genesis 1-11 might well be saying, is not what God has already decided to do, but with what freedom he can respond, in mercy or judgment, to man's decisions,[4] creating good from evil and swallowing up wrath with mercy.

Though this is the major thrust of the primeval history, as I see it, there are some secondary elements that belong to the realm of predestination.

First, the creation story of Genesis 1 plainly envisages God creating everything with a *purpose*. The sun is created in order to rule the day, to distinguish day from night, to act as a marker of time. Man is created in order to rule on earth as God's viceregent. All living things are created according to their kind, that is, what they are and can be is a determinate part of the created order. God has not created an aimless, formless, indeterminate world, but a world of beautiful order where everything has a destiny: to be what God made it to be. Predestination in this sense, then, is an aspect of the doctrine of creation. Needless to say, this is not a predestination to salvation or damnation, but an affirmation of God's purposiveness in creation.

Secondly, there is a predestinarian type of idea in God's selection of Noah and his family to be saved from the flood. The story of Noah fits the pattern of the other narratives of the primeval history in that after the judgment upon man's sin is announced, grace intervenes and mitigates the punishment. But the Noah story is unlike the preceding narratives in that God's act of grace toward sinful humanity does not extend to all those who have sinned, but only to a chosen family, in whose salvation the human race will be kept alive. But why does God choose Noah to survive? It is not that Noah is the one righteous man on earth, to whose righteousness God can respond with salvation. For it is significant that God's favor rests on Noah (6:8) *before* any word is spoken of Noah's righteousness (6:9).[5] Here the form predestination takes is unmerited election.

Thirdly, from the perspective of Genesis 12, it becomes clear that a predestined goal was shaping the course of the primeval history. What would otherwise be a collection of unconnected episodes in Genesis 1-11 is seen from the standpoint of Genesis 12, to be a *sequence* that leads to Abraham. The primeval history itself has had no interest in stressing God's control of history, for its interest has been in God's freedom to respond to human decision. But in its setting in the book of Genesis the primeval history takes on a new significance: the primeval history is but the prelude to the story of the promise.

II. The Wisdom Literature

A. *Proverbs*

The heart of the theology of Proverbs is that good or bad deeds bring appropriate reward or punishment from God.

> A perverse man will be filled with the fruit of his ways and a good man with the fruit of his deeds. (14:14)
> The righteous is delivered from trouble, and the wicked gets into it instead. (11:8)
> He who is steadfast in righteousness will live, but he who pursues evil will die. (11:19)

That is, the destiny of men is determined by their own behavior. The *form* which predestination takes, then, in Proverbs' theology of reward is human self-determination. It is not God who decides whether a man shall be counted among the righteous and the wicked; it is his own actions that determine that. Thus Proverbs contains not only predictive proverbs, of the kind I have quoted, but also descriptive proverbs about what constitutes wickedness, folly, wisdom, sloth, prudence, generosity, deceit, so that a man may recognize himself and know his destiny.

Predestination in Proverbs is not contradictory to or incompatible with predestination as we have seen it in Genesis, but the emphasis is very different. Proverbs is not denying the promise to Abraham and his seed, but neither does it find it necessary to affirm it. When it is a matter of how a man should live his life, Proverbs is saying, *divine* predestination is not the point; what counts is how a man is destining his own future. No doubt there are ways in which divine predestination could be relevant to ethics: another Israelite teacher might well have exhorted his hearers to "walk worthy of the vocation with which you are called" (Eph. 4:1). But Proverbs does not choose that route. Proverbs of course does not claim to be the whole of Scripture, and it would be a mistake to regard the theology of Proverbs as the only valid way of looking at the question of ethics. But it is a legitimate position, and as such receives confirmation in the New Testament (see Rom. 2:6-10), even by Paul, whom most would regard as the New Testament's chief apostle of divine predestination.

Already something has been said about the *role* of predestination in Proverbs: in the sense of human self-predestination, it is central to the teaching of the book. But the role such predestination plays in the theology of Proverbs can be more carefully evaluated if we consider how God is related to this scheme of deed and retribution.

In the first place, it is clear that God is the one who brings reward or punishment. Yet it is noticeable that God's activity in this respect is not often explicit in Proverbs (10:29 is about the nearest Proverbs comes to saying it). More frequently good or bad seems to bring its own reward automatically: "The work of a man's hand comes back to him" (12:14).[6] It is not of course denied that this is God's doing, but the emphasis does not lie there. Secondly, and more important, God's relation to men's destiny is that he creates the path of life, which is wisdom, and summons men to follow that path. If a man is righteous, that is, in the terminology of Proverbs, if he has wisdom, it is not because he has inherently a good streak in him, but because he has been amenable to the teaching of the wisdom that is a gift from God. "Folly is bound up in the heart of a child, but the rod of discipline drives it far from him" (22:15). That "discipline" or "instruction" is ultimately "the Lord's discipline" (3:11), and the wisdom which the maturing child develops is regarded as "given" by God (2:6). So while growth in wisdom and goodness is a matter of effort and discipline, Proverbs' concept of wisdom as essentially God's creature (cf. 8:22-31) makes it impossible for a righteous man to regard his wisdom as his own achievement. In a word, a man prepares his own destiny, but if his destiny is life, he has God to thank, and not himself. But if a man is headed for destruction, he has only himself to thank for that.

Finally, having observed where the emphasis lies in Proverbs' teaching about predestination, we are perhaps in a better position to understand some sentences which apparently set forth a rigorous divine predestination:

> The LORD has made everything for its purpose, even the wicked for the day of trouble. (16:4)

Here might seem to be presupposed a doctrine of "double predestination," but what is really involved is the usual teaching of Proverbs about appropriate retribution. The word translated "purpose" is actually "answer," so a better translation would be:

> The LORD has made everything with its counterpart, so the wicked will have his day of doom.[7]

That is, the wicked man is on his way to his appropriate fate. However, this does not mean that his destiny is fixed and irreversible; iniquity *can* be atoned for (16:6), he need not remain wicked.

Again, when we find:

> The king's heart is a stream of water in the hand of the LORD; he turns it wherever he will (21:1),

we do not have some doctrinaire assertion that a king never makes any decisions of his own and is only a puppet in God's hand. That would be contrary to the general outlook of Proverbs, though the proverb in isolation could doubtless mean that. Rather, what is taught here is that God, the world's governor, cannot be thwarted even by kings, who are accustomed to having their own way. It is a variation on the theme of 21:30:

> No wisdom, no understanding, no counsel, can avail against the LORD.

Similar proverbs are:

> A man's mind plans his way, but the LORD directs his steps. (16:9)
> The plans of the mind belong to man, but the answer of the tongue is from the LORD. (16:1)
> The horse is made ready for the day of battle, but the victory belongs to the LORD. (21:31)

Our English equivalent is: "Man proposes, God disposes." Anyone who believes that God rules the world is bound to say as much. He does not mean that God always sets aside human plans or that it is only divine decisions that matter; that plainly is not what the book of Proverbs as a whole is saying. But when it comes to conflict between God and man, undoubtedly it cannot be man who wins the day.

B. *Ecclesiastes*

Ecclesiastes is surely the leading Old Testament exponent of predestination. Life is essentially for him a matter of God's "allotment" or "gift" (3:13; 5:18; 6:2; cf. 7:13). Everything in life happens according to its allotted occasion (3:17); so he says in his most famous lines:

> For everything its season, and for every activity under heaven its time:
> a time to be born and a time to die;
> a time to plant and a time to uproot;
> a time to kill and a time to heal. (3:1-3, NEB)

That does not mean that there is an appropriate time for every human activity, which a man must recognize and fall in with; this is not an ethical precept, but a global statement about the nature of human existence, that the variegated experiences of life do not occur by human design but when their "time" arrives.[8]

Once again, however, it is valuable to consider the form and role of Ecclesiastes' idea of predestination.

As for its *form*, we can observe first that Ecclesiastes is not thinking about differentiated destinies for man after death. For him, good and bad alike meet the same ultimate destiny— death. If there is any hereafter, Ecclesiastes does not reckon with it; he simply asks, "Who knows whether the spirit of man goes upward and the spirit of the beast goes down to the earth?" (3:21). His horizon is the span of a human life.

Secondly, Ecclesiastes is not thinking about a predestination to good or evil deeds. He believes that there is a distinction between the righteous and the wicked (e.g. 8:14),[9] and that men ought to be righteous, fear God, and keep his commandments (12:13). He is not arguing that the righteous and the wicked are so because of any predestination.

Yet, thirdly, there is something predestined for every man— that is, his death. Death is undeniable "in the hand of God": "the time to die" (3:2) is appointed by God as the conclusion of these "days of life which God gives" man under the sun (8:15), when man's "spirit returns to God who gave it" (12:7).

Ecclesiastes is not viewing death as a punishment, or as a tragedy, but as a most significant factor in the created order. Men are mortal; it is God who has made them so; the time when they succumb to their mortality is likewise of his making.

Now, fourthly, God's sovereign freedom over death becomes for Ecclesiastes the paradigm example of God's freedom over all reality: "I know that whatever God does endures forever; nothing can be added to it, or anything taken from it" (3:14). He is not speaking of God's initial creation, but of the multifarious activities which go on upon earth (3:1-8), all upon the occasion appointed for them (3:17). To put it rather crudely: all that life adds up to is death, so if death is destined by God, all that life is is equally destined by God.

Death is plainly a nodal point in Ecclesiastes' theology. Probably he is an old man himself, who, as he faces the prospect of death, asks what "profit" there has been in life. Death negates all the values that men strive for in life; pleasure, fame, success, possessions, even wisdom and righteousness, are empty in the face of death (cf. 2:1; 9:11; 4:7f.; 6:1-2; 2:12-17; 8:14). This realization brings him into conflict with the ideals of wisdom teaching, as they are to be seen especially in Proverbs. Wisdom offers life, but what about when life itself is no longer desirable (12:1), or when life has been overcome by death?

The fact of death is a constituent element of the created order; it is part of *God's* world, God has made things like this. Then he too has created the relationship between the values of life and the fact of death. It is God who has created a world in which all values add to zero and what is crooked cannot be made straight (7:13; 1:15). Weeping, laughter, seeking, losing, silence and speech, war and peace (3:1-8) are real, but each has its time, and one is superseded by the other without any discernible progress or any measurable profit. So the catalogue of the "times" concludes: "[But] what gain has the worker from his toil?", or better, "What does the doer [of these] add by his effort?" [10] And that is the world God has made; that is his destined order of things, so argues Ecclesiastes.

Fifthly, we may note that predestination for Ecclesiastes does not mean that the particular acts of individuals are fixed in advance by God, but rather that the possibilities open to man and the value of human activities are settled in advance by the framework of God's created order, which terminates everything human with death.

When we come to enquire about the *role* that these ideas of predestination, so difficult to nuance correctly, play in Ecclesiastes' book, we may be surprised that Ecclesiastes is not impelled by this view of life to advocate suicide or despair. Ecclesiastes is, however, far from pessimistic; his message is life-affirming to a remarkable degree: "There is nothing better for a man than that he should eat and drink, and find enjoyment in his toil. This also, I saw, is from the hand of God" (2:24).

There are two reasons for Ecclesiastes' positive attitude.

First, Ecclesiastes does not doubt that God knows what he is doing. "It is an unhappy business that God has given to the sons of men to be busy with" (1:13), when looked at from a human perspective. Yet God has "made everything beautiful in its time" (3:11), he says, echoing the repeated phrase of Genesis 1: "And *God* saw that it was good." It is simply that God's purpose is inaccessible to man; he has so made man that he "cannot find out what God has done from the beginning to the end" (3:11), that is, he cannot understand the totality of God's purposes nor how the individual event is related to the totality. "As you do not know how the spirit comes to the bones in the womb of a woman with child, so you do not know the work of God who makes everything" (11:4; cf. 8:16f.; 9:1; Prov. 30:3). God is inscrutable. In so saying, Ecclesiastes holds up a needful warning sign before the teachers of wisdom who claimed they could know how and when God would act, ever faithful to the principle of retribution.[11] Job knows well that retribution is only a general rule, not an infallible one: the righteous may suffer. The Psalmists too experience the prosperity of the wicked and the victimization of the innocent, quite contrary to the principle of retribution. So also Ecclesiastes; his extremism, neglectful of God's actual revelation of himself to Israel, is because he is working stolidly from a theology of creation. To Ecclesiastes, God is essentially Creator (cf. 12:1); and a creator must be wise, he must know what he is about, even if we can know nothing of his purpose. This is a world away from a belief in a blind fate or a capricious Deity.

Secondly, as a theologian of creation Ecclesiastes must accept that what *is* is "from the hand of God." And part of what *is* is happiness, work, wisdom, righteousness, the commandments. Since they exist, they were created, and to deny them would be to deny, or "forget," one's Creator. Whatever else the world is for, it is given to man for his enjoyment (2:24; 5:18f.); therefore let a man busy himself with his work and his pleasure (3:12f.; 8:15; 9:9; 11:9). Precisely because these "goods" have been created, they are approved by God (9:7). Whatever one's hand finds to do (9:10) is what one is intended to do.

What we find, then, in Ecclesiastes, is a radical awareness

of a divine predestination which encompasses the whole of human activity but which, just because it is inscrutable, imposes no constraints on men, nor weakens their self-determination, but rather points them from the mystery of their existence to the mystery of the Creator God.

III. The Prophetic Literature

In the prophets, predestinarian ideas take on two major forms: the concept of God's election of Israel, and the concept of divine purposes in history.

(1) The first major *form* which predestination takes on is that the people of Israel has been *chosen* by God to be his people. That is a predestination because it is not just an act of grace or salvation but an act which establishes Israel's future destiny, and an act that defines what it will mean to be Israel.

The occasion of this election is not for the prophets an eternal decree but a historical act: the election took place at the exodus from Egypt (Ezek. 20:5f.). It was then that Israel was "chosen," "formed" (Isa. 43:20f.), "called" (Hos. 11:1), "wooed" (Hos. 2:14f.), "known" (Amos 3:1f.). All these terms belong to the election vocabulary, for they all point to the divine action which constituted Israel.

The nature of this election is expressed by many images of Israel found in prophetic poetry.[12] Israel is God's vineyard, planted and tended by him (Isa. 5:1-7); God's bride, whom he took to himself in Egypt (Jer. 31:32), led through the wilderness (2:2), and lavished gifts upon (Hos. 2:7f.); God's servant, whom he has chosen (Isa. 41:8f.; 43:10; 44:1f.) and "formed" (44:21) and destined to glorify him (49:3); God's adopted son, called by him from Egypt (Hos. 11:1).

We should also enquire about the *role* of the idea of election in the prophets, that is, why should the election of Israel be mentioned at all by the prophets? The major emphasis of the pre-exilic prophets is the announcement of imminent judgment upon Israel. Sometimes it is said that repentance is still possible, and the doom can be averted (e.g. Hos. 14:2). At other times it appears that it is too late for repentance (e.g. Amos 8:2), but in either case the focus is upon the heralded doom. The role of election in such a context is to highlight the contrast between God's grace and Israel's sin. Election in the prophets is no guarantee of eternal security. Amos is characteristic of prophetic theology when he proclaims this word from God:

> You only have I known of all the families of the earth;
> therefore I will punish you for all your iniquities. (3:2)

God's "knowledge" of Israel here is clearly identified with his election of them in Egypt; the word is spoken "against the whole family whom I brought up out of the land of Egypt" (3:1).[13] And it is precisely because of the prophet's belief in election that he can be sure that Israel's iniquities will not be overlooked by God. Elsewhere this same connection is apparent: the picture of Israel as God's vineyard is introduced in order to denounce Israel's sin:

> For the vineyard of the LORD of hosts is the house of Israel, and the men of Judah are his pleasant planting; and he looked for justice, but behold, bloodshed; for righteousness, but behold, a cry! (Isa. 5:7)

and to announce its destruction:

> And now I will tell you what I will do to my vineyard. I will remove its hedge, and it shall be devoured; I will break down its wall, and it shall be trampled down. (5:6)

Likewise in Jer. 2:2 Israel's marriage to the Lord is the backcloth to the Lord's current controversy with his people, and in Hos. 11:1 Israel's call to sonship is but the preface to the irony of election:

> The more I called them, the more they went from me.

It is noteworthy also how often in Isaiah Israel is referred to as God's people in the context of its disobedience or its impending destruction (e.g., Isa. 1:3; 2:6; 5:13, 25). The role of election theology, then, is to heighten the gravity of Israel's sin and to guarantee that there is no escape from the consequences of their guilt.

However, the doom of Israel, though the major preoccupation of the pre-exilic prophets, is not their only concern. They, together with the prophets of the exile and beyond, also deliver prophecies of hope. In this setting the role of election is different. Here election takes on the character of promise, assurance that Israel will become what she was called into being to become. Israel must respond to the prophetic reminders about election with courage, faith, work. Thus we find:

> But you, Israel, my servant, Jacob, whom I have chosen, the offspring of Abraham, my friend; you whom I took from the ends of the earth, and called from its farthest corners, saying to you, "You are my servant, I have chosen you and not cast you off"; fear not, for I am with you, be not dismayed, for I am your God. (Isa. 41:8ff.) (Cf. also Isa. 43:1f.; 44:1ff., 21f.; Hos. 2:14ff.; Hag. 2:4f.)

(2) The other major *form* which prophetic predestination takes on is the idea that events of world history are planned by God.[14] A clear example is Isa. 14:24-27:

The LORD of hosts has sworn: "As I have planned, so shall it be, And as I have purposed, so shall it stand, that I will break the Assyrian in my land, and upon my mountains trample him under foot . . ." This is the purpose that is purposed concerning the whole earth; and this is the hand that is stretched out over all the nations. For the LORD of hosts has purposed, and who will annul it? His hand is stretched out, and who will turn it back?

Other references to God's "purposes" or "plans" or "thoughts" occur in Isa. 25:1; 46:10; Mic. 4:12; Jer. 23:20; 29:11; 49:20; 50:45; 51:11. And of course the whole rationale of prophetic prediction is that God has plans or intentions, whether of judgment or salvation, which are so sure of fulfillment that they may be announced in advance.

Almost all of the specific references to God's plans have in view a particular event or a limited series of events, for example, "his purposes against the land of the Chaldeans" (Jer. 50:45). Furthermore, it is not a matter of a *single* divine plan; various passages speak of various intentions, and some references are in fact to God's plans in the plural. So it cannot be shown that the prophets believed in a fixed divine plan that extended from the beginning to the end of world history. When they spoke of God's plan they referred to the obvious truth that God is purposive in his actions. As for the prophetic predictions of what God is going to do, it can be freely acknowledged that they are extremely varied in their scope, comprehensiveness, and time-range. But they do not amount to a claim that all the events of history move towards a divine goal. They are rather an assertion that within history God is working his purposes out.[15]

The *role* of this form of predestination must be defined in terms of the main foci of the prophetic message. Characteristically the announcement of God's "plan" is an announcement of doom, whether against foreign nations (Isa. 14:26; Mic. 4:12; Jer. 49:20; 50:45; 51:11, 29) or against Israel itself (Jer. 23:20-30:24; cf. Isa. 5:19). On one occasion, it is a promise of the future welfare of Israel (Jer. 29:11). That is, the predestinarian element functions as an assurance that the prophetic message will take effect. It is not an expression of a broad philosophy of history so much as an affirmation of the inescapability of God's wrath or the certainty of God's blessing. The same is true of the predictive or predestinarian aspect of prophetic oracles of judgment or hope, even when terms for God's "plan" are not used.

IV. Other Old Testament Literature

We can here only glance at some of the other Old Testament writings.

The so-called *"Court History"* of David (2 Sam. 9 to 1 Kings 2), a complex narrative of events in both the personal and national spheres. Throughout, the story moves on the level of human intrigue, ambition, lust, revenge, vacillation, magnanimity, and the narrator does not pause to indicate where God's hand may be in this *mêlée* of incidents. However, the frame within which the story is set leaves us in no doubt that this is not a purely human story, but a story of God's doing. Before the narrative begins, 2 Samuel 7 recounts God's assurance through Nathan that David is his chosen king (7:8), and God's promise that David's son will succeed to the throne and will build the temple (7:12f.). And after the court history has concluded, 1 Kings 3 records Solomon's acknowledgment that his succession is due to God (3:7), and 1 Kings 5 records Solomon's intention to build the temple (5:5). How the history can be both human and divine the story itself does not divulge.

A similar outlook is held by the *Chronicler* of the post-exilic era. To mention only one example, at the completion of the rebuilding of the temple, the Chronicler observes that what has come about is the doing both of God and of the Persian emperors: "They finished the building by command of the God of Israel and by decree of Cyrus and Darius and Artaxerxes king of Persia" (Ezra 6:14). The divine and human are artlessly conjoined. *How* God's purpose becomes also the emperor's purpose the Chronicler does not precisely say; he only knows that somehow "the LORD . . . had turned the heart of the king of Assyria to them" (6:22), or that he had "stirred up the spirit of Cyrus" (1:1).

In *Deuteronomy* we have an important exposition of the truth that Israel is God's *chosen* people.[16] In this book the focus is on the relation between God and Israel as a whole, and in that context the question is raised: Why should there be any relation at all between God and Israel? The reason for God's choice cannot be that Israel was more numerous than other nations (7:7), any more than the reason why Israel is given the land can be that they were more righteous than its former inhabitants (9:4ff.). The only possible reason is that "the LORD loves you, and is keeping the oath which he swore to your fathers" (7:8), that is, there is no cause for Israel's election outside God himself. Here the *form* which predestination takes is the unmerited election of the people. Its *role* is to establish the ground of the relationship which the book is setting forth.

In *Daniel* we find the nearest approach the Old Testament makes to the idea of a fixed divine plan that determines the course of history. The scheme of successive world empires (Dan. 7-12), whose fortunes demonstrate the truth of the programmatic utterance, "The Most High rules the kingdom of men and gives it to whom he will" (4:32), would seem to go beyond the prophetic conception of particular divine goals in history. Yet it would be mistaken to see in Daniel some of the more dogmatic predestinarian teaching developed by later apocalyptic literature,[17] and it is noteworthy how much of Daniel's visions merely predict what human rulers will do (e.g. Dan. 11), while God's determination of events is restricted to those which impinge most closely on the people of God (e.g. 7:25ff.).

Summary

Though it does the rich and varied teaching of the Old Testament on predestination an injustice to attempt to summarize it within a few propositions, perhaps we should make the attempt nevertheless.

(1) The Old Testament knows nothing of a divine predestination that determines in advance the particular acts of an individual.

(2) Nor does it affirm a predetermined destiny for individuals in an after-life.

(3) When it speaks of God's purposes, they are usually specific and comparatively short-range. There is no thought of a detailed blueprint for history.

(4) There are, however, long-range promises whose fulfillment God sees to.

(5) Besides divine predestination the Old Testament wants to affirm a human predestination (Proverbs).

(6) Predestination in whatever form usually plays a role subsidiary to that of the full and (to all intents and purposes) undetermined relationship of God and man.

And as far as our method goes in approaching the Old Testament's teaching, we may summarize:

(1) Our method cannot be via the accumulation of proof texts drawn indiscriminately from the whole Old Testament, but rather we should move via the appreciation of the total message of each part of the Old Testament to the particular *form* which predestinarian ideas take on there.

(2) Even more important than deciding what is *true* in this subject is to decide how *important* various truths are. No doubt there are many reasonable inferences that may be made from biblical statements about predestination, but to be faithful to the Bible means in part to follow the Bible's emphases and not erect mere inferences into essential biblical doctrine. This is an appeal for sensitivity to the *role* which predestinarian ideas play in the Old Testament writings.

NOTES

1. The type of approach I am rejecting is exemplified in L. Boettner, *The Reformed Doctrine of Predestination* (Eerdmans, Grand Rapids, Ill.; 5th edn, 1941), 26-29, 81 f., etc.

2. The imperative of verse 1 "does not . . . have any kind of conditional undertone, as if the promise of Yahweh were dependent on the obedience of Abraham. Rather, it sounds like a summons to receive the repeatedly promised gift" (H. W. Wolff, *Interpretation* 20 [1966], 138).

3. It should be noted that the usual translation of 12:3 "the families of earth shall be blessed" is not certain; the text may rather mean that they will mention Abraham's name when pronouncing a blessing, praying that they may be blessed just as Abraham was (so RSV; for the idea, cf. Gen. 48:20; Ruth 4:11; elsewhere the promise is formulated as "they shall call down blessing on themselves" [Gen. 22:18; 26:4]). For discussion see G. von Rad, *Genesis* (SCM, London; 2nd edn, 1972), 166; B. Albrektson, *History and the Gods. An Essay on the Idea of Historical Events as Divine Manifestations in the Ancient Near East and in Israel* ([Gleerup, Lund; 1967], 78-81). However, this alternative translation still retains some sense of an overflow of the divine blessing beyond the Abrahamic family.

4. Cf. the view of G. Fohrer, that the Old Testament is not so much a history of salvation (*Heilsgeschichte*) as a history of decisions, in which man decides for or against God ("Action of God and Decision of Man," in *Biblical Essays. Proceedings of the Ninth Meeting of 'Die Ou-Testamentiese Werkgemeenskap in Suid-Afrika'* [1966], 31-39).

5. See W. M. Clark, "The righteousness of Noah," *Vetus Testamentum* 21 (1971), 261-280.

6. For an exposition of the "act-consequence relationship," see G. von Rad, *Wisdom in Israel* (SCM, London; 1972), 128-33.

7. Thus R. B. Y. Scott, *Proverbs. Ecclesiastes* (Anchor Bible; Doubleday, Garden City, N.Y.; 1965), 104. Similarly W. McKane, *Proverbs* (SCM, London; 1970), 497.

8. Cf. O. S. Rankin, "The Book of Ecclesiastes. Introduction and Exegesis," *The Interpreter's Bible* (Abingdon, New York/Nashville; 1956), vol. 5, 41ff.; G. von Rad, *Wisdom in Israel*, 263f.

9. Though he realizes that it is not an absolute distinction (7:20).

10. R. B. Y. Scott, *Proverbs. Ecclesiastes*, 220.

11. "Ecclesiastes is the frontier-guard, who forbids wisdom to cross the frontier towards a comprehensive art of life" (W. Zimmerli, "The Place and Limit of the Wisdom in the Framework of the Old Testament Theology," *Scottish Journal of Theology* 17 (1964), 158).

12. See G. A. F. Knight, *A Christian Theology of the Old Testament* (SCM, London; 1959), ch. 15.

13. " 'To know' approaches the sense of 'to choose' (cf. Gen. 18:19; 2 Sam. 7:20; Jer. 1:5; Hos. 13:5)" (E. Hammershaimb, *The Book of Amos. A Commentary* [Blackwell, Oxford; 1970], 56f.).

14. Most helpful on this subject is B. Albrektson, *History and the Gods*, ch. 5 "The Divine Plan in History."

15. "In so far as it is at all possible to speak of a divine plan it concerns a definite chain of events and a limited goal" (Albrektson, *op. cit.*, 87). Sim-

ilarly, G. Fohrer, *History of Israelite Religion* (SPCK, London; 1973), 275.

16. See R. E. Clements, *God's Chosen People. A Theological Interpretation of the Book of Deuteronomy* (SCM, London; 1968), especially 45-49.

17. See L. Morris, *Apocalyptic* (IVP, London; 1972), 48f., 76-81.

7

Predestination in the New Testament

I. HOWARD MARSHALL

Our first task in this essay will be to set out the New Testament evidence relating to predestination (I). We shall then examine how this sort of language is used on a human level (II) as a prelude to observing the difficulties which arise when it is applied to God (III). This will lead to a consideration of the causes of these difficulties (IV) and then to a final statement of what predestination language is meant to do and what it cannot do (V).

I. The New Testament Evidence

The verb "to predestinate" occurs in the KJV (AV) a total of four times as the translation of the Greek verb *proorizō* (Rom. 8:29, 30; Eph. 1:5, 11). The same Greek word also occurs in Acts 4:28 (translated "to determine before") and 1 Cor 2:7 ("to ordain"). In accordance with its policy of always translating any Greek word by the same English word if possible, the ASV (RV) has "to foreordain" in all six passages. Later translations adopt a variety of renderings. The RSV has "to predestine" in Rom. 8:29, 30; NIV uses the same translation in these two verses and in Eph. 1:5, 11.

The Greek *word* is thus comparatively rare in the New Testament,[1] but of course the *idea* is much more widespread, and a larger word-field demands investigation. "*Pre*-destination" in English, as in Greek, refers to an act of decision prior to a later action; one decides beforehand what one is later going to do. This means that all *pro*-verbs which refer to God purposing or choosing in advance must come into our field of interest. Such verbs can of course be used of human purposing. Thus Paul speaks of the Corinthians making their gifts each "as he has made up his mind" (*proaireomai*, 2

Cor. 9:7), and of course there are many such verbs which simply indicate that one action preceded another. Prophets can *fore*-see what is going to happen, i.e., see it before it happens, and *fore*-tell it or "*fore*-write" it (e.g., Acts 2:31; Gal. 3:8; Acts 1:16; Rom. 9:29; Heb. 4:7; 2 Pet. 3:2; Jude 4). In the same way God (who was of course the inspirer of the prophets) can have foreknowledge of what is going to happen (Acts 2:23) or of particular people (Rom. 8:29; 11:2; 1 Pet. 1:2); a special case is where Jesus and his career are said to be foreknown by God (Acts 2:23; 1 Pet. 1:20).

But God also prepares things beforehand for his people (Heb. 11:40), and chooses people beforehand for various tasks (Acts 10:41; 22:14; 26:16; cf. 3:20 with reference to the Messiah). The verb *protithēmi* can be used in this way with the meaning "to propose" or "to plan beforehand"; in Rom. 1:13 it refers to a purpose of Paul which had been thwarted, and in Eph. 1:9 it is used of God's purpose of salvation.[2] The corresponding noun *prothesis* ("purpose, plan") is more frequent, and refers to God's purpose in Rom. 8:28; 9:11; Eph. 1:11; 3:11; 2 Tim. 1:9. Finally, we may note that the preposition *pro* ('before') can be used to refer to things that God planned, promised or did before the creation of the world (John 17:5; 1 Cor. 2:7; Eph. 1:4; 2 Tim. 1:9; Tit. 1:2; 1 Pet. 1:20; Jude 25).

In many of the above texts the use of *pro-* is strictly unnecessary, since it is obvious that willing and purposing *must by their very nature precede* the action willed and purposed. (We may perhaps compare the increasing use of "pre-" in such phrases as "pre-packaged vegetables"; pre-packaged vegetables are identical with packaged vegetables when they reach the shopper's table.[3]) But this means that all texts in which God is described as willing, planning and purposing must also come within our survey, since here too we are concerned with acts of *pre*-destination. So we must note the use of *thelō*, "to will" and of *thelēma*, "will." This verb can be used to express what God *desires* (Matt. 9:13; 12:7; Heb. 10:5, 8) and what God actually *wills* to happen (1 Cor. 12:18; 15:38; Col. 1:27); sometimes the dividing line between these two is not absolutely clear (cf. John 5:21; Rom. 9:18, 22; 1 Tim. 2:4).

What God thus desires or purposes can stand in opposition to the desires of men and even of his Son (Mark 14:36; cf. Matt. 26:42 and Luke 22:42). What men purpose stands, therefore, under the condition "if the Lord wills it" (Acts 18:21; 21:14; 1 Cor. 4:19; James 4:15; 1 Pet. 3:17). The noun can stand for what God wishes that men should do (Matt.

7:21; 12:50; cf. 21:31); so Jesus did the will of the Father and not his own will (John 4:34; 5:30; 6:38-40). God's plan of salvation can be spoken of as his "will" (Acts 22:14; Eph. 1:5, 9; Col. 1:9), as can his plan in creation (Eph. 1:11; Rev. 4:11). The life of the church in detail—the choice of apostles and the actions they perform—follows the purpose of God (e.g., Rom. 1:10; 15:32; 1 Cor. 1:1); and his purpose for men is that they should obey his will in ethical action and holiness (e.g., Rom. 2:18; 12:2; 1 Thess. 4:3; 5:18).

A very similar picture is presented when we look at the synonymous verb *boulomai*, "to wish"; and the noun *boulē*, "plan." The former is used of God's will that can stand over against man's (Luke 22:42), and of his plan of salvation, whether only intended (2 Pet. 3:9) or actually carried out (James 1:18; cf. Heb. 6:17); it is also used of the way in which the Son reveals the Father to those whom he wishes (Matt. 11:27; cf. Luke 10:22). As for the noun, it can be used in general terms of God's plan that he wants men to follow for their lives (Luke 7:30), of his plan of salvation (Acts 20:27), and of his purpose which is accomplished in the death of Jesus and the lives of other men (Acts 2:23; 4:28; cf. 13:36). God is the one who accomplishes all things according to the purpose of his will, says Paul as he piles up the expressions for rhetorical effect (Eph. 1:11).

Other words are also used for what God appoints to happen. Thus *horizō* has a similar meaning to *proorizō*. The life of Jesus and his future activities were appointed by God (Luke 22:22; Acts 2:23; 10:42; 17:31; cf. Rom. 1:4), and God appoints the times at which things happen in the world (Acts 17:26), and the day of salvation (Heb. 4:7). Similarly, *proorizō* is used of Herod and Pilate acting in accordance with God's plan in the condemnation of Jesus (Acts 4:28). God made a plan before the ages for our glory (1 Cor. 2:7). He foreordained certain people to be like his Son (Rom. 8:29, 30), and indeed to become his sons (Eph. 1:5) and his portion (Eph. 1:11). Again, the verb *tassō*, "to appoint," can be used of rulers (Rom. 13:1), those appointed to eternal life (Acts 13:48), and the details of an apostle's career (Acts 22:10).

Finally in this catalog, we have the verb *eudokeō*, "to be pleased," and the noun *eudokia*, "pleasure, will," which often bring out the element of God's pleasure in doing certain things or choosing certain people. He delights in his Servant, Jesus (Matt. 3:17; 12:18; 17:5; cf. Col. 1:19). He delights to save believers by the preaching of the word (1 Cor. 1:21), to reveal himself to Paul (Gal. 1:15), and to bestow the kingdom on the disciples (Luke 12:32). It is his pleasure to reveal himself by the Son (Matt. 11:26; Luke 10:21); salvation is for the men on whom his favor rests (Luke 2:14), and the carrying out of his plan expresses his favor to them (Eph. 1:5, 9).[4]

II. The Language of Predestination—as Applied to Men

This summary of the terms used to express predestination in the New Testament may have been tedious, but it is necessary. It is not complete, for it has omitted words referring to calling and election, discussed elsewhere in this symposium. But it is comprehensive in that an attempt has been made to cover the whole vocabulary of predestination and to indicate in broad terms how it is used. The concept of God's plan as it affects his Son, the creation of the world, the redemption of mankind, and the individuals who compose the church, is clearly present in the New Testament, and it is no part of our purpose to obscure this fact by hiding any of the evidence; our task in this volume is to be true to Scripture.

But it is one thing to *state* what Scripture says; it is another to *understand* it and to bring it into relation with the rest of what Scripture says. Here there are real difficulties, and we must now try to deal with them. A recent study of this problem was criticized for confining itself to exegesis and not tackling the problem theologically.[5] We hope that we shall not be criticized for turning to theology and philosophy in order to perform our exegesis better.

When we use the language of predestination and speak of God as willing and purposing, we are using human language to describe God in personal terms. If God is a person, we must use personal language to describe him—which is what the Scriptures do. That he wills and purposes is one aspect of the fact that he is a person. (We may recall that one argument for the personality of the Holy Spirit is that he wills certain things: 1 Cor. 12:11.) But the Scripture is using a human analogy when it describes God in this way, and we have to be very careful when using analogical language. We have to find out how the language is used when applied to men, and what similarities and differences must be noted when it is applied to God.

(1) We observe first that, willing and purposing is an *essential* attribute of persons. They can make plans, form intentions, and then act to carry them out; if they could not do so, they would fall short of being real persons.

(2) We can distinguish between the elements of *"desire"* and *"resolve."* The former is the wish to do something without necessarily being able to carry it out or even intending to

carry it out (for example, because we prefer to follow some other wish). The latter is the actual decision to do something, and it entails at least attempting to put it into effect. For example, there is a difference between my present *desire* to read a novel instead of typing this essay, and my *resolve* to remain at my desk.

(3) It is of the essence of both human desires and resolves that *they may not be fulfilled*. Paul wished to visit Rome in a particular way, but was not able to do so (Rom. 1:13). Circumstances prevent us doing all that we want to do, and these circumstances may include our own mental and physical limitations.

(4) More important, there may be *a clash between* the *wills* of two or more people, so that one of them does not achieve his desire or resolve. While I may not be tempted from my desk by the lure of my unfinished novel, I may be forced away by a persistent knocking at the door and the need to obey somebody else's command.

(5) A particularly tricky situation arises when we ask whether it is possible for somebody to *predict* infallibly and in detail what I shall will and do. I am writing these words on the eve of a British election. It is possible for somebody who knows me well to make a good prediction of how I shall vote in the light of my general character, statements that I have made, and so on. He might even know the physical state of my brain and all the factors that will influence it over the next few hours, so that he can predict confidently what I will do. (The practical impossibility of anybody possessing such knowledge is of course overwhelming.) Does this mean that my behavior is predetermined, so that I am not able to choose freely? There is one case at least where this is not so. If somebody says to me, "I predict that you will vote for X," I know that I am free to falsify his prediction by voting for Y. For if he tells me what he predicts, this changes the situation on which the prediction is based and thereby makes it invalid.[6] It would seem to follow that I may be acting equally freely even when somebody makes such a prediction without telling me about it.

There are, of course, situations in which I am not free, and my behavior is predetermined. The most obvious is that of a post-hypnotic suggestion. Here a person is hypnotized and told to perform a certain act at a given time. He is then released from hypnosis, and the experimenter can know confidently that he will perform the act (assuming that it is not physically impossible or morally repulsive). But the subject thinks that he is performing the act freely, although it is in fact in response to hypnosis. If a person thinks that he is free, is he "really" free?

(6) If an outside observer cannot predict my behavior infallibly *and* inform me of his prediction, it follows that it is impossible for me to predict infallibly my own activity; for even if I can assemble all the information about myself, I can never dissociate my roles as observer and acting subject, and hence can always falsify my own predictions, if I want to do so. In principle I cannot predetermine my own future states of mind. The attempt is *logically inconceivable*, quite apart from its practical impossibility.

(7) Even more difficult to imagine is the possibility of my *predetermining a course of action involving myself and another subject:* "First I will say A to him, then he will say B to me, then I will reply with C, and he will respond with D. . . ." Naturally, this can be done to some extent: there have been games of chess in which one player has been able to force a predetermined sequence of moves on his opponent, leading to checkmate, but this assumes that the opponent is playing according to the rules of the game (which lay down a finite set of possibilities) and that he will respond intelligently to each situation. But on the level of free agents it is impossible. For in the chess illustration, the moves of the opponent are not "free" in fact or in his subjective consciousness. Moreover, we reach the situation that the "moves" of the person doing the predetermination also cease to be free. Having decided what he is going to do at each particular state (if, for the sake of argument, this is possible), he is then bound to that course of action and cannot change it himself, for if he does, then he must replan the other subject's responses.

(8) An interesting point arises if we consider the situation of *the author of a play* who invents his characters and has them perform their parts "in character," but so that his ultimate goal for the action of the play is achieved. We can then speak of the various characters acting "freely," but with the result that in their freedom they advance the action to the desired point, since the author has been able to foresee where their freedom would lead and to account for it in framing his plot. But when applied to real life this analogy breaks down at two points. One point is when *the author himself walks on stage* and becomes a participant. What happens then? D. M. Mackay admits that it lies beyond our conception. For then the drama becomes free and extempore, and the actors do not know what to say: the lines they learned do not take account of such untoward events, unless the appearance of the author as player is built into the original dialogue, in which case, as we have seen, the author has no freedom.

But the author point is perhaps more important. We have

spoken in terms of the *characters*, but the characters are played by actors, and the *actors* who are bound by the characters assigned to them and the lines that they have learned. There is no question of the "character" saying "I am free what to say"; this is an unreal question. He simply says what is in the script. But the actor too knows that he is bound by his lines, and his freedom lies simply in the way in which he says them; if he varies them, he ceases to be the character he is meant to be. A better possibility might be provided by a jazz band in which the various instrumentalists provide their own extempore harmony and counterpoint, yet in such a way that the piece does eventually come to a conclusion and has some sort of unity. But in this case the players collectively know roughly where they are going and their musical sense enables them to recognize where the music as a whole is going, and even to cope with changes in direction (if, say, the composer is playing the melody line and chooses to vary it). It is not so certain that sinful men are willing to cooperate with God in the same way.

The purpose of the above eight points has been to show something of what is involved in using the language of "willing" in respect of free human agents, and it has brought out particularly the problems inherent in talking about predicting the free decisions of another person or of myself or of both of us interacting with each other. It emerges that it is doubtful whether I can predict the willing of another free person; that it is impossible for me in principle to predict my own willing; and that (consequently) it is impossible for me to predict the pattern of an interaction involving myself. (Note that "predict" here means "predict infallibly.") Naturally, there are situations in which I can predict in broad terms what I am going to do, and what other people will do; a lover can reach the stage where he can determine that when he meets her tomorrow he will make a proposal of marriage and can predict with reasonable certainty that she will respond favorably; and the same thing happens in a host of other situations, but this is not the same thing as the strict determination that is at issue here.

III. The Language of Predestination—as Applied to God

A. *Factors in the Situation*

So now the question arises of what happens when we use this kind of personal language in order to talk about God. Let us first ask what exactly the Bible is using this language to express. We may list the following ideas:

(1) God is *personal*. He can will and purpose what he wants to do, and has freedom to do so.

(2) God is *sovereign*. Ultimately his purpose for the universe will be achieved, so that "God is all in all."

(3) God is *gracious*. The salvation of sinful men depends entirely upon his gracious initiative; no man can come to Jesus unless the Father draws him.

It would not be too difficult for the theologian to construct a scheme in which these three elements are preserved. But the problem is sharpened by the existence of three other equally real factors which stand over against the three points we want to preserve:

(1) *Men are personal* and have wills of their own. We face the problem of possible opposition to the will of God, and the difficulty of balancing human freedom over against divine predetermination.

(2) *Evil exists* as a factor which is contrary to the will of God, and of which God is not the author. We have the difficulty of fitting it into God's plan.

(3) *Some men are not saved*. The implication is that grace was not shown to them, and we then have the difficulty that grace has been bestowed arbitrarily.

B. *The Calvinist Solution*

The typical Calvinist approach in face of these factors admits the ultimate mystery of the problem with which we are dealing, but nevertheless attempts to come to terms with it. It plays down the fact of human freedom in two ways. On the one hand, it argues that divine predestination and prediction of human willing and acting and the subjective experience of human freedom are not incompatible, even if we find it impossible to explain how they can be compatible. (The important essay by D. M. Mackay is a major attempt to find a way of stating how they can be compatible.) On the other hand, so far as the limited area of faith in God is concerned, it asserts plainly that man has no freedom, not even to respond to the grace of God; he is dead in sins and must be given the capacity to believe by God (who gives this to the elect).

Second, the Calvinist allows that somehow even evil acts are included in the all-embracing purpose of God; he tolerates evil in his system so that good may come out of it. But while he allows men to commit evil, it is they who are responsible and bear the guilt for what they freely do, while God himself is not responsible and bears no blame.[8]

Third, the Calvinist insists that God is not under obligation to show grace to any guilty sinner, and therefore he does no injustice in merely showing grace to some, indeed (if many Calvinists are to be believed) to most sinners.[9] Moreover, no sinner need feel excluded from grace, because any person who looks for grace does so only because God has appointed him to do so; it is not possible that a person should seek for grace and yet find that he is not one of the elect.

In this way the Calvinist insists that he does justice to the antinomies which are found in Scripture. Moreover, he is able to do justice to the complete sovereignty of God and the apparent freedom of man. One difficulty which remains is that caused by statements which imply that God wishes all men to do what is right and to be saved. But this is solved by a distinction between the preceptive will of God and the *decretive* will of God. The former expresses what God wants men to do, while the latter (secret) will expresses what he in fact resolves will happen.

C. Difficulties in the Calvinist Solution

This package solution, however, is exposed to considerable objections.

(1) In the previous section we have explored the difficulties which arise when we try to think of a person foreordaining the course of a relationship between himself and another person. *This concept is logically self-contradictory*, like the mediaeval concept of a God who can do anything, and therefore can create a stone so big that he himself cannot lift it. The difficulty arises, as we have seen, as soon as the creator of the universe is himself a participant in it. This produces a self-contradictory situation. It can be argued that God is above logic, and that the rules of logic do not apply, just as in mathematics the normal rules for finite quantities do not apply in the realm of trans-finite numbers.[10] But this objection misses the point: we are not concerned with what God can do, but whether we can use *our* language of predestination to describe him without the language breaking down, and the point is that when this language is applied to divine-human relationships it *does* break down.

It is worth reflecting that, by applying the scriptural language of human generation to the relation between Father and Son, the Arians (and others of their ilk) ran into difficulties and tried to solve them by the solution that Jesus had a beginning in time; Origen rightly saw that this false solution arose because language was being misused, and introduced the necessary qualification by speaking of the "eternal generation" of the Son; here is a perpetual reminder that human language cannot be applied to God without qualification. It leads to results incompatible with other statements (as in the Arian controversy) or to self-contradiction. The Calvinist is using human language without observing that it breaks down when applied to God.

(2) *The problem of evil* also causes difficulties. The Calvinist view that God can cause evil and suffering through "free" human agents without himself being responsible is untenable. I am responsible for what my agent does.[11] One may, therefore, seek refuge in a modified sense of the word "cause," so that men are not the agents of God, following out his will when they commit evil. But this is another way of admitting that the model of thought we are using, in which God foreordains all things, is breaking down and will not bear the weight that we are putting on it.

(3) To say that God shows mercy to one sinner and not to the next, i.e., to adopt a doctrine of double predestination (as is done in orthodox Calvinism), is to land in *a moral difficulty*. In this case, divine mercy is not being understood in terms of divine justice. I cannot see how it can be just arbitrarily to save one guilty sinner and not another; and there can be no doubt that any human judge (for it is the pattern of the judge which provides the model) who behaved in this way, and *a fortiori* any human father who treated his sons in this way, would be regarded as falling below the standards of Christian justice. To this the reply may be made that we cannot understand the secret working of the mind of God, that he has freedom to show mercy or to harden, as he chooses, and that we must be prepared to trust the inscrutable will of God as being ultimately just, even if we cannot see it from our limited point of view. But again this objection misses the point which is that the use of the language has broken down; it does not explain, but leaves a mystery. Now there can of course be situations of this kind. There is the case of Job who does not know why he is suffering; the point of the suffering (from God and Satan's angle) would disappear if Job knew why it was happening. For God's aim is to show to Satan: Here is a man whom I allow to suffer very grievously, and yet he will not curse me. The point of the experiment is lost if Job sees that he has no need to question the ultimate goodness of God. Similarly, Paul endured his "thorn in the flesh" when it wasn't God's will to remove it, and then learned to experience the grace of God in a situation of human weakness. But it is one thing to attempt to reconcile experience with faith and another to have a faith which cannot reconcile an apparent contradiction in God himself.

(4) The contrast between the preceptive and decretive wills of God does not really help the situation. We should note that

in these two phrases we are really talking about two different things, for *the word "will" is being used in two different senses.* God's preceptive will is his desire that men should do certain things and that all men should be saved by responding to the gospel. It is God *commanding* men to do certain things. "This do, and you shall live." (For the Christian, "this do" means of course "believe in Jesus," John 6:28f.) But God's decretive will is the expression of his resolve that he will accomplish certain things by whatever form of *causation* leads men to act in accordance with it.

The problems that arise here are great. First, God's preceptive will is *not* always obeyed, and therefore his sovereignty is not fully obeyed. What he desires is not accomplished. So, second, we have to fall back on his decretive will. But this means that his preceptive will and his decretive will stand in contradiction to each other on many occasions. In the Calvinist view he gives a man the precept "believe in Jesus," and at the same time by his decretive will he resolves that this man is not one of the elect and therefore cannot obey his preceptive will. But such a self-contradiction is intolerable. The reason why the two wills do not coincide in their effects is of course because of human sin; but in the Calvinist view the decretive will of God embraces human sin, and the ultimate reason why some sinners are saved, and others not saved, rests in the secret will of God. If we say that it is God's will that not all will be saved, this stands in plain contradiction with his expressed desire that all men should repent and come to a knowledge of the truth. (The Calvinist way out of this difficulty is to deny that God does wish *all* men to be saved by reading an unlikely meaning into the verses and erecting a doctrine of limited atonement.)[12] So the sovereignty of God is not preserved by this distinction.

Worse still perhaps is the fact that it makes God out to be hypocritical, offering freely to all men a salvation that he does not intend them all to receive. Certainly, on the human level, all who wish to respond to the gospel can respond; nobody who wants to respond is excluded. But on the divine level, when we look "behind the scenes" at what God is doing, he is doing one thing with his right hand and another with his left.

From these considerations it becomes clear that the Calvinist attempt to use the language of predestination with respect to God lands in great difficulties, both logical and moral.

IV. The Causes of the Difficulties

(1) The basic difficulty is that of attempting to explain the nature of *the relationship between an infinite God and*

finite creatures. Our temptation is to think of divine causation in much the same way as human causation, and this produces difficulties as soon as we try to relate divine causation and human freedom. It is beyond our ability to explain how God can cause us to do certain things (or to cause the universe to come into being and to behave as it does). Predestinarian language must not be pressed so as to become a doctrine of "mechanical" causation.

(2) A second difficulty is *the fact of evil.* The Bible is clear that God is not the author of evil. Its origin is and perhaps *must* be a mystery. Its evilness lies in its lack of good purpose, and thus in its irrationality and opposition to the purpose of God. How it can have come to exist in a universe created by God is unknowable. We must be content to leave the question unresolved. The Calvinist falls into error when he ascribes the reason why some people are not saved to the decretive will of God; in effect, he is trying to *explain* evil. It is wiser to locate the reason why some people are not saved in the sheer mystery of evil. Admittedly, this way of looking at things also has its dangers; the Calvinist suspects that it conceals an ultimate and intolerable dualism, which Christian theology has in general rejected as a false option; biblical faith, however, insists that in the sovereignty of God evil will be brought to an end.

(3) A third difficulty is due to the existence of more than one type of language to describe God in the New Testament, or perhaps rather to *the existence of different types of relationship between God and his creatures.* The Calvinist approach regards all God's dealings with men as being expressed ultimately in terms of his decretive will, which means that his relationship to men is that of a dramatist to his characters; basically, what God does is to predetermine everything that men think, will and do. But this approach has the effect of denying the validity of the other type of language used to describe God. Here God is regarded as standing over against the wills of men. He can give commands to them which they may obey or disobey (his preceptive will). He expresses desires. He speaks of his love for them, demonstrates it in action, and looks for answering love. He can place his will over against their wills, as when he threatens that those who disobey his will shall endure his wrath. *This language is as real in the Bible as the predestinarian language, and it cannot be reduced to the latter or expressed completely in terms of it.* This should be obvious from the analogy of the dramatist which, as we have already seen, breaks down when applied to God. A dramatist may indeed say that he has come to love his characters (Sir Arthur Conon Doyle, it is said, came to hate Sherlock

Holmes!), but it is obvious that this is a special use of the term "love"; it does not include the possibility of the characters loving the dramatist, and, even if he makes them say "I love my creator" in his drama, this is not mutual love in the real sense. So too it makes nonsense of God's joy over the repentance of the sinner if the whole thing, joy and all, has been predestined by God. What the Calvinist approach does is to reduce all this language of interpersonal relationships to the expression of the decretive will of God; and to do this is to turn the story of creation and redemption into sheer farce.

The reason why the Calvinist does this is because he wants to insist that God is sovereign over all things and that his will is always done; he thinks that this can be done only by claiming that God predetermines *all* that happens. This solution does not work, because it creates a clash between what God desires (in his so-called prescriptive will) and what actually happens. It is not true that everything that happens is what God desires. But further this solution arises because the Calvinist cannot see any possibility of God's will being done other than by predetermination of all that happens. There is, however, another way in which God's will can be sovereign, and that is by reason of its superior power, so that God can place his will over against ours, and say, "You may want to do X, but you shall do Y." And this is how the Bible portrays the ultimate victory of God; he will be all in all when all creatures bow down before his will and obey it, willingly or unwillingly (not because their wills have been predetermined to obey it, but because they have to bow to his superior power).

A solution to the problem of predestination must do justice to the way in which the Bible speaks of God as one who places his will over against ours and acts like another person, rather than as a being who does not enter into real relationships with his creatures but simply treats them as the unconscious objects of his secret will.

This does not mean, however, that we can do away with predestinarian language. We may illustrate this point by referring to prayer. The Bible commands us to pray that God's will may be done, as if this was dependent on our prayers. Prayer influences God. (We can, of course, say that we pray because God wills that he should be moved to act in response to the prayers which he himself has moved us to make. But this reply reduces God to the level of the dramatist.)

But prayer also influences men, in that (for example) the work of preaching the gospel effectively depends upon the intercession of the people of God. The wills of men can thus be affected by prayer—or else we would not pray for them. *To believe in prayer is thus to believe in some kind of limitation of human freedom, and in some kind of incomprehensible influence upon the wills of men.* (This raises a problem of a different kind: does A have a better chance of salvation than B because X prays for A and not for B? But this is part of the general problem of theodicy, e.g., that a person in Birmingham or Boston has a better chance of hearing the gospel than one in Borneo or Bangladesh.) We must freely admit that there is an element of mystery here, and not try to tone down either aspect of the language of the Bible.

V. The Purpose and Limits of Predestinarian Language

(1) The New Testament clearly teaches that God has desires and acts to put them into effect. He is God, and he is free to do what he likes, choosing one person for a particular task rather than another. He is sovereign in that he is supreme. But we do not yet see all things under the feet of Jesus or the Father. The language of predestination voices the assurance that in the end God's sovereignty will be entire and complete, all opposition having been quelled and his plan of salvation having been accomplished.

(2) Predestinarian language safeguards the truth that *in every case it is God who takes the initiative in salvation* and calls men to him, and works in their hearts by his Spirit. Salvation is never the result of human merit, nor can anybody be saved without first being called by God. Men cannot in any sense save themselves. It must be declared quite emphatically that *the non-Calvinist affirms this as heartily as the Calvinist* and repudiates entirely the Pelagianism which is often (but wrongly) thought to be inherent in his position. When a person becomes a Christian, he cannot do anything else but own that it is all of grace—and even see that he has been affected by the prayers of other people. But whether we can go on to speak of an "effectual" calling of those who are saved is dubious. The terminology is not scriptural, and is due to an attempt to find the explanation why some respond to the call of God and others do not respond in the nature of the call itself. Rather, the effect of the call of God is to place man in a position where he can say "Yes" or "No" (which he could not do before God called him; till then he was in a continuous attitude of "No").

(3) Predestinarian language roots salvation in past eternity, "before the creation of the world." This leads to the temptation to think of God acting in terms of a blueprint prepared in

eternity past. But this is to misinterpret the language and leads to illogical consequences. It destroys the freedom of God who can, for instance, be grieved that he has created sinful men, and then decide what he is going to do next. *The Bible has the picture of a God deciding fresh measures in history and interacting with the wills of men alongside the picture of a God planning things in eternity past*, and both pictures are equally valid. Neither is to be subordinated to the other. Our difficulties in appreciating this arise from our inability to cope with the concept of eternity and its relation to time. The predestinarian language is meant to affirm that God's plan has all along been one of salvation, and that he created the universe in order to have fellowship with man.

(4) Predestinarian language expresses the fact that *God can foretell what is going to happen*, and can act to bring about his will. Somehow this truth has to be safeguarded despite the difficulties which attach to the idea of prediction. The answer may lie in the fact that in general individuals do not know about the existence of predictions relating to their willing and behavior and hence do not have the possibility of refusing to obey them; nor is the language of God predicting what certain individuals will do confused with the language of God himself entering into personal relationships with them; nor, or course, is the language of prophecy entirely unconditional, but many prophecies are conditional on the obedience or disobedience of the people concerned; nor again is all prophecy concerned with the predetermining in detail of how certain people are going to act.

(5) But now we must assert that *predestinarian language must not be used to make God responsible for evil.* Certainly he is able to make evil subserve his purposes, but this is not the same thing as being responsible for it. It follows that predestinarian language must not be used to assert that everything that happens is what God wants to happen. His preceptive will, i.e. his desires, are not always fulfilled in this present world, although the New Testament promises that one day his complete sovereignty will be revealed. At the same time the Christian confesses that in all things God works for the good of those who love him (Rom. 8:28), and can rest in the goodness of God.

(6) Predestinarian language must not be pressed to express *praedestinatio in malam partem*, the reprobation of certain individuals by the will of God. God wants the wicked man to turn from his wickedness and live; he has no delight in the death of the sinner, and that is his last word on the matter. We have no right to go beyond Scripture and assert that he determines otherwise in the secret counsel of his heart. He

is not willing that any should perish but that all should come to a knowledge of the truth and be saved (1 Tim. 2:4). "Whoever wishes, let him take the free gift of the water of life" (Rev. 22:17). That is God's *final* word on the matter.

VI. Conclusion

It will be clear that the writer of this essay believes in predestination; he cannot do anything else and remain faithful to the testimony of Scripture. Our purpose, therefore, has been to *explain* the meaning of the phrase, to point out the logical difficulties and moral dangers involved in its use, to place alongside it other types of language which are equally valid and important in understanding the biblical doctrine of God, and so to see how the phrase may legitimately be used. In the end, however, we have seen that we are confronted by mysteries which cannot be solved by the theologian, and it is here that he must confess his faith that, although he cannot solve the problems rationally, what he knows of the power and goodness of God revealed in Christ means that there are answers.

NOTES

1. It is not found in the LXX.

2. The meaning in Rom. 3:25 is different: "to display publicly."

3. The difference is presumably that "pre-packaged" vegetables are packed *before* they reach the shelves in the retailer's shop, while others are packed (if at all) at the time of purchase.

4. Most of these words are discussed in TDNT: I, 629-637 (G. Schrenk); II, 738-751 (G. Schrenk); III, 44-62 (G. Schrenk); V. 452-456 (K. L. Schmidt); VIII, 164-167 (C. Maurer). See further the discussions of calling (III, 487-496, K. L. Schmidt) and election (IV, 144-192, G. Quell and G. Schrenk).

5. R. T. Forster and V. P. Marston, *God's Strategy in Human History* (Wheaton, Ill.: Tyndale House, 1974). See the reply to this approach: S. Motyer, "Predestination in Biblical Thought," *TSF Bulletin* 70, Autumn, 1974, 10-15.

6. See especially D. M. Mackay, "The Sovereignty of God in the Natural World," *Scottish Journal of Theology,* 21, 1968, 13-16; *The Clockwork Image: A Christian Perspective on Science* (London: Methuen, 1974).

7. D. M. Sayers, *The Mind of the Maker* (London: Methuen, 1941), appears to be a major modern influence on the use of this analogy.

8. The danger of this type of argument should be noted. A. G. N. Flew has argued (orally) that if God is omnipotent, and can create beings who while free will do what he intends and predicts (as in the analogy of post-hypnotic suggestion), then he could have created them so that they would freely choose good instead of evil, and thus would have avoided all the pointless suffering in the world; but since there is suffering, it follows that God is

not omnipotent—or not good—or simply does not exist. Flew favors the last possibility.

9. B. B. Warfield, *Biblical Foundations* (London: Tyndale Press 1958), pp. 246-309, especially p. 304.

10. A similar point has been made by C. Sampson (in a letter dated 19/11/74) in which he points out how a circle can be defined as a conic section which passes through two points on the line at infinity. These points are both "real" and "imaginary" (in the nonmathematical sense of these terms). The rules of logic do not apply in the normal way when we are dealing with the infinite, and here we must recognize that logic has limitations when applied to the relations between man and God.

11. Admittedly, the Jews argued that if a principal ordered an agent to do something illegal, it is the agent who carries the sin on his own shoulders; in this situation, there is no "agency." But this ruling was designed to prevent agents hiding behind their superior authority if they acted wrongfully. J. D. M. Derrett, *Law in the New Testament* (London: Warton, Longman and Todd, 1970), pp. 52f.

12. See the essay by V. C. Grounds, pp.

13. It should not be necessary to point out that the writer of this symposium would emphatically reject universalism in the sense that all men will be saved. The offer of the gospel is indeed for *all* men, but not all accept that offer.

8

Soteriology in the Epistle to the Hebrews
GRANT R. OSBORNE

Perhaps the most enigmatic work in the New Testament is the epistle of the Hebrews. Both authorship[1] and destination are unsolved problems, and the perspective of the book as a whole is vigorously debated. The general view is that it had a Jewish Christian provenance; in fact, the strong dualism and the figures employed (angels, Melchizedek, etc.) have led some to posit an Essenic background.[2] Other have noted an Alexandrian hermeneutic and have hypothesized a Philonic origin.[3] On the other hand, many scholars recently have argued for a Gentile destination, especially since the early church considered itself to be the New Israel, and the Old Testament was authoritative for Gentile as well as Jew.[4] In fact parallels to gnosticism, such as the dualism throughout, the concept of the "wandering people of God," and the speculative Christology, have led some to postulate a Hellenistic provenance.[5] With regard to the present state of the question, it may be best to assume that the work was written to a mixed group of believers, possibly at Rome (13:24).[6] The Essenic, Philonic, and Hellenistic elements are all seemingly present and may be due to the background of the author himself as well as the addresses. The danger to which the epistle speaks, then, would be a relapse into the old way of life, whether Jew of Gentile. In countering this danger, the author points to the overwhelming superiority of Christ.

Most writers believe the theology of the epistle centers on Christology, especially upon Jesus' high priesthood.[7] However, we would agree with Marxsen's statement that while "it is true that in many respects [the writer's Christology] is unusual ... we would be interpreting the author's message wrongly, or at least in an unbalanced way, if we were to assume that he was interested in christological speculations.

His approach is far more from the soteriological angle." [8] In this epistle Christology is presented from a soteriological perspective, i.e., with a soteriological purpose.

Indeed, it is the writer's overriding soteriology which determines the contents of his epistle. His purpose has been defined in various ways: to demonstrate the superior priesthood of Christ, to warn Jewish Christians about apostasy, to demonstrate the universalism of Christianity as a world religion, to show that the Christian life is a pilgrimage, to establish the finality of the gospel.[9] All of these, which are legitimate purposes, reflect the writer's soteriological concern. He views the Christian life as a dynamic process, and salvation is seen to be a day-by-day walk with Christ. The believer dares not lapse into an apathetic Christianity, for his very "life" is at stake. This theology will be the focus of this study.

Before we can proceed further, however, we must determine the spiritual condition of the readers: were they actual Christians or not? Many have argued they were not believers; Calvin, for instance, believed they were outward followers but were not among the "elect," [10] and Kosmala says they were members of Qumran who had not yet accepted Jesus as Messiah. However, it seems far more likely in light of 3:1f.; 6:4f.; 9f.; 10:23, 26; 12:22f. that they were believers. They showed every evidence of being Christians, were called "brothers" (2:11, 12, 17; 3:1, 12; 7:5; 8:11; 10:19; 13:22, 23) and were in danger of apostatizing "from the living God" (3:12). It is doubtful that a good case can be made for denying the reality of a faith described in such terms as 6:4-6 (see below).

I. Sovereignty and Free Will

W. C. Linss[11] has noted the presence of divine necessity in the terms of 2:1 ($\delta\epsilon\hat{\iota}$), 2:10 and 7:26 ($\check{\epsilon}\pi\rho\epsilon\pi\epsilon\nu$), 2:17 and 5:3 ($\check{\omega}\varphi\epsilon\hat{\iota}\lambda\epsilon\iota$), 9:26 ($\check{\epsilon}\delta\epsilon\iota$), and 8:13 and 9:16, 23 ($\dot{\alpha}\nu\dot{\alpha}\gamma\kappa\eta$). He also finds traces in the warning passages (6:4, 18; 10:4, 11; 11:6) which discuss the impossibility of reconversion for the apostate. When we examine the passages teaching sovereignty, we find that the overwhelming majority concerns the necessity of Christ's sacrifice. The only exceptions are 5:3 (on the old covenant practices) and 2:1 (on the need for "greater attention" on the part of these apathetic Christians). There is no mention of predestination in a Pauline sense. As Marshall says regarding 11:40,[12] "The idea here is not that of the predestination of particular people to salvation, but rather of the fulfilment of God's promises in due time.... The key word in Hebrews is not predestination but promise. Such promises may be pre-temporal, but their fulfilment depends, in each case, upon the faith and obedience of the recipients (Heb. 4:2; 6:11f.; 10:36)."

In this epistle we see the God of the covenant, the God who is faithful to his promises. The keynote is reflected in 13:5, which uses Deut. 31:6, 8, "I will never leave you or forsake you," as the basis for Christian contentment. There God's faithfulness is seen to be more precious than riches; in verse 6 this becomes the antidote to fearful anxiety. At the same time these promises can only be realized by those who take them by faith. The sovereign power is available, but only to those who appropriate it for themselves. On this basis we see here a perfect balance between sovereignty and free will, with the emphasis being placed on the latter due to the particular problem to which the epistle is addressed, namely the willful apostasy of some from the faith.

II. The Possibility of Apostasy

The key to the purpose of this epistle is 13:22, which describes it as a "word of exhortation." The extensive passages on the superiority of the person, ministry and death of Christ all point to this and set the scene for the "exhortation" or warning passages. Bornkamm argues that a familiar baptismal confession has been employed to highlight the present privileges of the readers (cf. 3:1; 4:14; 10:19f.), [13] and he may be right. At the very least these are catechetical elements used to stress the foundation of the readers' faith and to provide a further backdrop to the warning passages.

Pay attention, lest you drift away, 2:1-4—The first chapter had shown that Christ was superior to the angels, who possibly had been objects of worship among at least a segment of the addressees. [14] These verses draw the conclusion from this (οὖν) and show that the purpose for the exalted Christology of chapter 1 was exhortatory. The overwhelming preeminence of the Son demands decision, and the readers must change their lives accordingly. They dare not allow themselves to "drift away" from the teaching of the gospel regarding such a One. This warning is important enough that the author includes himself in it, "We must pay more attention to what *we* have heard, lest we drift away. . . . How shall *we* escape if *we* neglect so great a salvation."

"Drift away" is a nautical term which metaphorically pictures indifference as an uncharted boat drifting out to sea and death on offshore rocks. [15] Apathetic "neglect" [16] of the Christian truths, which were confirmed by eyewitnesses, "signs and wonders," "mighty works," and "gifts of the Holy

Spirit" (vv. 3b, 4), lead to a condition from which there is no "escape." The tone is eschatological, looking to the final judgment, and the believer is warned that present indifference will result in final retribution. "Salvation" here is similar to that in 1 Peter rather than Paul (see further below), looking to the future reward of the people of God. As such, its attainment is based on persevering growth in the truths of the gospel; this is seen in the "pay more attention" of verse 1.

Do not harden your heart, lest you fail, 3:1-19—This passage follows the discussion of Jesus' high priestly activity and begins by asserting Jesus' superiority to Moses (vv. 1-6), implying thereby that rejection of Jesus is correspondingly more serious than Israel's rejection of Moses. In keeping with this theme, the author uses the wilderness wandering as an illustration of the danger (vv. 7-19). At the outset, the writer stresses their position as the true Church, the New Israel—"holy brethren" (v. 1), "partakers of Christ" (vv. 1, 14), Christ's "house" (v. 6), "brethren" (v. 12). These are called upon to persevere, to "hold fast . . . firm unto the end" (vv. 6. 14), and this is to be accomplished by "hardening not your hearts" (vv. 8, 15) and by "exhorting one another daily" (v. 13). He also emphasizes that as a result of "unbelief" one can "fail to enter God's rest" (v. 19). One must conclude that the reward is conditional[17] upon perseverance in "boldness and pride in our hope" (v. 6) and in "the beginning of our confidence" (v. 14). The danger envisaged here is that the deceitfulness of sin can progressively harden one's spiritual resolve and that this evil, unbelieving condition can cause one to "fall away from the living God" (vv. 12-15). In this context this denotes the results of active rebellion against God.[18]

Wilderness typology was quite prevalent in the early church as illustrative of both judgment and reward. Both 1 Cor. 10:1-13 and Jude 5 make it a warning against the dangers of sin. The obvious inference in all three passages is that one dare not trust his original "deliverance" from sin and lapse into apathy, but must persevere in his walk with Christ. Ps. 95:7b 11, used by the writer as the basis for his splendid *midrash* here, was sung by Jews as part of their sabbath worship in the temple. The readers probably understood it in this fashion, especially since verses 1-7a of the psalm consist of a call to worship. The obvious inference is that one must listen to God—"Today if you shall hear His voice" (vv. 7, 15)[19]—and that this listening includes obedience.[20]

Fear, lest you fall short, 4:1-13—This passage is an extended explanation of the "rest" theology of 3:11, 19. Here the writer adds the "reward" imagery from the "wilderness" typology

of 3:1-19. To the Jew the "rest" of God referred to his "promises" which were still "open" to his people, i.e., they extended
beyond the "Promised Land" of Canaan. Israel failed to appropriate these promises and so failed to "enter" God's "rest."
This is an eschatological concept which implies that the believer proleptically shares the "rest of God," i.e., the kingdom
blessings of peace and security promised for the "last days."
This rest is still promised God's people, but they must "enter"
it themselves (4:9, 10). In Jewish exegesis, the "Sabbath rest"
referred to "the world to come" (Gen. R. 17:12a).[21] Here
the writer uses it in the sense of inaugurated eschatology, for
the believer lives in a state of tension between the present
promise and future realization. It is meant for "today" for
those who obey and do not "harden" their hearts (4:6, 7 repeat-
ing 3:7-8, 15), and yet it is a heritage which they can only
claim by faith and which points forward to the next life.[22]
The believer is responsible for his perseverance in that "rest."
Therefore in this epistle salvation merges with the concept
of rewards, and the realized aspect of the reward (present
faith) merges with the final aspect (future hope). Eschatology
becomes a part of soteriology.

   Press on, lest you fall away, 5:11-6:12—After a further section on Christ's high priesthood, this time centering on his
superior qualifications and Melchizedekian office, the writer
discusses his readers' immaturity and need for spiritual
growth. 5:11 and 6:12, combined with the plea for hearing/
obedience in 3:7-8, 15; 4:7, shows that the problem had not
yet gone so far as apostasy. What we see here is a spiritual
deafness which may be called "spiritual laziness." [23] The
readers were not listening to God or seeking to grow nearer
to him. This would fit the picture of spiritual apathy we noted
in 2:1-4. Though they had been believers for some time, they
were still "babes" in Christ who had not learned even the
"fundamentals of the first principles" (5:12). Far from being
ready for the advanced doctrine of Jesus' high priestly
ministry, they needed to be retaught the ABC's of the faith.
They had retrogressed rather than progressed and so are given
a strong rebuke.

   With this in mind, the author lays down the "foundation"
teachings from which they must advance (6:1-3).[24] The
doctrines mentioned in these verses are taken by many[25]
to represent early prebaptismal catechesis, and it seems
probable that this is so. The similarities between the doctrines
and Jewish teaching (see fn. 24) may be a deliberate attempt
by the writer to remind them that they were little different
from Jews in their current state.

The danger itself is described in verses 4-6. There have been many attempts to explain this from the Calvinist perspective, and these fall into two major categories: 1) Calvin himself (fn. 10) believes the "tasting" was only partial, and these people were not among the elect; they exhibited many of the characteristics but only externally, never internally.[26] 2) Others believe the warning is only hypothetical and is not actually possible; due to the severity of the issue, the author overstates his case in order to help them remain steadfast.[27]

Both of these are doubtful. First, the powerful phraseology used of the endangered ones makes it certain that he believed they were true believers: 1) "once enlightened," a strong phrase describing conversion, with both terms used in the New Testament of the salvation which Christ wrought;[28] 2) "tasted the heavenly gift," which must mean they had fully experienced [29] the salvation blessings (cf. 2:9); 3) "partakers of the Holy Spirit," which could hardly describe anyone other than believers (cf. 1 Cor. 12:13; 2 Cor. 13:13; Phil. 2:1);[30] 4) "tasted the goodness of the Word of God and the powers of the age to come," which must mean an experience of both the Word and the kingdom blessings. "Age to come" is part of the eschatology of this epistle (see below and on 4:1-13) and speaks of the present possession of messianic glory. In conclusion, we must say there is no more powerful or detailed description of the true Christian in the New Testament.

Against the "hypothetical" theory of many Calvinists, we must note that there is no hint of such a possibility in this epistle (nor in the New Testament as a whole!). The language could hardly be more explicit; and while hyperbole is a possibility, this is not equivalent to a hypothetical, imaginary danger. The participial structure of verses 4, 6 favor the translation of the NASV, "For in the case of those who . . . and *then* have fallen away. . . ." The best interpretation is to take the Greek directly, as expressing an actual possibility;[31] in fact, some think the language favors the theory that the writer is speaking of something which had already occurred (although, as we have already pointed out, this is doubtful).

The question of reconversion is related to the two parallel participles if verse 6b, which are usually taken to be causal, i.e., reconversion is impossible "because they recrucify [32] to themselves the Son of God and expose Him to public shame." The usual explanation by those who accept the possibility of both apostasy and reconversion is reflected in the RV's margin, "the while they crucify. . . ." The present participles are taken to mean "as long as they continue" in such apostasy.[33]

However, this reads too much into the passage, and Bruce correctly says the author "distinguishes (as did the Old Testament law) between inadvertent sin and wilful sin, and the context here shows plainly that the wilful sin which he has in mind is deliberate apostasy." [34] The point the author makes is that such a person will continue in that state and will enter such a condition that he cannot repent.[35] He says nothing regarding whether such a person can ever cease his apostate state.

Finally, the writer proceeds to a point of encouragement (vv. 9-12), showing his confidence that the readers are headed for "better things." However, he is not overconfident, for this assurance includes his "desire" that each one persevere "in the fulness of hope" by throwing off their "sluggishness" and becoming "imitators" of those who have already "inherited the promises." The eschatological language of this epistle continues the theology of the Christian life as a future-oriented perseverance. The language of chapters 3-4 is repeated in a context of encouragement rather than exhortation.

Hold fast, lest you die, 10:19-39—This follows the strong doctrinal section (6:13-10:18) on Jesus' high priestly activity both in his person (7:1-28, the Melchizedekian priesthood) and in his work (8:1-10:18, the perfect sacrifice). Again the conclusion is drawn in terms of strong admonishment. As is common in the New Testament (especially Paul), didactic passages are followed by ethical commands. The same is true here, though the imperatives are couched in stronger modes due to the more serious problem to which the epistle is directed. Many of the same themes seen in 5:11-6:12 are reintroduced here. The believer's confidence is again combined with his need for perseverance, and the danger of apostasy is repeated, here in the language of Old Testament sacrifice.

Also, we once more have the readers described as actual believers. The first person plural (cf. ch. 6) dominates the exhortatory introduction (vv. 19-25), introduces the warning section (v. 26), and concludes the closing section on the past suffering for Christ and present need for a steadfast faith (v. 39). Moreover, they are described as having "received knowledge of the truth" (v. 26) and "enlightened" (v. 32). The first phrase is found often in the pastorals (1 Tim. 2:4; 2 Tim. 2:25, 3:7; Tit. 1:1) and the Johannine corpus (John 8:32; 1 John 2:21) and certainly refers to experiencing the salvific force of God's revelation.[36] Moreover, they are described as "sanctified" by the "blood of the covenant" (v. 29).[37] Both terms in the context of this epistle speak of Christian regeneration. "Sanctified by the blood" in 9:14 speaks of the power of Jesus' redemption; in 10:10, of Jesus' "once-for-all" sacrifice; in 10:14, of the believer's perfection; and in 10:19, of Christian worship (see further on the discussion of "perfection"). It is obviously a key phrase in the author's concept of salvation and stems from the *verba Christi* (Mark 14:24; Matt. 26:28; Luke 22:20; cf. 1 Cor. 11:25).

Indeed, the whole previous section (vv. 19-25) speaks of the believer's confidence in entering God's presence *via* the High Priest. Interlaced within this summary statement are a series of exhortatory passages, encouraging the believers to "enter the holy place" (v. 19), "draw near" to God in worship (v. 22), "hold fast the confession of hope" (v. 23), and constantly "encourage" each other in the faith (v. 24). Verse 22 is especially crucial, speaking of both outward and inward cleansing in language reminiscent of levitical ceremonial ablutions (Ex. 29:4 for priests, Lev. 16:4 for the high priest) and also of the messianic promise in Ezek. 36:25, which also combines the two: "I will sprinkle clean water upon you, and you will be clean; I will cleanse you. . . . A new heart I will give you, and a new spirit I will put within you." The author undoubtedly considers his readers to be actual believers who had a vital experience of the living Christ.[38]

The apostasy itself is described in very strong terms as a willful turning to sin.[39] Three phrases stress the severity of the act (v. 29): 1) "trampled under foot the Son of God," a phrase which shows open contempt and deepest scorn (cf. Zech. 12:3 LXX; Matt. 5:13, 7:6); 2) "considered the blood of the covenant an unholy thing," which may involve eucharistic sins[40] but more likely refers to the attitude of the apostate, who makes Jesus' blood a "common" thing, i.e., of no account; 3) "insulted the Spirit of grace," which is at least as strong as "grieving the Spirit" in Eph. 4:30 and may well refer to the "unpardonable sin" of Mark 3:29 and parallels. One must say that such a sin involves the complete rejection of Christ, and so the conclusion, like 6:4, is that "no further sin-offering remains." In this epistle this must mean that no further forgiveness is possible; the apostate has become an "adversary of God" and all that "remains" is "a fearful expectation of judgment," "a fierceness of fire" (v. 27).[41]

Again the writer turns after this powerful warning to encouragement (as in 6:9-12). Verses 32-34 provide the setting for this warning (and probably for the others as well). Under threat of persecution[42] they were being pressured to renounce their faith. They had come through one such experience and were being asked to persevere through another. However, in verse 39 he shows his confidence in them: "We are not among those who draw back to perdition; we are of the faith and obtain life." This is taken by many (see fn. 27) as further evidence for hypothetical thrust of the warnings (cf. 6:9f.). However, again this hardly supports such a view, since the argument is simply, "You haven't done this yet; I don't think you will," rather than a prophecy regarding their final perseverance.

Be careful, lest you fall short, 12:1-17—The best-known passage in this epistle is found in the intervening material between these two exhortation passages. Chapter 11, of course, contains the famous discussion of faith. Again, the doctrinal section has a soteriological purpose, the conclusion is that in the face of the data one must persevere. Most scholars agree today that the "cloud of witnesses" in 12:1 refers back to the list of faith-heroes in chapter 11. So "faith" also has an exhortatory thrust (see below for the writer's view of faith).

Heb. 12:1-11 calls for a general submission to God's disciplinary process, and 12:12-17 is a call for action. The warning passage itself is found in 12:15-17, but the exhortations in verses 1-14 build up to it. Verse 3b concludes the section on Jesus' example for perseverance (vv. 1-3a) and commands that they "not tire, losing heart" (Montefiore's translation). The imagery continues the athletic metaphor of verse 1, picturing the runner collapsing before the end of a race. The following ten verses compare the sufferings of the readers to the discipline of a father (God) for his children (the Christian). The theology of the passage teaches that God does not superficially allow trials but does so out of love, for the good of his children, so that they may learn discipline. He always has our best in mind, desiring that we might "share his holiness" (v. 10) and that this might "yield the peaceful harvest of righteousness" (v. 11). This section also closes with a general exhortation (vv. 12-14), again based on athletic imagery but couched in Old Testament language (Isa. 35:3f.). The idea is that the spiritually crippled should brace themselves first and then help the "lame" to come for healing. There is added here the concept of responsibility, not only for one's self but also for fellow believers.

These general exhortations point to a danger which they must avoid. Again that danger is apostasy (v. 15—"fall away"; v. 17—"rejected"). The possibility that some will do so is strongly suggested[43] and there are three areas within this danger: 1) "falling away from the grace of God," which echoes the active apostasy of 6:4f. and 10:29f.; 2) "root of bitterness," which "springs up and troubles you," looking back to Deut. 29:18 (cf. 1QH 4:14) and stressing the dangerous results of apostates in the community who "defile" many others;[44] 3) "immoral and unspiritual people, like Esau," which draws upon Jewish tradition regarding his immorality and profane character[45] in selling his birthright as an example of the finality of apostasy (he "had no opportunity to repent" [46]). Therefore, we must again conclude that the writer considers apostasy to be not only a viable possibility but also a definite danger for his readers. Again the severity of the danger is presented in the strongest terms.

Conclusion—Several points have been clarified in this discussion: 1) the writer was addressing actual believers; 2) these believers were in danger of apostatizing from the faith, probably as a result of pressures placed upon them in the form of persecution; 3) such apostasy, if experienced, is irredeemable, for the person involved places himself beyond the possibility of repentance;[47] 4) the only remedy is a constant perseverance in the faith, and a continual growth to Christian maturity; this latter antidote must be accomplished not only individually but also corporately, i.e., every member must help and encourage one another in the faith; 5) the author is convinced that they would not become apostates and encourages them thereby to further growth in Christ.

In terms of the last two points, we must note that the major soteriological purpose of the epistle is not warning but encouragement. As Marshall notes,[48] this is accomplished in three major ways: First, they are reminded of the basic gospel truths which they had learned, to which they must cling, and from which they must develop (2:1-4; 3:6, 14; 10:35-39). Second, a living faith is made the earnest of the future hope (see further below) and leads to an obedient perseverance which triumphs over sin. Third, he calls on them "to assist each other by mutual exhortation on their pilgrim journey" (3:13; 10:24f.; 12:12f.; 13:17). These are all given as means of encouraging them to ensure their perseverance in light of the threat of apostasy.

III. The Atonement and Repentance

In this epistle the atonement is seen as a radical, once-for-all provision given by the sovereign God. This is seen especially in the writer's use of ἅπαξ (found here 8 of the 14 New Testament occurrences) and ἐφάπαξ (found here 3 of its 5 New Testament occurrences). Four of the former and one of the latter occur in chapter 9 (vv. 7, 26, 27, 28; and v. 12), which centers on Jesus' "once-for-all" sacrifice in contrast to the continuous "once a year" sacrifices of the high priest. "Eternal redemption,"[49] according to verse 12, came through Jesus' "once-for-all" entrance into the Holy Place with "his own blood." Here and in 11:35 redemption is seen as the eternal gift[50] procured by Christ's once-for-all sacrifice.[51]

The connection between atonement and repentance is seen in 6:4f., where the once-for-all provision is connected to the impossibility of a second repentance. J. Behm says Hebrews "emphasizes the seriousness of the total change implied in conversion when this is considered in relation to the obvious danger that Christians will grow slack in their Christianity and sink into dull indifference." [52] The conclusion is that Hebrews makes repentance a total commitment, a total surrender of the whole person at conversion, and that this can only be negated by a total apostasy. In light of the finality and vast superiority of the redemption Christ provided, repentance must also be a once-for-all decision. Due to the nature of the epistle—it addressed believers in danger of apostatizing —it says little regarding the "first" repentance; e.g., it does not comment on the nature of repentance, whether or not man's free will plays a part, and whether or not he is sovereignly "elect" of God. All the attention is given to Christian exhortation, and the author's soteriology as a whole must be found in his view of faith and implied from his view of repentance.

IV. Salvation and Eschatology

This epistle, like 1 Peter, gives salvation an eschatological orientation. It therefore must be seen in light of the inaugurated eschatology already discussed (cf. p. 7). Many have noted the primitive Jewish-Christian apocalyptic seen throughout the epistle and have argued that it provides the fundamental perspective of the epistle.[53] There is indeed a futuristic apocalyptic here; Christ awaits the day of victory over his enemies (1:11; 10:13, 25) when he will "appear a second time" (9:28), and God has already "subjected the world to come" unto him (2:5). The writer expected the imminent return of Christ (10:25, 37) which would see the fulfillment of God's promises for his people.

Indeed, the word "promise" provides a bridge between eschatology and soteriology, showing that the basic eschatological perspective is indeed "inaugurated" and is seen in a soteriological sense. "Promise" occurs fourteen times and is connected with the rest of God (4:1), the inheritance of the saints (6:12; 9:15), Abraham and the old covenant (6:15, 17; 7:6; 11:9, 13, 17), faith (11:33, 39), and the salvation Christ has provided (8:6; 10:36). It is therefore a soteriological term which looks to salvation as a present possession of the future hope. It is a "heavenly" promise (11:16) which links "the longed-for homeland of 11:16 and the heavenly Jerusalem of 12:22," "the unshaken Kingdom (12:28) and the city to come (13:14)." [54] This is both a future promise and a present experience; Christians "have come" already to these (12:22f.).

A second word which connects the two doctrines is "hope," which adds the present aspect to the futuristic "promise"; the believer accepts the promise as a living hope. As a "better hope" (7:19) it is especially connected to the command to persevere in the "confidence of our hope" (3:6; 10:23) or "full assurance of hope until the end" (6:11; cf. 6:18). "Hope" is both a present possession and a future possibility; in it there is a tension between the "already" and the "not yet" [55] which illustrates perfectly the problem discussed in the epistle. In our discussion of chapters 3 and 4, we pointed out the present and future aspects of the "Sabbath rest." [56] It appears also in the warning section of chapter 6, where the believer is described as experiencing the "heavenly gift" and "the powers of the age to come" (6:4, 5). The heavenly realm, or eschatological reality, has entered this age and become a part of the believer's life.

It is in this light that we will examine the writer's soteriology. It must be understood as the present possession of a future inheritance. W. Foerster says "σωτηρία denotes coming salvation. . . . In content this σωτηρία is defined by δόξα... but it is typical of Hebrews that the coming σωτηρία is viewed as already present." [57] It is seen as both a future inheritance (5:9) and a present reality (7:25). It is linked to the past provision of redemption through Christ (2:10), the present experience of its benefits (6:9), and the future finalizing of its rewards (9:28). Above all, it is connected with the encounter of Jesus' proclamation of eschatological salvation (2:3).[58] Foerster (fn. 57) connects it explicitly with δόξα; this is especially true when one combines 2:3 with 2:10, in which ἀρχηγὸς τῆς σωτηρίας is connected with the "glory" which God brings his sons.[59] Note again the juxtaposition of past (Christ as "pioneer"), present (sonship)[60] and future (glory) in salvation. Thus while there is security in our salvation (6:9, 10; 10:39) there is no guarantee. It is ours by virtue of repentance but can only be secured finally by means of perseverance.

Moreover, salvation in Hebrews is not separated from the life of holiness. The writer would agree with James' "faith without works is dead" theology. This is seen especially in the writer's use of ἁγιάζω in the epistle. Throughout (9:13; 10:10, 14, 29; 13:12) the term has its Jewish force of "purify,"[61] speaking of the process by which the ceremonially defiled were "cleansed" of their impurity. The Christian's present state as believer is spoken of as a consecration act. As Bruce says, "By His death they are consecrated to God for His worship and service and are set apart for God as His holy people, destined to enter into His glory. For sanctification is glory begun, and glory is sanctification completed." [62]

therefore the major motif is the present status of the believer as a consecrated one.[63] It is synonymous with, yet also builds upon, σωτηρία. At the same time there is a dynamic element in it. The presence of salvation within must lead to a "holy life" without. In 12:10, 14 the term is given the meaning it has in the Pauline corpus (cf. Rom. 8:18f.; 2 Cor. 1:12; 1 Thess. 5:23, etc.), i.e., holiness of life and conduct. To secure the final salvation, one must continue in a day-by-day holy walk with God.

V. Faith and Salvation

H. N. Huxhold has written that faith in Hebrews, especially in chapters 11-12, is more like Pauline hope than Pauline faith.[64] In this he is essentially correct, for the concept has an eschatological character in the epistle. No better definition of faith in this epistle could be given then that found in 11:1: "Now faith is certainty regarding things hoped for, evidence for things not seen." [65] ὑπόστασις translated "certainty" here, has both an objective and a subjective side in its other two occurrences in Hebrews. In 1:3 it is used objectively of God's "essence" and in 3:14 it is used subjectively of the believer's "confidence." Here it has nuances of both,[66] though the latter predominates, and "certainty" seems the best translation. ἔλεγχος "evidence," employs the metaphor of eyesight to illustrate spiritual faith. In the same way that our eyes provide "evidence" for physical reality, "faith" produces evidence for spiritual reality.[67]

In Paul, while faith and hope are similar and closely connected (cf. Rom. 4:18; 8:24), the basic meaning is personal trust and union with Christ. In John it is faith-commitment and personal belief (John 1:12; cf. 20:29). "In Hebrews faith is the faculty to perceive the reality of the unseen world of God and to make it the primary object of one's life." [68] The whole of chapter 11 relates to the writer's concept of salvation as a future-oriented gift. He uses the Old Testament faith-heroes as examples of his basic definition in verse 1 and as illustrations of his concept of salvation. They too had to persevere in accepting the future-thrust of salvation as a promise from God. They lived as though the future state was a present reality. Faith was simply accepting God's word, believing it, and living in that light.

The lesson is therefore obvious. Salvation must be secured by a persevering faith which grasps the future salvation and makes it a present reality. Faith must take hold of his promises in the midst of trials and suffering,[69] trusting God in light of the blessings Christ has wrought. The danger was that they might allow their faith to slip, lose sight of God's promises, and therefore fail to "keep their souls" and be "destroyed" (10:39). This last warning is couched in the language of encouragement and has led some to conclude that the author is actually certain that his readers will see the end of their faith whatever the persecution, i.e., that he teaches the final triumph of their faith.[70] While this is somewhat true, it cannot detract from the persevering aspect of this faith and the reality of this danger. This comforting thought must be read in the light of the warning passages, not vice versa. The whole pattern of soteriology in this epistle demands the absolute necessity of perseverance for final salvation.

VI. Perfection and Faith

One of the important teachings of Hebrews centers on the development of perfection, first in Christ and consequently in the believer. Heb. 12:2 links the two concepts—perfection and faith—in Jesus himself. He is called "the Pioneer[71] and Perfecter of our faith." The problem is how Jesus could be the "perfecter" when he himself was "perfected" (2:10; 5:9). Käsemann takes a literal view and interprets it in gnostic fashion that the redeemer needed to be perfected himself before he could bring others to perfection.[72] However, as Marshall shows, the dominant idea in both verses is suffering, not perfection.[73] It is not that Christ was imperfect but that he entered completely into the believer's experience of "perfection" through suffering. This was part of his high priestly ministry.

Behind this whole idea is the pattern of "obedience," a key part of the writer's perfection theology, as seen in 5:8-9.[74] Obedience to the Father can only be learned through "discipline" (12:5f.), and this is the path to maturity or perfection. Jesus was "perfected" by becoming "obedient unto death" (Phil. 2:8) and suffering as the one sacrifice. It is in this sense that he is "Pioneer and Perfecter." By his perfect sacrifice[75] he brought man to the possibility of perfection (10:14). He was both perfect provider and perfect example in bringing men to sonship and glory.[76]

A strong debate ensues over the question whether τελειόω and cognates[77] are cultic[78] or ethical[79] in thrust. Actually, it is best to note both ideas in the concept. The cultic-religious implications are seen in the tabernacle dualism of 9:9f.; the Melchizedekian priesthood emphasis (5:9); the imperfect law (7:19), and the mature-immature contrast (5:14). Yet within these very categories there are ethical implications; implicit within these is an ethical-moral sense. This is seen especially in the theological concept of the "pilgrimage" of believers, who are on a "wilderness journey" in search of God's "rest." This is also indicated in the general soteriology of the entire epistle. A march-forward (6:1f.), a perseverance in the essentials of Christian development, is at the heart of the writer's exhortation.[80] Salvation is the eschatological possession of a forward-looking faith. Of course, this does not mean there is a total flux in salvation, for there is a once-for-all foundation (7:27; 9:12) for the Christian's sanctification (10:10). [81] Nevertheless this foundation is not a static fact but rather a dynamic, life-producing force in which the believer must be actively involved "now" (2:8; 8:6; 9:24; 12:26).

Therefore perfection is more than an external, cultic experience; it is an internal life-changing "goal." [82] Wikgren defines the concept thusly: "The response of faith by the believer" is "in a sense proleptically *teleios* through initiation and participation in that community of faith which also constitutes this ideal goal (cf. xi. 40)".[83] The end is not finally attained or obtained; one must reach it by suffering as he suffered. The idea is the attainment of "completeness" or "maturity," and the Christian is pictured as one in progress toward that end. He must "press on toward perfection" (6:1) [84] on the basis of the "greater and more perfect tabernacle" (9:11; cf. 9:9). It is the promise which leads to perfection (11:39-40). Heb. 12:23 seems to connect this with the believer's death, which is the "completion" of his earthly pilgrimage.[85] Therefore we might conclude that perfection, as one of the major terms for salvation in this epistle (see also "repentance" and "sanctified": earlier) has a twofold thrust: 1) it speaks of the crisis experience of salvation, in which one receives the salvific gifts;[86] and 2) it speaks of the eschatological "goal" by which the Christian strives *via* his spiritual pilgrimage to enter that final "rest" with God. This latter element, which is identified with the doctrine of perseverance in Hebrews, is predominant in this epistle.

Conclusion

Many might argue that the soteriology of this epistle, as presented here, is given a semi-pelagian coloring.[87] This, however, is to misunderstand the perspective from which the author wrote, as well as the "word of exhortation" (13:22) within which his purpose is found. The readers were believers who were in danger of failure and apostasy, and so the writer does not spend time discussing their faith-decision. This is presupposed in his ἅπαξ– theology, which provides the background for his view of salvation as a pilgrimage, i.e., both a present possession and a future hope. His perspective, then, is the other side of the salvation-coin, salvation as the eschatological goal, not only a present experience but also a future gift, which can only be obtained by perseverance in Christian development. The writer argues against a static Christianity which is content to dwell in the assurance of final inheritance. Such a faith is not faith at all; it inevitably stagnates into immaturity (5:13-14; 6:1) and leaves itself open to apostasy (6:4f.).

Some might also charge that such a doctrine teaches salvation by works; but here we must note that Hebrews presupposes the faith-decision and relates to perseverance in that new condition. Moreover, we would add that there is no sense here of a perseverance by works. The writer frequently connects perseverance with the sovereign power of God, and there is a definite sense of security (see above). However, this security itself is a present possession rather than a future guarantee. 10:14 and 2:11 use "timeless present" participles to describe the perfecting and sanctifying work of Christ. 12:28 says we have received "a kingdom which cannot be shaken" and 9:12 says Christ obtained "eternal redemption." However, this must be seen as present "promise" rather than as absolute certainty (9:15) and as subject to the dangers discussed in the epistle. Therefore, we would conclude that for the writer perseverance is not a "work" but is rather a yielding to the sovereign power of the Holy Spirit within.[88]

Hebrews and John—A comparison of these two key works will help clarify the doctrine of perseverance as we have defined it, for the two represent opposite sides of the same truth. Both teach a combination of security and responsibility in salvation, with John stressing the former and Hebrews the latter. In John 6:37-40 and 10:29-30 the believer's security is stressed in emphatic language (but note responsibility in the present participles of 6:35, 40 and in the "hear-follow" terminology of 10:27),[89] while in Hebrews the believer's responsibility to persevere is stressed (but note security in the passages just mentioned as well as in 6:9f. and 10:39). The promise of God's support provides security, but the Christian must avail himself of this promise "lest he fail to enter God's rest." [90]

New Testament passages on apostasy—If this epistle was the only place in the New Testament where the doctrine of perseverance and the possibility of apostasy were taught, we would wonder if our exegesis might be wrong or if Hebrews perhaps was not a part of the canon. However, it agrees with many other passages in the New Testament, and we must see it in the light of the theology of the New Testament as a whole. Several passages teach what we may call "conditional salvation," i.e., salvation which can only be received finally when man meets certain God-ordained conditions. Rom. 8:12-14 makes sonship conditional upon our continual participation in the leading of the Spirit; while the Spirit does the work (so Owen) the believer must continually yield to it. 1 Cor. 15:1-2 says that one must "hold fast" to the truths of the Word, lest his belief be "in vain"; this must mean perseverance is the only guarantee against an "emptying" ("in vain" is "to no avail" rather than "thoughtlessly" or "rashly") of one's salvation in apostasy. John 8:51 makes obedience to his Word the condition for eternal life ("never see death"). Col. 1:21-23 says the believer will be presented "blameless" only "if [he] continues in the faith" and is "not moved away from the hope of the Gospel" (cf. Acts 14:22). 2 Pet. 1:8-11 warns against forgetting the salvation experience (apostasy) and exhorts the readers to "make your calling and election certain." Perseverance is also seen in the phrase, "as long as you practise these things, you will never stumble." Finally, 1 John 2:23-25 says that one will only abide in the Father and have eternal life "if what [he] heard from the beginning abides in [him]."

There are also several passages stating the danger of apostasy. Matt. 24:4, 5, 11, 13 and 2 Thess. 2:3 prophesy a general apostasy which will precede the tribulation period. Only "he who endures to the end" "will be saved." It should be noted that this speaks of the time preceding the tribulation and not of the tribulation itself. 1 Tim. 4:1, 16 says some will apostatize and exhorts Timothy to persevere so as to ensure his salvation and that of his flock. 2 Pet. 3:17, 18 calls for diligence and exhorts the readers to guard themselves against the error of those who "fall from [their] own steadfastness"; the phrases "led away" and "fall from" show this is a real, not hypothetical, danger. In 1 Cor. 9:27, Paul's statement that he may become "castaway" must mean "rejected" rather than just "disqualified"; in Rom. 1:28; 2 Cor. 13:5; 2 Tim. 3:8; and Tit. 1:16 it means "reprobate" and refers to those who are outside the kingdom of God. James 1:14-16 and 5:19, 20 warn against the danger of "erring" and thus "dying" and equate "erring" with "straying." The death here is more than just physical death but must refer to eternal condemnation. 2 Pet. 2:20, 21 is quite similar to Heb. 6:4f. and 10:29f. Those who have "escaped the pollutions of the world by the knowledge of the Lord" and "are again entangled and overcome" are in a worse state than before. Again these must be believers, and again they have apostatized from the faith. Finally, Rev. 22:19 shows that some can have their names "removed from the book of life." These passages show that the position of the writer to the Hebrews with regard to apostasy fits the mainstream of New Testament teaching.

NOTES

1. Guesses, in addition to Paul (which few hold anymore), have involved Barnabas (Tertullian), Apollos (Luther), Clement of Rome (Eusebius), Luke (Origen, Calvin), Philip (W. M. Ramsay), Aquilla (H. Alford), or Priscilla (Harnack.)

2. See Yadin, Schnackenburg, Betz., Danielou, Kosmala, Bowman. Bruce, on the other hand, believes these are Jewish sectarians in general rather than Essenes in particular.

3. See Spicq and Montefiore, who argue the author was converted from Philonism.

4. See Kümmel, who argues that since in the epistle Christ is made superior to the Old Testament rather than to Judaism, the readers are probably Gentile. See also Moffatt & Scott.

5. See Käsemann, Michaelis, Marxsen. Narborough, on the other hand, believes the readers were proto-gnostic Jews.

6. See Guthrie and Kümmel. Guthrie would see a stronger Jewish element, Kümmel a stronger Gentile element. We would follow Guthrie's position.

7. See F. F. Bruce, "To the Hebrews" or "To the Essenes"?, *New Testament Studies* 9 (1963), 217-32. lii; and G. E. Ladd, *A Theology of the New Testament* (Grand Rapids, Mich.: Eerdmans, 1974), p. 577f.

8. W. Marxsen, *Introduction to the New Testament*, tr. G. Buswell (Philadelphia, Pa.; Fortress Press, 1968 [Oxford: Blackwell]), p. 219.

9. See, respectively, Nairne, Bruce, Manson, Käsemann, and Marshall.

10. See his commentary on Hebrews, especially ch. 6; and his *Institutes*, I, 608-609.

11. W. C. Linss, "Logical Terminology in the Epistle to the Hebrews," *Concordia Theological Monthly* 37 (1966), pp. 365-69.

12. I. H. Marshall, *Kept by the Power of God* (London: Epworth Press, 1969), p. 147. Against Michel's claim that the "firstborn enrolled in heaven" in 12:23 teaches election, he asserts (p. 148) that it simply speaks of the "burgess role of the citizens of Zion" and says nothing about election.

13. G. Bornkamm, "Das Bekenntnis im Hebrärtntirg," *Studien zu Antike und Christentum* II (München: C. Kaiser, 1959), pp. 188f. However, we would not go so far as Hughes, who says the danger was the repudiation of the converts' baptism, also a once-for-all event (to repeat it would be to repeat Christ's crucifixion and thus to mock the cross). There is no basis for such an extensive reinterpretation of the apostasy passages.

14. So Manson, Bowman, and Montefiore.

15. Another metaphorical use of the same verb pictures a ring "slipping off" a finger and being lost.

16. This question (v. 3) is used by those who wish to deny that the readers were Christians. However, the use of "we" throughout plus the data already discussed favors the interpretation here.

17. The conditional particles in vv. 6, 14 are, respectively, ἐάν and ἐάνπερ which provide further evidence that the writer considers apostasy to be possible.

18. "Provocation" and "trial" in v. 8 and Ps. 95:8 (LXX) look back to Ex. 17:1-7, where Moses, exasperated at Israel's revolt because there was no water, renamed the place *Massah* (tempting) and *Meribah* (striving), because their "strife" "tempted" Yahweh's patience.

19. Bruce, *op. cit.*, p. 65, points out the messianic interpretation of this phrase in TB Sanhedrin 98a, where it is used to explain the coming of the Messiah to the gates of Rome. Messianic salvation is conditional upon hearing and obeying.

20. Both the Old Testament and New Testament concepts of "hearing" precluded one's obedience to the message. See G. Kittel, "ἀκούω," *TDNT*, I, pp. 218-20.

21. See H. Montefiore, *The Epistle to the Hebrews*, Harper's New Testament Commentaries (New York: Harper & Row, [London: Black], 1964), pp. 85f.; and Bruce, *op. cit.*, pp. 77f.

22. See C. K. Barrett's excellent discussion in his article. "The Eschatology of Hebrews," *The Background of the New Testament and its Eschatology*, ed. W. D. Davies and D. Daube (Cambridge: University Press, 1956), pp. 363-93.

23. νωθροί in 5:11 and 6:12 refers to a "dullness" of hearing which may well denote disobedience to God, in light of the "hearing" metaphor.

24. As Marshall, *op. cit.*, p. 135, notes, the writer does not deny the possibility of further attention to these rudimentary doctrines but says they must advance beyond them.

25. See Bornkamm, Montefiore, Hughes, Buchanan, Michel. Bruce, *op. cit.*, pp. 113f., argues that it refers to Jewish doctrines used as a foundation for Christianity (seen especially in the plural "baptisms," which he believes refers to "ablutions" in a Jewish sense. However, Buchanan and Montefiore explain this in terms of Jewish Christianity, as seen in examples like the Baptist's disciples (Acts 19). Whatever the explanation, it is doubtful in this context if it refers to anything but catechetical instructions.

26. See also Owen, 1f.; and H. C. Thiessen, *Introductory Lectures in Systematic Theology* (Grand Rapids, Mich.: Eerdmans, 1949), pp. 390-91.

27. W. Manson, *The Epistle to the Hebrews* (London: Hodder & Stoughton, 1951), pp. 106f.; J. W. Bowman, *Hebrews, James, 1 Peter, 2 Peter* Layman's Bible Commentaries (London: SCM, 1968), pp. 42f.; Barclay, pp. 57-59; W. G. T. Shedd, *Dogmatic Theology*, 3 vols. (Grand Rapids, Mich.: Zondervan, 1969 [originally 1894]), II, p. 558; and K. S. Wuest, "Hebrews Six in the Greek New Testament," *Bibliothecra Sacra* 119 (1962), pp. 45-53.

28. "Once"—1 Pet. 3:18; Jude 3, 5; and a key word in Hebrews (see below); "enlightened"—2 Cor. 4:4, 6; Heb. 10:32.

29. See the discussion in Marshall, *op. cit.*, pp. 137-38, of Calvin and Owen on this phrase. J. Behm, "γεύομαι," *TDNT*, I, pp. 675-76; and R. Shank, *Life in the Son* (Springfield, Mis.: Westcott, 1960), pp. 177f., favor this interpretation.

30. Those who argue against this, like Owen and Wuest, do so in the sense of Calvin's "common grace," that some are given the blessings of the Spirit who have never been the "temple of the Spirit."

31. As Marshall, *op. cit.*, p. 140, says "The element of hypothesis in the passage is not in that the danger is an imaginary one but in that it is only a possibility and not yet a reality in the lives of the readers."

32. We agree here with Marshall and Michel, *contra* Bruce, that the ἀνα-prefix of this verb in this context means "again" rather than "up" (i.e., reinforcing "crucify").

33. See Shank, *op. cit.*, pp. 309-29, for this view.

34. Bruce, *op. cit.*, p. 124. This is supported by the parable of vv. 7-8, where the land which refuses to yield a good crop, no matter what attention is given it, is considered derelict and meant for the "fire."

35. As to the oft-debated question as to the implied subject of "be renewed to repentance," whether God or man, Spicq believes it refers to man, Marshall to God. In light of the implied teaching of 12:17 (see below), we believe the most probable meaning to be that God will not renew them to repentance.

36. See Bruce, *op. cit.*, pp. 258f.; and Montefiore, *op. cit.*, p. 177; *contra* H. Kosmala, *Hebräer-Essener-Christen* (Leiden: E. J. Brill, 1959), p. 137 and T. Hewitt, *The Epistle to the Hebrews* Tyndale Commentary (London: Tyndale Press, 1960), pp. 165f.

37. See Marshall's arguments against Hewitt's attempt to say the sanctification here is merely external rather than internal (p. 142).

38. This is favored by the present tenses used throughout the hortatory passages here, which adjure continuing in their present state.

39. This is described in language reminiscent of sinning "with a high hand" (Deut. 17:12, Num. 15:30), which act resulted in being "cut off" from God without forgiveness.

40. "Blood of the covenant" was a eucharistic phrase (the passages mentioned above are all in eucharistic contexts) and may refer here to the same situation reflected in 1 Cor. 11:25f. See O. Michel, *Der Brief an die Hebräer*, Meyer New Testament Commentaries (Göttingen: Vandenhoeck, 1966 [12]), p. 236; Montefiore, *op. cit.*, p. 179.

41. In the Old Testament there was no forgiveness for willful sins, and Qumran made apostasy an unpardonable sin (1QS 2:13f.; 3:4f.).

42. This, along with 12:4, is a major text in dating the epistle. It is not possible to enter this difficult discussion at this time. However, Bruce, *op. cit.*, pp. 267f., uses it to argue for an early 60's date, and this would fit the eschatology of the epistle.

43. The phrasing says, "Be careful to make certain that no one falls away from the grace of God."

44. See Bruce, *op. cit.*, pp. 365ff.; and Marshall, *op. cit.*, pp. 143f., who demonstrate that the imagery of the Deuteronomic passage speaks of a man who leads Israel into idolatry, saying that person will not find forgiveness but only "the curses written in this book," and "the Lord will blot out his name from under heaven" (Deut. 29:20).

45. We might note the degree of vilification in the Jewish allegory of Esau. He becomes the symbol not only of immorality (Gen. R. 65, 70d, 72a) but also a prime example of unrepentant sinners (Philo's Leg. All. 3:2 and de Migr. Abr. 153).

46. The metaphor itself does not mean God refused to forgive Esau but rather that the decision, once made, was final. Esau was "disqualified" and lost his "birthright." "Repentance," then, as in NEB, would refer to "second thoughts," i.e., Esau found no way to rectify the situation and regain his birthright. See R. T. Watkins, "The N.E.B. and the Translation of Hebrews xii. 17," *Expository Times*, 73 (1961-62), pp. 29-31 and also fn. 47.

47. Note here that the author in 12:17 went even further into this question. In the case of a person actively "seeking" reinstatement, the author seems to say God may deny him the "opportunity," i.e., may not allow him to be reconverted. However, it must be kept in mind that the author speaks throughout of active rather than passive apostasy. It is the one who "willfully" apostatizes who is discussed.

48. Marshall, *op. cit.*, pp. 146-47. See also E. Käsemann, *Das wandernde Gottesvolk* (Göttingen: Vandenhoeck, 1959 [3]), *passim*.

49. "Redemption" here is λύτρωσις, part of the New Testament "ransom" terminology. The synonym ἀπολύτρωσις occurs in 9:15 and 11:35. The basic meaning is seen in 11:35, where it speaks of "deliverance" from torture. Christ has procured man's deliverance from sin. As noted by J. Behm, "λύτρωσις," *TDNT*, IV, p. 351, there is no real "ransom" force in the use of this word here.

50. For the eschatology involved in the "promise" aspect of this provision (cf. 9:15) see the next section.

51. This is also seen in the "once for all" theology of 7:27 and 10:2, 10.

52. J. Behm, "μετανοέω," *TDNT*, IV, pp. 1005f. He believes 6:4f. states man cannot "bring them back" and 12:17 adds that God will not allow them the opportunity. As is already said in this study, we believe 12:17 gives the implied subject of 6:4.

53. See Barrett, *op. cit.*, pp. 363f.; Ladd, *op. cit.*, pp. 572f.; and W. Robinson, *The Eschatology of the Epistle to the Hebrews* (Birmingham, A. Selly Oak, 1950), *passim*. They argue that the apparent Philonic dualism between the heavenly and earthly realms, seen in chs. 8 and 9 is subservient to eschatology; when properly understood it is not Philonic as such.

54. Ladd, *op. cit.*, p. 574.

55. See O. Cullmann, *The Christology of the New Testament* (London: SCM, 1963 [2]), pp. 98f.; and Ladd, *op. cit.*, pp. 574f.

56. Barrett, *op. cit.*, p. 372, says, "The rest, precisely because it is God's, is both present and future; men must enter it and must strive to enter it."

57. W. Foerster, "σωτηρία," *TDNT*, VII, p. 996. See also C. E. Carlston, "Eschatology and Repentance in the Epistle to the Hebrews," *Journal of Biblical Literature* 78 (1959), pp. 296-302, who notes this same connection, though he takes a hypothetical view of the warning passages.

58. E. M. B. Green, *The Meaning of Salvation* (Philadelphia, Pa.: Westminster Press, 1965), p. 204, says salvation here "retains the characteristic New Testament eschatological tension. It is used as a general description of the Christian way (1:14; 6:9), but as both of these verses suggest, the emphasis is primarily future. Salvation belongs to the eternal world which our author contrasts with the empirical."

59. Montefiore, *op. cit.*, p. 60, defines this "glory" as the "splendour of ultimate salvation, which awaits the consummation of all things."

60. We might notice the presence of "many sons" here, which qualifies the universal atonement of Jesus "on behalf of all men" (v. 9). Christ died for "all," but only the "many" are sons.

61. G. W. Buchanan, *To the Hebrews*, Anchor Bible (Garden City, N.Y.: Doubleday, 1972), p. 32, uses this meaning of the term as major evidence that the epistle was directed to Jewish believers.

62. Bruce, *op. cit.*, p. 45.

63. This is probably the meaning of "holy brethren" in 3:1 and "saints" in 6:10.

64. Huxhold, 657f. In this same sense, Delling, "τελειόω," *TDNT*, VIII, 86 n3, says, "In Hb. πίστις is not be equated with σωτηρία, since it does not specifically denote the content of Christian faith."

65. The form of the Greek shows that this is a formal definition of "faith."

66. Faith accepts a future possibility as if it had present "substance" (AV). Therefore it is both objective and subjective in thrust. See Bruce, *op. cit.*, pp. 277-79; Michel, *op. cit.*, pp. 98-100, Marshall, *op. cit.*, p. 148.

67. Similarities between this definition and Hellenistic thought lead Grässer and Käsemann to conclude that the concept of faith here is taken from gnostic teachings. Others, like Bruce, see similarities with Philo. In light of previous conclusions regarding the Jewish background, the latter is much more likely.

68. Ladd, *op. cit.*, p. 584.

69. *Ibid.*, p. 585, shows how the writer was careful to make his list apply to the present situation. In vv. 35-39 he lists those who had faith in the midst of torture, "refusing to accept release, that they might rise again to a better life." These are seen in 12:1 ("witnesses") as an example for the present situation.

70. See P. M. Bretscher, "Faith Triumphant—Echoes from the Epistle

to the Hebrews," *Concordia Theological Monthly* 31 (1960), pp. 728-39, and also the discussion of that passage, p. 13.

71. On this term, see the discussion of 2:10 earlier. In this context it probably means that Jesus has pioneered the new age of faith. As Marshall, *op. cit.*, p. 149, says, he "supplies the impetus" and example for faith (see 12:3).

72. Käsemann, *op. cit.*, pp. 82f. Spicq, *op. cit.*, I, pp. 64f., notes Philonic parallels; and Michel, *op. cit.*, pp. 76f., sees a cultic flavor.

73. Marshall, *op. cit.*, p. 150. See also Bruce, *op. cit.*, p. 44.

74. "Learned obedience through suffering" (5:8) was a favorite saying in both Hellenistic (where it was a popular aphorism) and Jewish circles. In its application to the Son of God, however, it speaks of incarnation and divine purpose (cf. Phil. 2:8).

75. This is seen in 12:3, where he is "Pioneer and Perfecter" in the sense that he "endured the cross." Delling (fn. 64) says "the two terms refer primarily to the passion of Jesus on its personal side."

76. This does not dispute the sense seen by B. F. Westcott, *The Epistle to the Hebrews* (Grand Rapids, Mich.: Eerdmans, 1973 [originally 1892]), p. 397; and Bruce, *op. cit.*, p. 352, that it means "in Him faith has reached its perfection." Rather, both ideas are present; one has reference to him, the other to his followers.

77. τελειόω (2:10; 5:9; 7:19, 28; 9:9; 10:1, 14; 11:40; 12:23), τέλειος (5:14; 9:11), τελειώτης (6:1), τελειώτης (12:2), τελείωσις (7:11).

78. See O Moe, "Der Gedanke des allgemeinen Priestertums im Hebräerbriefe" *Theologische Zeitschrift* 5 (1949), pp. 161-169, Delling, pp. 82-83; Michel, pp. 76f.

79. See A. Wikgren, "Patterns of Perfection in the Epistle to the Hebrews," *New Testament Studies* 6 (1960), pp. 159-67; Cullmann, *op. cit.*, p. 92; Marshall, *op. cit.*, p. 150. All, however, recognize the presence of the cultic in the term.

80. Note Käsemann's title, *Das wandernde Gottesvolk*, which is an excellent example of a key element in Hebrews. Käsemann describes the readers as "pilgrim people of God" who are traveling the road of salvation. While his discussion of origins is highly suspect, his insight into theology must be applauded.

81. See p. 16 for this viewpoint.

82. Wikgren, *op. cit.*, p. 160, takes this sense of τέλος to be the basic use of the concept in this epistle.

83. *Ibid.*, p. 162.

84. The verses just before this (5:13-14) contrast the "mature" to the "babe"; the mature are those who by "practice have their senses trained to discern good and evil."

85. See Bruce, *op. cit.*, p. 376; and Wikgren, *op. cit.*, p. 160. The application is to the whole community of saints in the Old Testament and now, who are united through Christ. It especially has in mind the Old Testament saints of ch. 11 (cf. vv. 39, 40). Wikgren points to its use for martyrdom in IV Macc. 7:15; cf. Wisd. 4:13, Luke 13:32.

86. Green, *op. cit.*, p. 204, says, "Whilst, however, the main thrust of the teaching of Hebrews on salvation points to the future, it does not do so exclusively. In 5:9 we are told that Jesus became 'the procuring cause' of salvation. Clearly this is something that is already achieved."

87. One of the tragedies of our current situation in evangelicalism is the emotive code-words or labels which we attach to certain positions and which enable us to automatically reject the totality of that position on the basis of the label. One of the worst of these "code-words" is "semi-pelagian" which means automatically that the position is a-biblical, and that the data within need not be studied further. To many strong Calvinists any Wesleyan-Arminian position is automatically "semi-pelagian."

88. The Holy Spirit is seen in this epistle as giver and witness. 2:4 and 6:4 look to the believer's experience of the gifts of the Spirit at salvation (cf. 10:29); and 9:18, 10:15 (cf. 3:7) look to him as witness, speaking through Old Testament fulfillment and testifying to the efficacious sacrifice of Christ (cf. 9:14).

89. See the discussion of these and other Calvinist texts in "Exegetical Notes on Calvinist Texts," also within this volume.

90. Green, *op. cit.*, p. 206, says God "will certainly keep the trusting soul. . . . But that does not mean that he will keep the man who does *not* want to be kept."

9

Exegetical Notes on Calvinist Texts

GRANT R. OSBORNE

Many of the difficulties between Arminianism and Calvinism would disappear if scholars were to abandon the common practice of "proof texting." The problem is that in the past systematic theology has by and large taken passages out of context, grouped them together in a logical order, and in many cases made them say things not intended by the original authors. This error is common to both sides in the debate. The answer is to be found in the methods of biblical theology, whereby we take every passage in its own context and interpret it in light of the author's intended meaning. We do not place a verse from John next to a verse from Hebrews and interpret one by the other; rather we allow John to speak for himself and the writer to the Hebrews to speak for himself.

For this reason, we are not going to arrange the discussion according to theological categories (i.e., according to the so-called "five points") but rather according to book, and we hope to shed new light on the subject in this way. For those who are interested in the "five points," however, we will provide a "key" to the passages below, arranging the verses systematically:

Total depravity—John 6.44, 65, 8.44; Rom. 3:9-12; 1 Cor. 2:14; Eph. 2:1-3, 4:17-19;

Unconditional election—John 6:35-40, 15:16; Rom. 8:28-30, 33 [1]; Eph. 1:3-12; 1 Pet. 1:1, 2; 2:8, 9; Phil. 2:12, 13

Limited atonement—John 6:35-40; 10:14-18, 24-29; 17:1-11; Rom. 5:32-34

Irresistible grace—Matt. 11:25-27, 13:10-16; John 6:44-45, 64-65; Acts 13:48; Eph. 2:8, 9; Rom. 8:30

Perseverance (final) of the saints—John 10:27-30; Rom. 8; Phil. 1:6 (1 Cor. 1:7-9); Eph. 4:30; 1 Pet. 1:3-5

I. The Synoptic Gospels

Here, of course, we will be considering the *Logia Jesu*[2] as these shed light on the relationship between sovereignty and responsibility in salvation. At the outset, we would note that Jesus reacted against the Jewish stress on responsibility and so emphasized the divine activity in salvation. However, this must be interpreted in light of his eschatology, which contained both elements. The future aspects of the kingdom called for responsibility and perseverance (Matt. 6:33, 24:13; Luke 18:29f.), and the present aspects were grounds for security (Matt. 11:25f.; 13:10f.). The answer is then to be found in this tension between the present possession and the future hope regarding salvation, which reflects the eschatological tension between the already and the not yet throughout Jesus' teaching and the New Testament as a whole. As Marshall says,[3] "As far as the outlook of Jesus is concerned, entry to the kingdom of God is something which takes place in the future, although men can participate in the blessings of the kingdom." It is in this light that we must interpret the evidence.

Matthew 11:25-27—This passage, paralleled by Luke 10:21-22, is used by many Calvinists to teach a combined doctrine of election and irresistible grace. Here it is said that "God makes known to His chosen ones the secrets of the kingdom through the inward personal revelation given by the Spirit," [4] and that therefore this revelation has the divine seal. Those to whom "the Son chooses to reveal" (11:27) the Father are given a special inward call which they cannot resist. This passage is indeed important for an understanding of Jesus' unique sonship[5] and parallels the many statements in the Johannine corpus that the only true revelation of the Father comes through the Son. The election motif is an important element in the theology of Jesus and transforms the corporate identity of Israel's view to the individual thrust of Jesus' view (note the "anyone" of v. 27).

Nevertheless, we must ask exactly what this doctrine entailed. Does it mean that God irresistibly draws to himself those he chooses and guarantees their salvation? This is certainly not the emphasis here, for Jesus centers on the revelation aspect, not the election aspect, of salvation. The latter doctrine is used by Jesus to stress the redemptive activity of God, and the place of the Son as the means of the effective outworking of that divine plan. Therefore, election is taught in this passage, but irresistible grace is not.

Matthew 24:24—The Olivet Discourse is the only place in the Gospels where "elect" is used of Jesus' followers (cf. Mark 13:20, 22, 27; Luke 18:7; also Matt. 24:22, 31), and so it is important to understand Jesus' use of the title here. In the

Old Testament the title is used to designate the people of God (Ps. 105:6, 43; Isa. 65:9f.), and many scholars have noted that in the Old Testament as well as the New Testament, election "is conditional upon (one's) desire to retain it," [6] i.e., that God's choice of a person does not occur irrespective of his will and does not guarantee that he will never deny God's gift of salvation. This certainly seems to be indicated here, where Christ warns that the deception of the Antichrist will be so severe that "if possible, even the elect" will apostatize. The interpretation hinges on the meaning of "if possible," which many say teaches the impossibility of leading the elect astray. However, this need not be true; in fact, the force of Mark 13:13 and Matt. 24:13 provies the *crux interpretum* for the passage, indicating that some will fail to "endure to the end," i.e., be "led astray." [7]

It is difficult to make a case that the context of Mark 13:13 does not indicate true believers, since Christ was talking to the disciples. Dispensational Calvinists[8] argue that the passage speaks about Israel in the tribulation period and so cannot be applied to believers now. However, this fails to consider the constant emphasis throughout the New Testament on the church as New Israel. It would be difficult to show that all Jesus' teachings to the disciples applied only to Israel, not the church. While this passage does apply to the specific conditions of the final tribulation, it applies to general problems believers have faced in every general "tribulation" and must teach a genuine danger for the believer. Mark 13:13, then, takes "salvation" in the same sense as the writer to the Hebrews, as expressing the final gift of salvation rather than the present possession of eternal life (see the chapter on Hebrews in this compendium). It is interesting here to note the other synoptic parallel to Mark 13:13—Luke 21:18, 36—which stresses security in the midst of endurance. The danger is real, but Christ here promises God's protection; yet that protection can only be realized *via* prayer and perseverance. The security makes the danger slight, but it is nevertheless a real warning.[9]

II. The Johannine Corpus

The theme of all these writings is redemptive history, with the Gospel representing (from John's viewpoint) the past basis, the Epistles the present application, and the Apocalypse the future hope. The Gospel, even more than Paul, stresses divine sovereignty in salvation. Here Jesus is seen, even more than in the synoptics, to be the sovereign over history, and God's salvation plan is assured. Numerous passages in John stress this crucial element in salvation, stating that men come only when drawn to Christ by him. These provide the strongest New Testament evidence for the Calvinist claim that God's salvation is final, achieved by his sovereign choice, and so is ultimately guaranteed to the elect.

Boettner,[10] for instance, believes that there is a dualism of mankind into two separate classes, the elect and the non-believers, and that there can be no cross-over between those two distinct divisions, i.e., the unconverted cannot become elect. However, this is certainly not true for John. One of the major characteristics which distinguishes John from the synoptics lies in his dualism; in the synoptics it is horizontal (i.e., this age vs. the age to come), but in John it is vertical (heavenly vs. earthly).[11] Thus there is no true ground for Boettner's horizontal view in John. This is best seen in a study of κόσμος in the fourth Gospel. The "world" is pictured as mankind in general (7:4, 12:19, etc.) and is seen in a twofold relation to Christ. Primarily it denotes those who have rebelled against God (17:25) and have followed their "ruler," Satan (12:31; 14:30; 16:11); as such it is dominated by wickedness (7:7) and has rejected Jesus (1:10) and his disciples (15:18, 17:14). On the other hand, however, it is still the object of God's love (3:16) and salvation (3:17; 12:41), and Jesus came to provide life for it (1:29; 6:33). The disciples are to continue Jesus' salvific mission to the world (17:17-19). Therefore, the dualism which Boettner theorizes is simply not true. There is a dynamic relation between the world and the believer, and it is possible to move from one to the other. Let us look at the key passages for Johannine soteriology.

John 6:35-40, 44-45, 64-65—The question here is not whether this passage teaches divine sovereignty in the salvific decision but rather what this means. In this passage three Calvinist doctrines are discovered—predestination, irresistible grace, and eternal security. Murray[12] sees in this passage a progressive development—they will not be cast out, they were given, they will not be lost, they will be raised up at the last day—and asserts that election is the basis for the believer's final perseverance. The theme of God "drawing" the elect to Jesus in verse 44 and their "coming" to Jesus in verse 45 seems to reenforce this by stressing the sovereign power behind that "inevitable decision." Morris[13] points out that the verb ἐκλύω here implies resistance to the drawing power, but that there is no instance in the New Testament where that resistance is successful. "Always the drawing power is triumphant, as here." The same thought is expressed in verses 64, 65, which say no one comes unless the Father gives him the ability to do so; "left to himself the sinner prefers his sin." [14]

While there is some truth to the above statements, they for the most part neglect John's other emphasis, man's responsibility. In each of the above passages this is forcefully brought out. Verses 37-40 are based upon verse 35, where we see that eternal life is dependent on coming and believing. Moreover, the present tenses of the participles indicate it does not speak about a crisis faith-decision but rather about persevering in those two states. As Brown says, "The stress in verse 37 that God destines men to come to Jesus does not in the least attenuate the guilt in verse 36 of those who do not believe . . . with all John's insistence on man's choosing between light and darkness, it would be nonsense to ask if the evangelist believed in human responsibility." [15] This is not to denigrate the strong emphasis on the sovereign will in this passage; it is rather to point out that the sovereign force considers human responsibility before moving.

There are four major words in these three sections of John 6, organized into two sets of synonymous pairs—drawing = giving and coming = believing. They illustrate the two sides of the salvific act, God's part in drawing, man's part in coming. Here we must ask if God's drawing determines man's coming and if man's coming thereby is an act apart from the decision of his will. In 6:44 this certainly seems to be the case, but the verse must be taken in light of John's entire "draws" theology, which stresses the attraction itself, not the certainty of it. In 12:32, Jesus says that as a result of his death,[16] he will "draw all men" to himself. In itself, then, it does not teach irresistible grace but rather God's universal salvific love. Moreover, the context of those verses presupposes responsibility, for verse 45 says that only those who have "heard and learned" will "come" to Christ.[17] As Marshall concludes:[18]

> The purpose of the predestinarian language in John is not to express the exclusion of certain men from salvation because they were not chosen by the Father . . . but to emphasize that from start to finish eternal life is the gift of God and does not lie under the control of men. A person who tries to gain eternal life on his own terms will find himself unable to come to Jesus because it has not been granted to him by the Father (John 6:65); he has in fact been resisting the leading of the Father.

10:14, 14-18, 27-30—Verses 11, 14-18 are used along with Mark 10:45 as primary texts for the Calvinist doctrine of limited atonement. Many assert that Christ died for "many" not all [19] and for "the sheep" not those who are wolves, etc. This is especially seen in comparison with passages like "you are not my sheep" and "you are from your father, the devil."

However, this is to misunderstand Jesus' teaching here. The primary principle for interpreting any parabolic saying is that one must not go beyond the central teaching (see Jeremias' or Dodd's studies of the parable); especially, one must not base doctrines on what it does *not* say. Here Jesus is teaching about his death, not the efficacy of it; in this context he could hardly have said he laid down his life for all the animals! This must be interpreted in light of the other Johannine passages which connect Jesus' death with "all" or with the "world" (1:12, 29; 3:16; 12:32). In short, Jesus here teaches that he shows his love for his sheep by dying for them but nowhere limits his death to them alone.[20] To use his imagery, he died so that "all" may become "sheep." Calvinists who argue it is sufficient for all but efficient only for some are correct, but the criterion for the latter group is not a rigid predestination, as we have just argued, but rather the faith-decision of the individual. This, in fact, is the central theme of the fourth Gospel.

Verses 27-30 are the major proof text for eternal security, since it in a sense promises the double protection of the believer by both Christ and the Father. As Boettner argues,[21] this grounds security in God's omnipotence and in effect removes the believer from ultimate spiritual peril. Calvinists base their interpretation on three points here: the presence of eternal life (cf. 5:24), the phrase "shall never perish" (with the emphatic οὐ μή), and the promise of God's omnipotent protection (cf. Col. 3:3). The result is that nothing can remove the believer from his elect position.[22]

To understand the thrust here we must identify the theological meaning given to "eternal life" in the fourth Gospel. John stresses the realized aspect and makes it a present possession secured under the power of God. The verses herein are a part of that present thrust. Nonetheless, there is a future aspect to the gift of salvation, and it must be secured by perseverance. This has been noted in 6:35, 45 and is seen in the present tense verbs of verse 27, "hearing," "knowing," and "following." To be sure, these are not conditions for salvation *in this context* (*contra* Shank), but they are conditions in light of John's total theology. This is especially seen in the vine and branches *mashal* of 15:1-7. There we are told that those branches which stop abiding in the vine and cease bearing fruit will wither, be stripped from the vine, and be thrown aside for burning. In spite of all attempts to assert otherwise,[23] this gives a valid warning to the believer regarding the consequences of failure to "abide" in him. So we can conclude that while eternal life is a present possession, it is not a future certainty. One must add perseverance to the security before one can be certain of that future attainment.

Marshall[24] in this respect notes the Johannine themes of discipleship and faith. John stresses two types of disciples and two aspects of faith, one continuing to abide and having a dynamic inward relationship to Christ, the other having a superficial relationship to Christ and only a partial faith. However, we must note that John nowhere denies that this partial faith is real. In fact, the close connection between partial faith and John's signs theology (cf. 2:23-25, 10:38, 14:11) shows there is validity in it. Jesus' works are insufficient in themselves to produce faith but can become a valid first step to an understanding of Jesus' person. The best example of this is Judas. While many have noted that he is called a "betrayer" in 6:64 long before his actual act of betrayal,[25] we may note that this is an editorial aside which looked ahead to what Judas would become (not what he was then). The significant phrase is found in 17:12, which says, "I kept them in your name, whom you gave me; I have guarded them, and none of them is lost but the son of perdition." Here we have some of the major terms of security—"given," "kept," "guarded"— used with relation to Judas, who was "lost."

Chapter 17—Christ's intercessory prayer here (and his present intercession mentioned in Heb. 7:24, 25) is said to be evidence for the final perseverance of the elect. Jesus' prayer here is justly labelled his "high priestly prayer," for he both consecrates his coming sacrifice and intercedes on behalf of the people. It may be divided into three sections: (1) prayer for glory, verses 1-8; (2) prayer for the disciples, verses 9-19; and (3) prayer for future believers, verses 20-26. Chafer[26] notes two themes as indicative of security—the intensity of Christ's love and his dependence on the Father's protective power. Gromacki[27] finds the presence of security in the stress on Christians as (1) gifts to the Son, verses 2, 6, 9, 11, 12, 24; (2) possessions of the union between Father and Son, verses 9c-10a; (3) possessing eternal life, verse 2; and (4) objects of Christ's prayer for their preservation, verse 11, and eternal dwelling, verse 24.

However, again we must ask what this is really saying. Certainly Christ's prayer is given entirely with the disciples in mind. Even the prayer for glory (vv. 1-5) is given not for his own sake but that his followers may have life (v. 2). Security is indeed the teaching; the divine name is pledged as the basis of the disciples' protection (v. 12a). Nevertheless, we must continue to remember that security does not mean an absolute guarantee. In the same context with the promise of protection (v. 12) we have the example of danger. In itself, of course, we dare not make too much of Judas, for some have called him "the exception which proves the rule." However, the conclusion here fits the data noted above.

In conclusion, John's major emphasis is definitely upon sovereignty and security. However, this does not contradict the doctrine of perseverance; rather it strengthens it by adding the aspect of God's promises and aid in accomplishing it. It is certainly "not by might, nor by power, but by his Spirit," but this is the promise side of the perseverance, not the totality of perseverance.

1 John 5:11-13—As might be expected, 1 John continues the same themes as the Gospel, especially the possession of eternal life (5:13) and abiding (2:24-25). At the same time, however, John stresses perseverance in sinlessness (3:6f.; 5:16f.) and in prayer (1:8-10). Of course, in the first instance, it is not freedom from individual acts of sin but rather the absence of persistent sinning which is commanded. Christ in 2:1 is called the "advocate" (Paraclete) for those who do sin, and security is again seen to be the major concomitent of perseverance. Indeed, the two cannot be separated and are interdependent.

III. The Book of Acts

Several passages in Acts seem to teach the doctrine of unconditional election and indicate to many that Luke had a predestinarian theology. Acts, like John, defines the basic message of Christ and the church as one of salvation. The basic events all relate to the soteriological message of the church, as the followers of Jesus fulfilled his commands and promises relating to mission. In relating this, Luke in Acts is careful to show that all was accomplished under divine impetus and occurred as part of his redemptive plan. It is God who at each critical node intervenes directly to guide the church in its salvific purpose (cf. 1:8, 24f.; 5:19f.; 8:26f.; 9:3f.; 10:10f.; 13:2f.; 15:7f.; 16:9f., 25f.). So God is the prime mover in salvation for man, and this leads to those verses which seem to extend this to a predestinarian salvation:

11:18—This verse culminates the Cornelius episode (ch. 10) and Peter's report to the "apostles and brethren" (11: 1-17); they concluded, "Then to the Gentiles also God has granted repentance unto life." Here, God is the principal actor in redemption (cf. 5:31), but we must ask whether this is an unconditional choice on his part, and whether man's volition plays a part. The passage, of course, does not say, but there is some evidence that the latter is more probable. Cornelius was a "God-fearer" (10:2), a Gentile who worshipped God but had not taken the final step of circumcision.[28] As such he was a "devout man" and was open to God's call.

13:48—Here is the major election passage in Acts; Luke here says of the Gentiles in Antioch of Pisidia, "As many as were ordained to eternal life believed." Calvinist theologians[29] say the force of "ordained" here dare not be toned down; election must precede man's faith and form the basis for it. However, while we agree that the basic thrust is divine election,[30] this does not negate the presence of human volition, as seen in the context.[31] The preceding passage, especially verse 46, notes the responsibility inherent in salvation. There the unbelieving Jews were rejected on the basis of their personal decision: by their action they "judged themselves unworthy" in the presence of God. The best thrust for the perfect passive "have been ordained" is that combination of divine election and human volition which has already been noted in John, with stress on the former aspect here.

This is especially seen when one notes the passages on perseverance and the danger of apostasy in Acts. In 20:30 it says false teachers will arise who will seek "to draw away the disciples after them." This does not mean backsliding but apostasy, as seen in the term "draw away." The warning was real and involved heresy and apostasy. Also, we have examples of apostasy, possibly Ananias and Sapphira[32] but probably Simon Magus. He "believed and was baptized" (8:13) but later tried to buy his way into a miraculous ministry. As a result Peter tells him he no longer has a part in the kingdom. Here again the key is the "word of grace" which edifies the believer (2:42; 4:33; 15:31f.) and the means is exhortation (11:23; 13:43; 14:22). Therefore the believer must persevere in order to inherit eternal life.

16:14; 18:10-27—These minor texts all relate to the above and are used to further state the election of the believer *via* efficacious grace. Steele and Thomas[33] declare, "Faith and repentance are divine gifts and are wrought in the soul through the regenerating work of the Holy Spirit." Acts 16:14 speaks of Lydia, saying, "The Lord opened her heart to give heed." Here, however, we must again note the context; she was a "worshipper of God" and had already been seeking the truth. Acts 18:10 says, "I have many people in this city" and 18:27 speaks of "those who through grace had believed." Once again, however, we must note that this speaks of divine election and grace but does not teach that these are final acts. Acts 18:10 speaks of future believers rather than current Christians (18:8), but this speaks of foreknowledge more than unconditional predestination.[34] The same is true of verse 27, for this does not teach irresistible grace but rather the basis of salvation in general, God's grace. There is no hint of a rigid application to a select few only. In conclusion,

Luke in Acts stresses the divine activity behind salvation but does not identify this with a rigid predestinarian call.

IV. The Pauline Writings

The theologian *par excellence* of the early church is Paul. While his epistles are personal correspondence rather than treatises, and while Paul never made any real attempt to systematize Christian faith and doctrine, he nevertheless epitomizes the implications of Jesus' teaching for the church. There has been much debate regarding the central thesis of Paul's system. Since the Reformation, most have believed that justification by faith provides the key. However, apart from Romans and Galatians this is not the core of his thinking, and more recent scholars have tended to follow Schweitzer and Deissman that the "in Christ" motif is at the center. While this is one of the major Pauline themes, however, we might question whether it is broad enough to serve as the key to Paul's thought. The best answer is seen in the recent studies of Green and Ladd,[35] who have shown that eschatological salvation best summarizes Pauline theology. It is neither justification (past) nor "in Christ" (present) nor hope (future) but the inclusion of past, present, and future in the eschatological gift of salvation, the New Age in Christ.

Romans 3:9-12; 5:12; 6:20—These passages are bulwarks of the doctrine of total depravity, defined by Steele and Thomas[36] thusly: "The reign of sin is universal; all men are under its power . . . Men left in their dead state are unable of themselves to repent, to believe the gospel, or to come to Christ. They have no power within themselves to change their natures or to prepare themselves for salvation." Rom. 3:9-12 states that "all" are "under the power of sin" and concludes "none is righteous, no, not one . . . no one does good, not even one." This passage teaches the universality of sin and the power of sin.[37] Rom. 6:20 adds to this the fact that man has become "slaves of sin." Calvinists use this as a basis for their theory that man cannot ever choose to accept Christ; he will always choose sin. Only when God's elective love chooses to lift individual men out of their depraved condition can anyone be saved.

Before we can discuss 3:9-12, we must place it in its context. It concludes that important section on the universal guilt and condemnation of man (1:18-3:20) and sets the scene for Paul's discussion of the path to righteousness (3:21-5:21). In this section we find the best expression of Pauline anthropology, dealing with man's bondage to sin. Sin is deliberate rebellion and transgression against the commands of God (2:23f.) and is a falling short of God's standards (3:23); man's self-righteous attitude, especially for the Jew, led him to break the true law and become more guilty (2:17f.), and resulted in God's judicial wrath (cf. "God gave them up" in 1:24f.). The entire section deals with the pagans (1:18-32), the moral Jew (2:1-16), Jewish guilt (2:13-3:8) and concludes by bringing together both Jew and Gentile under one roof—universal guilt. Therefore we must conclude that the universality here deals with the quantity (all people) rather than quality (total sin) regarding depravity. There is no hint that depravity means man cannot accept Christ.[38]

Chapter 8—This passage is used by Hodge[39] exclusively to teach the doctrine of final perseverance and is indeed one of the important passages in determining Paul's view of salvation. Chapter 8 in a very real sense forms the Pauline victory cry after the seeming defeatism of chapter 7 and deals with the new life of the Spirit. In an eschatological sense it deals with the life of the New Age which the Spirit produces in the life of the believer.

(1) *No condemnation, v. 1f.*—The principle of "no condemnation" is taken seriously by Calvinists as the irreversible negation of sin and guilt. The believer is given a twofold promise here—he is "in Christ" and he has "the Spirit of life." The result is "freedom from the law of sin and death." However, while we agree that there is security and promise here, we must ask whether Murray[40] is correct when he calls the fact "complete and irreversible." We must also agree with him that the passage refers to freedom from the power of sin as well as from the guilt of sin; however; this does not mean that the Christian life is guaranteed for him. Perseverance is also taught in this passage, and it is a necessity for the freedom described here. There is still the choice between a carnal and Spirit-filled mind-set (v. 6), and the believer must "walk not after the flesh but after the Spirit" (v. 4). While these are not conditions, they are valid possibilities and cannot be lightly dismissed.

(2) *The Principle of life, vv. 11-13*—Hodge argues that the life principle within the believer is evidence of his security. The Holy Spirit "quickens" or enlivens the believer and is himself the foundation of his security. However in verses 11-13, this is seen to be conditional[41] upon the continual indwelling of the Spirit, and "mortification of the flesh." Both possibilities—death and life—are presented here, and the believer must choose which path to take—that of the flesh or that of the Spirit. While the victorious side is stressed here, the other side is seen as a definite danger.

(3) *Sons of God, vv. 14-17*—Sonship is a further base for security. Calvinists argue that God would not cast "sons" out of his "family." The "Abba" motif is the key to Jesus' prayer theology in connection with his sonship, and is well connected with the "adoption" theology here. "Abba" was never used in prayer by Jews because it transmitted an intimacy which was foreign to them.[42] Jesus, because of his unique relation to the Father, gave his followers a new relationship to him, and it could not be expressed better than here. Nevertheless, we note the same possibilities as in verses 11-13, and the same need for perseverance. Verse 14 says "being led by the Spirit of God" is a prerequisite of sonship.

(4) *The purpose of God, vv. 26-30*—Here we see the juxtaposition of the Spirit's intercession (vv. 26-28) and the redemptive election by God (vv. 29-30). Both aspects are part of the Calvinist soteriology: Redemption is a gift of God and in no way an act of man: God will never fail to save those whom he has called.[43] The major question lies in the relationship between foreknowledge and election—which is prior? Murray[44] would make election prior, saying, "The faith which God foresees is preconditioned by his decree to generate this faith in those he foresees as believing." The term "foreknow," then, refers to God's elective love rather than to an actual foreknowledge of the believer's faith-decision. However, while we would agree that "foreknow" does contain in itself the idea of elective love,[45] we would not agree that the word itself indicates a predestinarian decree. We would state with Bruce that the two are simultaneous but separate aspects: "When God takes knowledge of people in this special way, He sets His choice upon them." [46]

There are two major approaches to the predestinarian sense of this paragraph by opponents of the Calvinist interpretation —corporate and individual. Shank [47] believes that election is corporate and refers to the sovereign choice of the church as a whole, while individual members must come to personal decision and must persevere in the faith. While this has a certain attraction, it is hardly the answer here. The phrase "conformed to the image of his Son" undoubtedly has a personal application and presupposes an individual thrust. Marshall [48] provides a better answer; the passage itself discusses believers, and not unbelievers (cf. v. 28). Therefore the election here is not unto salvation but unto conformity. We would add to this, however, that in every aspect foreknowledge and election are two aspects of divine predestination. God's sovereign choice always takes into consideration the free will of the individual.[49]

(5) *The love of God, vv. 31-39*—This passage is used by

Calvinists to teach the doctrines of election (v. 33), limited atonement (vv. 32-34), and eternal security (whole passage). Calvin himself [50] calls this "that magnificent exaltation of Paul, in defiance of life and death, of things present and future; which must necessarily have been founded in the gift of perseverance." Regarding the doctrine of the atonement, Murray[51] declares, "The succeeding context specifies just as distinctly those of whom the apostle is speaking—they are God's elect (v. 33), those on behalf of whom Christ makes intercession (v. 34), those who can never be separated from the love of Christ (vv. 35, 39). The sustained identification of the persons in these terms shows that this passage offers no support to the notion of universal atonement."

At the outset we must note the optimism of Paul which runs throughout this passage. Towards man he is pessimistic, but when he considers the Father and the Son his rapture knows no bounds. Man may fail, but God will never fail, and the love of Christ is not dependent on the vicissitudes of man. Here we might note the arguments of Arminius and Wesley.[52] This passage does not relate to perseverance but simply speaks of the believer's encouragement in the faith. Paul here states his confidence in God's part but elsewhere notes his own responsibility and danger (1 Cor. 9:27). Outside pressures can't separate us from God's love, but inward apostasy can. It is God's love rather than his divine decree which is discussed here. We might add that the context provides the solution. Again Paul is speaking to believers, and the "elect" must be interpreted in light of verses 28-30 (see above).[53] It states the same truth as seen in John 10: 28-29, that no outward force can separate us from God. The emphasis is on this, but other contexts provide the basis for the further thought (not discussed here), "Can we ourselves fail to use this promise?" We might conclude by saying that even the apostate—apart from those who have committed the unpardonable sin(s) of Mark 3:28f. and parallels, Heb. 6:4f., and 1 John 5:16b—is still loved and sought by God.[54]

1 Corinthians 2:14 This is a key verse in the Calvinist doctrine of total depravity. The "natural man," when convicted about "the things of God," can neither "receive" them nor "know" them; to him they merely seem "foolishness." Therefore, Hodge concludes,[55] only when man's inward state is changed by the Holy Spirit can he begin to comprehend spiritual truth. "If our gospel is hid, it is hid to those who are lost." However, this is to misunderstand the Pauline doctrine of faith. He is not contrasting free will and sovereignty here but the natural man and the spiritual man. Man's depravity is such that left to himself he could find nothing about God. However, he is not left alone, but is given the Spirit to aid him. Ladd[56] notes "the gnostic-sounding language that sets forth a very ungnostic theology," i.e., the unveiling of God's hidden wisdom (2:6-13) in the historical act of the cross (1:18, 2:2). This can be understood only when the Spirit reveals it; but there is no hint here that the Spirit works only among the elite, i.e., the elect. Rather, his convicting work is universal, but man must yield to it before they can "discern" spiritual truth.

Ephesians 1:3-12—This important passage relates both to unconditional election and final perseverance. Next to Rom. 9-11, this is the most important passage for the Pauline doctrine of predestination. Here we are told that "before the foundation of the world" God "chose us in him," "destined us in love to be his sons," and "appointed [us] to live for the praise of his glory." Boettner[57] uses this passage to refute the Arminian doctrine of foreknowledge, since this "makes faith and holiness to be the consequents, and not the antecedents, of election (Eph. 1:4, John 15:16; Titus 3:5)." The phrase "before the foundation of the world" is a Hebraism for "from eternity" and refers to God's eternal decree of redemption. That decree is eternal and immutable.[58]

Yet there are striking similarities to Rom. 8:29-30. In both passages Paul is speaking to believers, and the "we-you" terminology in both is paralleled by the election itself, which is not to eternal life but to "holy and blameless" lives (v. 4), to sonship (v. 5, note the parallel to "conformed to the image of his son," Rom. 8:29), and to living "for the praise of his glory" (v. 12). While redemption and forgiveness are a central part of this passage (v. 7), the election itself looks at believers only and does not consider election out of unbelief, i.e., election here looks at the benefits of the salvation act, not at the act itself.[59] A further point is noted by Dibelius,[60] who sees a twofold contrast here: 1) between the part in accomplishing salvation and the human part in hearing and believing; and 2) between "we" or the church and "you" or the one-time pagan readers of Paul's epistle. In both contrasts the benefits are seen on both sides. Election in this respect is not a guarantee given to the privileged few and does not relate to the faith-response as provided only by the overwhelming call of the Spirit. Rather, it refers to God's gracious providence and purpose for those whom he chooses and who respond to the gospel. It relates to privilege as well as status.

Ephesians 1:13-14, 4:30—Both these passages (see also 2 Cor. 1:18-22) relate to the "seal" placed upon the believer by the Spirit. Calvin[61] defines the "earnest" of verse 14 as a security or promise of the remainder "which, therefore, is not taken back, but kept till the residue is paid to complete the whole sum." The Holy Spirit, then, is the "guarantee" of the believer's future inheritance. Strombeck[62] notes three aspects to the seal here—sealed as to position (eternal salvation), as to ownership (purchased by his blood), as to future (eternal life). Therefore, Calvinists argue, the seal of the Spirit does not rest on the continuance of man's faith; belief is the antecedent but not the grounds of the sealing.

The "seal" as such does indeed denote authentication, possession and protection, and the "earnest" refers to the first installment which guarantees full payment later (cf. 2 Cor. 1:22; 5:5). There is a very real security in this passage. However, we must ask if this is an unconditional, final security. Personal responsibility parallels divine protection in 4:30, where the Christian is warned not to "grieve" the Spirit (cf. 1 Thess. 4:8). Ladd[62b] relates this to Pauline eschatology, noting that "the presence of the Holy Spirit in the church is itself an eschatological event." This is certainly true, for Pentecost in the early church was viewed as an eschatological event (note the Joel prophecy) which became the presence of the New Age in the believer, Paul, like the other writers we have noted, interpreted salvation in terms of the tension between the "already" and the "not yet," and the present possession of security is held in tension with the need for future perseverance. The "day of redemption" is secured here, and God's protection is promised, but the believer dare not assume he plays no part. The danger of apostasy is real, and he dare not "grieve" the Spirit.[63]

Ephesians 2:1-3; 4:17-19—These two passages contrast the ignorant, rebellious course of the heathen to the enlightened walk of the true follower of Christ. The pagans are "children of wrath" who are "darkened in their understanding" and "alienated from the life of God" "due to their hardness of heart." Many think that these powerful passages, growing out of the death-to-life metaphor of 2:1, teach the impossibility of human response, God must override man's propensity to evil as he sovereignly chooses, thereby bringing the "dead" to "life" *via* elective love. Yet we must ask if this is really what Paul is trying to say. He is not denying man's faith-response to the salvific call; it is in every way the response of individual volition to God's love and the Spirit's convicting work.

Ephesians 2:8, 9—Closely connected to this is the important passage which provides the Pauline definition of the salvific act: "For by grace you have been saved through faith; and this is not your own doing, it is the gift of God—

not because of works, lest any man should boast." This has long been a major Calvinist proof text against the "error" of Wesleyan-Arminianism. The latter, they say, teach a salvation by "works" and thereby deny the "grace" of God in redemption. Henricksen,[64] for instance, believes that *toûto* in verse 8 refers not to "grace" or to "saved" but to "faith," saying that anything else would amount to needless repetition. In this respect, then, the believer's faith does not come from within him but itself is an external gift from God. If faith-decision were an act of human volition, it would become works and lead to self-boasting.

There is another approach to the passage, one which does greater justice to the context and to the neuter force of *toûto*. That is to take the latter term as referring to the whole previous phrase rather than to any particular part within it. Salvation is the cover term which has two aspects— God's grace and man's faith. All come within the category of "gift." This is not to say that man's faith is not really man's but originates from the activity of the Spirit; rather, it is a volitional yielding to the activity of the Spirit within. The gift is not forced upon man but must be received on the part of man "by faith." It is not "works" because it is from God; man is the passive recipient because he yields to the Spirit in faith-decision.[65]

Philippians 1:6; 2:13—Berkhof[66] takes these two verses with John 6:37-40 as illustrating the "covenant of redemption" which finalizes the gift of salvation; it is both final and eternal. Phil. 1:6 relates the apostle's confidence that God would safeguard his "good work" among them and "bring it to completion at the day of Jesus Christ," and 2:13 says God works within his follower "both to will and to work for his good pleasure." The first verse also relates to 1 Cor. 1:7-9, which says God will "sustain you to the very end."

In both cases, Paul is speaking to the church as a whole in his customary "thanksgiving" section, and the context favors a corporate rather than individual interpretation, i.e., the church will be sustained, but individuals will be protected only so long as they remain in the church. However, we would agree that this dare not be taken too far (as, for instance, Shank tends to do), as an answer to the predestination problem. Paul does intend that the promise extend to the individual. He will be kept by God with a view to the final salvation,[67] but this does not obviate the need for perseverance. That necessity is noticeable in 2:12, 13. The promise of verse 13 is related to the command of verse 12, that each person must "work out [his] own salvation with fear and trembling." Once again we have that combination of corporate and individual thrust, with probably a stronger hint of individual application due to the presence of "your own salvation" here.[68] Verse 13, then, is not a promise that the perseverance of verse 12 will be assured. Phil. 2:16 states the possibility of failure; they could negate his activity among them by failing to "hold fast the word of life."

In conclusion, Paul stresses security and election in his writings, but this never removes human responsibility and the place of perseverance in one's life. Election is related to those who have believed and promises God's strength in bringing them to a life of holiness and to final salvation. At the same time Paul realizes the personal responsibility involved in perseverance. While the Christian is promised God's power, he still must continue to avail himself of that strength. Paul alludes to the danger of apostasy in Rom. 8:12-14; 1 Cor. 9:27; 15:1-2; Col. 1:21-23; 1 Tim. 1:18-20; 4:1, 16 (on these passages, see the short discussion at the close of the article on "Soteriology in Hebrews"). This was a very real danger, and the only antidote was perseverance; while the Christian is promised God's help and protection, he is not given a guarantee.

V. I Peter

The stress in this epistle is upon joy and hope in the midst of persecution. As such, it gives good coverage to both aspects of salvation, i.e., promise and responsibility. The opening tone catches this spirit, speaking of the readers as "sojourners and aliens" who are "elect ... according to the foreknowledge of God" (1:1-2). Their "living hope" consists of an "inheritance" which is "kept in heaven" for them, and they are "guarded" by God "unto salvation" (1:3-5). The stone imagery (2:4-10) especially emphasizes their chosen position, likening them to the "elect cornerstone," Jesus, and calling them a "chosen race." The Christian life in this epistle is eschatological, lived in present stress but looking forward to the fulfillment of the hope at the manifestation of Christ in glory; to that end God is strengthening and helping them (1:5-9; 2:12; 4:13, 17f.; 5:10).

At the same time Peter is aware of the dangers to faith which persecution brings. It is interesting that just as in Hebrews "salvation" in Peter is eschatological, looking forward more to the final reward than the present experience (1:4, 5, 13; cf. 4:13f.; 5:1, 40), although the present aspect is seen proleptically (1:9-10) on the basis of Jesus' bringing in "the end of times" (1:20). For this reason the readers were called upon to persevere in their faith-belief (1:5, "through faith") and to strengthen their hope *via* sober thinking (1:13). They must stop living according to sinful man's standards (2:1, 11f.; 3:11; 4:1) and start seeking a pure and holy life (1:15; 2:12, 21; 4:2). A special word in Peter is "do good," found in his epistle four times as opposed to none in Paul (cf. 2:15, 20; 3:6, 17); this aspect of the Christian life was not just "good works" but persistence in righteous conduct, following Christ's example (2:21) in the face of pagan persecution (3:13f.) and involved submission to all aspects of authority, whether the state, the slave-master relationship, or the home. Satan is active and seeks to lead believers astray (5:8), and so the follower of Christ must persist in his walk (5:6f.) and be steadfast in God's grace (5:12c). As in Paul we note the beautiful blend of optimism and exhortation. Election is not a guarantee but rather an encouraging promise.

Conclusion

It is the conclusion here that the New Testament writers each stress differing nuances of the salvation-truth. John and Paul stress the sovereignty side while Hebrews stresses the aspect of responsibility. Yet all are in agreement that there is both sovereignty and responsibility, both security and perseverance. The time of eschatological salvation had begun, and the church was indeed the chosen people of God. Yet at the same time this was a proleptic gift, looking forward to the final salvation which would be secured at the eschaton. There was security in the sovereign bestowal of eternal life in the present and yet responsibility in the human need for perseverance with regard to the future. With this in mind we will attempt a reinterpretation of the fine points at the Synod of Dort.

(1) Man is totally depraved, i.e., he can do no good in himself and cannot choose Christ over sin. However, this does not mean he has no volition, for the Spirit convicts all men equally and enables them to come to faith-decision, i.e., to the point of yielding to the Spirit's convicting power.

(2) Believers are elect or predestined to a life of holiness and conformity to the Son. This salvific choice is concomitant with foreknowledge and does not amount to an ineffable call to a chosen few but rather is the accompanying force with man's faith-decision.

(3) The atonement is universal, i.e., for all men, and is limited only by man's failure to respond.

(4) The call of God's grace is not irresistible and limited to the elect; rather the "drawing" power of God is universally

applied but effective only for those who accept it by faith. God's grace and man's faith are separate aspects of the same salvific act.

(5) Perseverance is a necessity rather than a guaranteed, final promise. It relates to man's need rather than God's protection. Security is the other side of that need, for God does promise his protecting power. However, the believer must avail himself of that strength, lest he slip away and apostatize from the faith.

NOTES

1. Rom. 9-11 is discussed in a separate chapter of this symposium and so will not be covered here.

2. Of course, we are not going to get into the involved debate regarding the authenticity of these sayings. We will assume the conservative conclusions of scholars like Dodd, Cullmann, Moule, that they are basically trustworthy and will follow evangelicals like Marshall, Ladd and Pinnock who argue that they are indeed authentic. However, we would note that the question itself is unnecessary, since we are studying the church's theology itself. Cf. I. H. Marshall, *Kept by the Power of God* (Minneapolis, Minn.: Bethany Fellowship, Inc., 1975), pp. 34, and E. M. B. Green, *The Meaning of Salvation* (Philadelphia, Pa.: Westminster Press, 1965), pp. 96f.

3. Marshall, *op. cit.*, p. 36. In fact, it could be said that salvation is equated with the kingdom of Christ (Mark 10:17f. and par.) and the early church (Acts 8:12, 19:8, 28:23f.). That is, they contain both present (the kingdom blessings) and future (final salvation) aspects.

4. D. N. Steele and C. C. Thomas, *The Five Points of Calvinism* (Philadelphia, Pa.: Presbyterian & Reformed, 1963), p. 52.

5. G. E. Ladd, *A Theology of the New Testament* (Grand Rapids, Mich.: Eerdmans, 1974), p. 165, calls it "the most important passage for the study of synoptic Christology." This, however, is probably overstated, since the theology of this passage is more closely related to the Johannine emphases. The synoptics stress more the messianic tension of Jesus' ministry, reserving the sonship motif for critical points in the narrative (cf. Mark 1:11; 9:7; 15:39) or to indicate his power over the forces of evil (cf. Mark 3:11; 5:7).

6. Cf. Marshall, *op. cit.*, p. 52, who quotes H. H. Rowley on this point.

7. *Ibid.*, p. 54, believes the "if possible" clause expresses the mind of the deceivers ("Let us lead them astray if we can") rather than the comment of Jesus. The use of the first-class condition (ϵi) which normally assumes reality or valid possibility, would favor this interpretation.

8. See L. S. Chafer, *Systematic Theology*, 8 vols. (Dallas, Tx.: Dallas Seminary Press, 1947-48), III, p. 292.

9. Other synoptic passages which provide a warning of apostasy would be the parable of the sower (Mark 4:3-9, 14-20 & par., especially vv. 5-6, 16-17), where it says they "believed for a time"; the parable of the tares (Mark 4:26-29, elaborated in Matt. 13:24-30, 36-43) which shows the church contains both good and bad elements; the parable of the talents (Matt. 25:14-30), which seems to indicate that Christians who fail to show fruit will be "cast into utter darkness"; and Jesus' saying about "salt which has lost

its taste" in Matt. 5:13, which relates to judgment. See the discussions of these in Marshall, *op. cit.*, and R. Shank, *Life in the Son* (Springfield, Mo.: Westcott Publishers, 1960).

10. L. Boettner, *The Reformed Doctrine of Predestination* (Grand Rapids, Mich.: Eerdmans, 1958), pp. 109f., 291f. His style is typical systematic proof-texting, but much of his argument is taken from John.

11. See Ladd, *op. cit.*, p. 223; and R. E. Brown, *The Gospel of John* (Anchor Bible; Garden City, N.Y.: Doubleday, 1966), CXV-CXVi.

12. J. Murray, *Redemption—Accomplished and Applied* (Grand Rapids, Mich.: Eerdmans, 1955), pp. 196-97. Gromacki, *op. cit.*, p. 84, says, "Since every believer is a gift from the Father to the Son, everyone of these will come to Christ."

13. L. Morris, *Commentary on the Gospel of John* NIC (Grand Rapids, Mich.: Eerdmans, 1971), pp. 371n. He notes P. Borgen's conclusion in the latter's *Bread from Heaven*, 161, that the verb has the idea, "take possession of" and indicates divine selection and inevitable reception by the divine agent (Jesus).

14. *Ibid.*, p. 387. Steel and Thomas, *op. cit.*, p. 29, say, "Men left in their dead state are unable of themselves to repent, to believe the gospel, or to come to Christ. They have no power within themselves to change their natures or to prepare themselves for salvation." The classic work on this, of course, is Martin Luther's *The Bondage of the Will.*

15. Brown, *op. cit.*, p. 276. He adds, "It would be just as much nonsense to doubt that, like the other biblical authors, he saw God's sovereign choice being worked out in those who came to Jesus."

16. "Lifted up" is a Johannine term which speaks of Christ's passion as being "lifted up" on the cross (it results in being "lifted up" in glory). It is a strong salvific term looking back to Moses' "lifting up" the serpent in the wilderness (3:14-15; cf. 8:28). In conclusion, this verse would deny Morris' contention that "resistance is never successful." In fact, his discussion of this verse is particularly clumsy, for he still tries to interpret this word as teaching final salvation and so must wrestle with the question of universalism, i.e., the belief that all will be saved.

17. Note the parallel to 12:32 in this verse, "It is written in the prophets, 'And they shall all be taught by God,'" which is a free translation from Isa. 54:13 LXX. The drawing power is entirely God's, and that is universally applied; but the act of coming proceeds only when one "hears" and "learns."

18. Marshall, *op. cit.*, p. 177. R. Shank, *Elect in the Son* (Springfield, Mo.: Westcott Publishers, 1970), pp. 176-77, argues that God's drawing is "Compelling" but not "coercive," i.e., it is the call of salvation rather than the guarantee of salvation.

19. But note 1 Tim. 2:5, 6, which says Jesus gave his life a "ransom for all" in a clear paraphrase of Jesus' statement here.

20. The same is true regarding the picture of 12:40, where we have the picture of God "blinding the eyes" and "hardening the heart" of those who have disbelieved (v. 39). Some take this in a double predestinarian sense, but neither in Isa. 68:10 nor here has God moved in a vacuum. Rather, he has finalized the consequences of their own rejection. See Morris, *op. cit.*, p. 604.

21. L. Boettner, *The Reformed Doctrine of Predestination* (Grand Rapids, Mich.: Eerdmans, 1932), p. 198.

22. See Gromacki, *op. cit.*, pp. 76f.; J. F. Strombeck, *Shall Never Perish* (Chicago, Ill.: Moody Press, 1966), pp. 2-3. Both declare that "they follow me" is a statement of fact rather than a condition and expresses a guaranteed aspect of the salvation process.

23. There are three Calvinist approaches: 1) Murray, *op. cit.*, *Redemption*, pp. 190-91, and Calvin, *John*, 108, assert that this refers only to professing believers who have the external resemblance but not the internal life; however,

we must agree with Westcott, 216-17, that the branches are definitely "in Christ" and are receiving nourishment from him. 2) Chafer, *op. cit.*, III, pp. 289-98, believes that what it teaches is that the Christian can lose his communion (fellowship) with Christ but not his union, i.e., it is their testimony, not their soul, that is lost; however, this does not fit the imagery of the passage, which hardly speaks of a testimony—it is the branch itself, not just the bark, etc., which is burned. 3) W. N. Clarke, *An Outline of Christian Theology* (New York: Scribner's Sons, 1911), pp. 421-22, takes this as a hypothetical possibility, i.e., God uses these very real warnings as the means of ensuring the final perseverance of his saints; against this approach see the discussion on "Soteriology in Hebrews" in this symposium (especially on 6:4f.).

24. Marshall, *op. cit.*, pp. 279-81.

25. See Chafer, *op. cit.*, III, p. 286; Morris, *op. cit.*, p. 386. On this point Marshall, *ibid.*, p. 179, is in agreement on the grounds that this was John's belief.

26. Chafer, *op. cit.*, III, p. 332.

27. Gromacki, *op. cit.*, pp. 49-50.

28. F. F. Bruce, *The Epistle of Paul to the Romans* (TNTC; Grand Rapids, Mich.: Eerdmans, 1963), p. 216, says, "it was such God-fearers who formed the nucleus of the Christian community in one city after another in the course of Paul's missionary activity."

29. See Bruce, *ibid.*, pp. 283n; and Boettner, *op. cit.*, p. 102.

30. It is interesting that two other scholars take opposite sides from their normal positions, with Marshall, *op. cit.*, p. 84, agreeing with Bruce on linguistic grounds, while J. O. Buswell, *A Systematic Theology of the Christian Religion*, 2 vols. (Grand Rapids, Mich.: Zondervan, 1962), pp. 152-53, agrees with Alford that it should be translated "as many as were disposed to eternal life." Here we would have to agree with the first three, for divine election rather than human volition is certainly the topic here.

31. See the extensive discussion in R. Shank, *Elect in the Son* (Springfield, Mo.: Westcott Publishers, 1970), pp. 183-87. He is wrong in arguing for the translation "disposed" but correct in noting the context of the verse.

32. This is a doubtful parallel, because one cannot know whether they knew Christ beforehand and, more importantly, because their death most probably was physical rather than spiritual.

33. Steel & Thomas, *op. cit.*, p. 53.

34. See Marshall, *op. cit.*, p. 85.

35. Green, *op. cit.*, pp. 152-53; Ladd, *op. cit.*, pp. 373-75.

36. Steel & Thomas, *op. cit.*, pp. 28-29.

37. J. Murray, *The Epistle to the Romans*, NIC; 2 vols. (Grand Rapids, Mich.: Eerdmans, 1965), p. 104, summarizes, "To state the thought of verse 11 both negatively and positively it is that as respects well-doing, there is not one, as respects evil-doing there is no exception."

38. Here we must qualify ourselves. We do believe that man's depravity is such that he cannot come to faith-decision of his own volition. However, we also believe in the universal salvific will of God; the Spirit convicts "the world" (all men—John 16:8f.) and each man has the opportunity of yielding to the "drawing power" of Christ in the spirit. Therefore, we would basically agree with the doctrine of total depravity but stress that this does not lead to the doctrine of unconditional election and irresistible grace.

39. C. Hodge, *Systematic Theology*, 3 vols. (Grand Rapids, Mich.: Eerdmans, 1946 [originally 1871-73; Eerdmans]), pp. 110-113.

40. Murray, *op. cit.*, p. 274 (see 274-82).

41. While the particle in verse 11 is εἰ, assuming reality (perhaps equivalent to "since") the present tense verbs of the passage and the use of in both sections of verse 13 point to an actual condition throughout the passage. We cannot be too rigid in our grammatical categories in the New Testament,

since the classical distinctions were disappearing in first century Koine Greek. See also F. L. Godet, *The Epistle to the Romans*, trans. A. Cusin (Grand Rapids, Mich.: Zondervan, 1969 [originally 1883]), p. 307.

42. See the excellent discussion of this in Jeremias' *The Prayers of Jesus*.

43. See Hodge, *op. cit.*, III, p. 111.

44. Murray, *op. cit.*, *Romans*, pp. 316-17.

45. Note the use of this term in 1 Pet. 1:2, where it is used as a synonym for election. The word "know" is used often for God's gracious love in the Old Testament—cf. Gen. 18:19; Ex. 33:12; Jer. 1:5; Amos 3:3; Hos. 13:5; and in the New Testament, 1 Cor. 8:3; Gal. 4:9.

46. Bruce, *op. cit.*, p. 177.

47. Shank, *op. cit.*, *Life*, pp. 365-67.

48. Marshall, *op. cit.*, p. 93.

49. Ibid., p. 93, notes Wesley's comment here that the passage never says the same number are called, justified, and glorified. It simply describes the salvation process. Nothing said removes the necessity for perseverance or makes faith a God-given commodity only for the elect.

50. J. Calvin, *Institutes of the Christian Religion*, III (Grand Rapids, Mich.: Eerdmans, 1957), xxiv, p. 10. G. C. Berkouwer, *Faith and Perseverance* tr. K. D. Knudson (Grand Rapids, Mich.: Eerdmans, 1958), pp. 9-10, speaks of the timelessness of the doctrine of final perseverance, founded on "the richness and abidingness of salvation."

51. Murray, *op. cit.*, *Romans*, p. 325.

52. J. Arminius, *The Works of James Arminius*, 3 vols. (Grand Rapids, Mich.: Baker, 1956 [1853]), p. 191; J. Wesley, *The Works of John Wesley*, 14 vols. (Grand Rapids, Mich.: Zondervan, 1958-59), X, p. 291.

53. This also provides the answer to Murray's thesis that limited atonement is taught here. "Us" does refer to the "elect," but these are believers, and the nonelect have no part in the discussion. This must be balanced by the other Pauline statements regarding the universal salvific will—Rom. 5:18; 11:15; 1 Cor. 15:22; 2 Cor. 5:19; Col. 1:20; 1 Tim. 2:4, 6; 4:10—and the two aspects are found in Pauline theology in the same way as already noted in Johannine theology.

54. See Shank, *op. cit.*, *Life*, pp. 309-29. While he is wrong in saying the apostasy of Heb. 6:4f. is redeemable (see the chapter on Hebrews in this symposium), he is correct regarding apostasy in general.

55. Hodge, *op. cit.*, *Corinthians*, p. 44.

56. Ladd, *op. cit.*, p. 490.

57. Boettner, *op. cit.*, p. 98. See also Chafer, *op. cit.*, III, p. 174: "men are not first holy and then elect; but they are first elect and that election is unto holiness."

58. Buswell, *op. cit.*, II, p. 145, says in this regard, "If God has unconditionally elected to save a people, and if He has provided atonement which makes their salvation certain, it follows by inevitable logic that those whom God has elected to eternal salvation will go on to eternal salvation."

59. Arminius, *op. cit.*, III, p. 490, argues that in Eph. 1 faith is presupposed as the basis of predestination (cf. John 1:12).

60. Dibelius, p. 72f., as noted in Marshall, *op. cit.*, p. 96, who concludes, "Nothing is said which would deny that certain people heard the Gospel and did not believe, and it is not suggested that such people did not believe because they were not predestined to believe. All that we are told is that God foreordains those who believe to become holy and to be His sons."

61. Calvin, *op. cit.*, *Ephesians*, p. 209. See also Berkouwer, *op. cit.*, p. 212.

62. Strombeck, *op. cit.*, pp. 58f.

62b. Ladd, *op. cit.*, p. 484.

63. "Grieving" the Spirit is probably taken from Isa. 63:10, which speaks

of Israel's rebellion against God, who "turned to be their enemy" as a result. Hendricksen, *Exposition of Ephesians* (Grand Rapids, Mich.: Baker, 1967), p. 222, calls this the first step on the downward path to resistance (Acts 7:51) and then to quenching the Spirit (1 Thess. 5:19). We would go further and note this as a definite warning to a church which would later foster apostates (i.e., the false teachers noted in the epistles to Timothy).

64. Hendricksen, *op. cit.*, pp. 121-23. He argues against Robertson who relates it to grace, i.e., God's grace and man's faith; and against Grosheide (with whom we agree), who says it relates to the whole phrase. In the latter sense, however, Hendricksen's arguments are directed more against the application to "saved."

65. The rigid external interpretation of many Calvinists is exactly the reason many modern scholars have objected to the doctrine of "substitutionary" atonement (e.g., V. Taylor in *The Atonement*, 60, as noted in Ladd, *op. cit.*, pp. 426-27), namely, because they make it entirely outside of and apart from man's decision so that man can do nothing. However, there is both an objective (Christ's substitution) and subjective (man's response) side to salvation.

66. L. Berkhof, *Systematic Theology* (Grand Rapids, Mich.: Eerdmans, 1956), p. 547.

67. Again we see the concept of eschatological salvation. Paul placed his greatest emphasis on the present aspects of salvation, i.e., justification and sanctification. However, the future aspect was still noted, and while Paul was confident he nevertheless stressed the necessity for perseverance (see below).

68. Marshall, *op. cit.*, p. 113, gives a cogent argument (*contra* R. P. Martin, *The Epistle of Paul to the Philippians*, TNTC [Grand Rapids, Mich.: Eerdmans, 1959], pp. 110-11) for an individual rather than corporate interpretation here. While "salvation can mean corporate "health" (Acts 27:34), it is always used in Paul in a spiritual sense.

10

God's Promise and Universal History:
The Theology of Romans 9
JAMES D. STRAUSS

2 Corinthians 1:20—All promises are yes in Christ.
2 Peter 1:4—He has granted to us his precious and very great promises.

Ours is an age that would have sent the Greeks to their oracles. Cultural fragmentation in the form of paralyzing pluralistic pragmatism causes many in the last quarter of the 20th century to despair of God's presence in any dimension of reality except "the depth of being" and this only begrudgingly, if at all. Here he is privately locked out of the physical, biological, social, and historical processes of the universe. God's transcendence over the universe has been seriously challenged since the 17th century astronomical revolution.[1] This challenge to God's providential guidance of the universe was later intensified by the Hegelian dialectical view of all reality which claimed to answer the question: What is the total purpose of the world? It is especially relevant at this juncture in human history to challenge the dominant rumor of angels which is only a very immanent rumor.

The first time the gospel according to Romans was heard, the world was in a cauldron of misery where life was intolerable and death unbearable, men turned to demons, astral deities, Zeus, fate (contra grace and freedom), Caesar (god manifest), Apollo, stoicism, gnostics, hermeticists, aesthetism, neo-platonism (mysticism). (Seneca's note of despair—"Where will you find him whom we have been seeking so many ages?") Venerable systems collapsed; customs and conventions were caught in a flood of change. It was a bewildering new age, before the rising of the "Son" with healing in his wings. Men were seeking deliverance from the Republican wars and

Civil wars, devastating earthquakes, frequent famines, gradual extermination of the middle class, universal misery, atrocious tax systems, political crises, barbarian invasions, world weariness and pessimism.

Then the glory of God appeared in the night of the mind, the night of morals and the night of Graeco-Roman culture (Rom. 1:18ff.). God appeared in the night to take away man's "darkness at noon." This light prevailed for a millennium and a half, then crises severed Europe's nerve. This third great failure of nerve within Western Christian civilization set the stage for a secular revolution; instead God's Word created the greatest spiritual revolution since the day of Pentecost. Europe was saved from a moral and cultural plague by the power of the gospel according to Romans. Now as we plummet toward the 21st century, the voice of God has been stilled in many areas of the West, at least, by the voice of futurologists who are busy planning our future by choosing "the best of all possible worlds" out of an infinite number of possibilities. From Parmenides to Moltmann the watchword is: We shall choose a world out of the infinite number of ontological possibilities; then we shall rise up and build it. This attitude would be more than difficult to harmonize with the theology of universal history in Romans—under the sovereign control of the creator-redeemer of the fallen universe.

Historically, the theology of sin in Romans 5 from both the Catholic and Protestant perspective had consistently suggested a view of sin which made any conditional element in the receiving of the saving grace of God impossible. Though this is not our concern in this essay, our theological judgment concerning the nature of sin and whether or not the saving grace of God has any contingency, we believe that the scripture suggests, in both Old and New Testaments and especially in Romans 9, 10, and 11, that men are responsible for the sinful violation of the will of God, and we believe that it pleased him to make faith and obedience contingencies of his saving grace.[2]

In order better to hear God's word from Romans 9, we propose a brief sketch of three "contexts" in which we find this profound chapter: (1) God's Total Eschatological Promise; (2) The Obedience of Faith: Missionary Framework of Romans; (3) Cosmic Purpose of God in Romans 9-11; then from these three perspectives a study of the theological claims of Romans 9. Our concern is—What does Romans 9 say, not whether or not it fits some preconceived theological notions about the nature of sin, faith, grace, God's sovereignty, etc. In this way we might reduce the dangerous possibilities entailed in isolating any verse or pericope of scripture from its larger context.[3]

As we examine these three contexts and Paul's argument, especially in Romans 9, we will test three operating assumptions: (1) The creator-redeemer is sovereign; (2) man, even in a fallen state, has a range of freedom, thus responsibility; and (3) no man can be saved apart from God's grace, and that is conditioned by man's obedient faithfulness to God's will as revealed in Christ and Scriptures.

I. God's Eschatological Promise

God created and ordered the universe; then man rebelled against God's order and the disorganizing power of sin required the intervention of the creator-redeemer, the Lord of nature-history. The first glimmer of God's glory appears in Gen. 3:15. Here we are given both the positive and negative dimensions of God's promise. What or who is that seed? "Now the promises were spoken to Abraham and to his seed." He does not say, "And to seeds," as referring to many, but rather to one, "and to your seed," that is, Christ (Gal. 3:16). Next the promise comes to Abraham (Gen. 12:1ff.). The seed is promised to Abraham, Sarah, Isaac, and Jacob (Gen. 13:14ff.; 15; 17:6-7; 26:3-4; 28:3-4; 35:11-12; 48:3-4). The promise is later renewed to Israel and David (Israel—Ex. 6:7; Deut. 29:12-13; House of David, 2 Sam. 7:1; 1 Chron. 22:9). The promise of David parallels that to the patriarchs and Israel of the exodus. In God's great mercy he extends the promise through the prophets and Psalms (Ps. 89; Isa. 55:1-3; Zech. 14:16-21) to all who believe in Yahweh's purpose. Then ultimately, the promised Messiah comes as a light to the nations. He is the kingdom bearer—the bearer of "the last days" and calls all to repentance—Jew and Gentile alike.

II. The Obedience of Faith

The concept of Israel,[4] as a people of God made up of true believers, was fundamental to Jewish proselytism. The Hebrew word for a foreigner who had been accepted in Israel was (gēr)—Abraham was called a gēr. This phenomena must be understood before a clear evaluation of Paul's theology of Israel in Romans and Galatians can be made.[5]

It is of inestimable value to keep in mind that Romans is Paul's declaration of the nature of the gospel and he is its bearer. Paul is an evangelist establishing the "body of Christ," primarily beyond the context of his ancient heritage. He is on the way to Jerusalem, then on to Spain. He has been called ". . . to bring about the obedience of faith among all the Gentiles, for his name's sake" (Rom. 1:5). After showing us the glory of God through our need for redemption and its availablity in Christ; then he reveals his broken heart over his disobedient kinsmen (Rom. 9-11).

III. Cosmic Purpose of God: Romans 9-11

The fundamental problem about which Paul bears both the heartbeat of God's cosmic purpose and his own broken heart results from the unbelief of his brothers according to the flesh. Next he defends God's purpose in the course of human history (9:6-18). Israel's unbelief is not proof that God's word of promise has failed. God's faithfulness is to the patriarchs whom he elected (9:6-13). God's choice of Moses and Pharaoh is proof of his justice. God's justice is personal and not necessarily legal. As Paul continues his close argumentation, he responds to an objector to God's ways with man (9:19-24). The objector misunderstands the entire nature of God's sovereign power. God does not treat man merely as an object to be manipulated for his ultimate purpose. Paul magnificently makes this point by presenting God's choice of the nation as an act of grace which does not preclude a remnant to Israel (9:25-29). Throughout his defense of God's sovereign grace, freedom, and mercy, Paul is heartbroken because of Israel's unbelief (9:30-33).

Israel's unbelief is not grounded in genuine knowledge of God's purpose (10:2-3). Surely Israel has heard that faith comes by hearing (10:14-18). But the historic tragedy is now before us. Israel did not accept the ultimate promise of God, Jesus Christ (10:19-21). Does this present rejection frustrate the effectiveness of God's promises? God's apostle-prophet now declares that Israel's disobedience is partial (11:2-10) and not permanent and it is for the everlasting benefits of the Gentiles (11:11-24). The ultimate solution for Israel's present unbelief is now affirmed to lie in our coming to understand the mystery of God's gracious mercy, his creative and saving word which will work good out of Israel's present disobedience (11:25-32). What more can Paul now do as he stands in awe before his sovereign Lord than conclude these theological claims with a praise to the ever-healing help of God's wisdom? (11:33-36).[6]

IV. God's Universal Purpose and Israel's Unbelief

Paul is deeply involved in Israel's present unbelief (vv. 1-5). His feelings and conscience (*sunedesis*, literally to see together where integration or wholeness is attained)[7] are

vividly "aware before God" of the scandalous disobedience
of the Nation of Israel, even within the historically visible
"light of the world." Yet, he stands in God's presence as
a believing seed of Abraham under excruciating agony for
his people, like Moses (Ex. 32:32). If Paul believed that God
arbitrarily chooses "some to life" and others to condemnation," his emotional state is hardly appropriate, even as their
biologico-historico kinsman.

In resolving this crisis of faith, Paul will seek to penetrate
the mystery of God's saving activity as creator-redeemer of
the universe. Neither problem nor the solution is given pro-
ventialistic perspective, rather we are brought face to face
with the purpose and promise of our sovereign Lord who is
working out his will within the space/time categories of human
history, universal human history.[8]

How can Israel's historic defection be harmonized with the
gift of God's gracious election? How can Israel disregard
all her privileges which includes "sonship," God's presence
(Hebrew kobad; doxa—LXX and New Testament) the cove-
nants, the word of God given to Abraham, Moses, and David,
which spells out the will of God for fallen creation, Israel
and nations? All of Israel's history is set out for microscopical
observation by Paul in 9:5, ". . . whose are the fathers, and
from whom is the Christ according to the flesh, who is over
all, God blessed forever, Amen."

V. The Promise: Neither Frustrated Nor Failed

Paul's doxology (v. 5) is his firm basis for the following
theological consideration of the dialectical tension between
fulfillment/nonfulfillment of the promise of God. First, Paul emphatically denies that God's Word has failed or that his gracious manifestation of justice can be impugned. Paul next
reasons from historic illustrations of how God has worked
in Israel's past to bring to fruition his efficacious promise.
No man can lay claim to the promise on his own. God's promise
becomes visible in history where his justice is observable in
the lives of his obedient children (Rom. 3:21-5). God's purpose
is salvific. His election is based beyond human standards of
moral achievement (vv. 9-13), and the exodus deliverance (vv.
14-18). Human responsibility for the covenant relation with
God is clearly revealed throughout Israel's history (note the
basis of denial in v. 6). In Paul's overall perspective, God's
"call" is ordered to his final glory. (Compare God's presence
in the tabernacle, temple, and God's departure from the temple
because of Israel's unbelief. Compare Ezek. 48:35, "Yahweh
shall be there," and Rev. 21). Paul's perspective is from God's

acts in salvation history, not from all eternity "prior" to the creation of heaven and earth. In man's *de facto* condition, he cannot become righteous, only God's righteousness graciously extended through Christ can reconcile man to God.

Paul's consideration of Jacob, Esau, Moses, and Pharaoh is not occupied with their ultimate personal salvation, but rather with their role in the historic working out of the promised blessing. Paul is only concerned with the details in each person's life which radically effect the historic working out of the salvific promise of God. Paul's major emphasis in Romans 9 is the understanding of God's word and justice as achieved through men but neither are realized because of men's actions. The true people of God are not as such biologico-historico Israel, but rather are those who believe the promise of God and that he will ultimately fulfill what he has promised. Paul next explains the relationship of God's sovereign promise, justice and mercy by examining a series of events centering around persons involved in vital periods of Israel's history.

VI. God's Ultimate Concern

Paul sets forth the doctrine of the remnant [9] (v. 6) which obviates the charge that the promise of God has failed. "... it is not as though the Word of God has failed" (*ekpeptoken*—perf. tense, ind. voice—not permanently failed). Israel[10]—why hasn't the word permanently failed? Because in the first place, "They are not all Israel who are descended from Israel" (v. 6—*ou gar pantes hoi ex Israel, houtoi* Israel). "They certainly are not children because (causal *hoti*) they are Abraham's descendants, but (contrastive *all*) in Isaac shall your descendants be named" (*en Isaak klethesetai*—fut. ind., passive—*soi sperma*), verse 7. Paul here declares that not all of Abraham's seed are called, only those that descend from Isaac. This election was a sovereign choice of God. The ultimate purpose of this free choice of God was that "all the nations of the earth shall be blessed" because of God's promise to Abraham (Gen. 12:1ff.).

The mere fact of being a child in the historic family of Abraham does not make one a child of the promise (*alla ta tekna tes epangelias logizetai EIS sperma*—here Paul uses *logizetai*, which is the same word he employs in speaking of our righteousness in Christ), verse 8.

The emphatic word in this verse is promise (*epangelias*), verse 9. God's purpose becomes more visible in this promise to Sarah (Gen. 18:10-4). Only God could enable a woman of Sarah's advanced age to have the son of promise. God alone could know that it would be a son, the very son which would be received back as from the dead (Heb. 11:17-19). Abraham's response to Isaac on Mt. Moriah reveals the sovereign activity of God in history. Abraham answers Isaac, "Yahweh will provide himself"; the Hebrew text contains a reflexive form. The Hebrew grammar entails the great sacrificial activity of Yahweh. Yahweh shall provide himself—ultimately with his own Son on the cross. Finally, the purpose of the blessing of the nations will be accomplished. Paul's examples of Jacob and Esau enables him to illustrate that the moral stature as well as their biological potential are not the determining factors in God's choice of the younger over the older as the instrument for further realizing this promised blessing. Also, the example completely inverts the cultural behavioral pattern of the Near East, i.e, that the younger always serves the older. Paul quotes from Mal. 1:2-3, which is a discussion of the prospective nations—not the individuals, Jacob and Esau. The context from which Paul draws his pointed example states that "the oracle of the word of the Lord to Israel by Malachi. 'I have loved you,' says the Lord. But you say, 'How hast thou loved us?' 'Is not Esau Jacob's brother?' says the Lord, 'yet I have loved Jacob but I have hated Esau; I have laid waste his hill country and left his heritage to jackals of the desert.' . . . 'Great is the Lord, beyond the border of Israel!' "

Hosea also mentions Jacob in a corporate sense, not as an individual in Hos. 12:2ff., "The Lord has an indictment against Judah, and will punish Jacob according to his ways, and requite him according to his deeds." In fact, historically the individual Esau never did serve the individual Jacob, only the Edomites as a nation served Israel as a nation. If Paul had wished to discuss Jacob and Esau as elected individuals, one to salvation and the other to condemnation, it is strange that he chose a passage of scripture which reveals the exact opposite as his Old Testament proof of God's sovereign act. The phrase "Jacob I loved, Esau I hated" comes not from Genesis but from Malachi at a time in their history when the nation as a whole was under consideration. The phrase is a Semitic idiom of sharp contrasts; it does not reveal God's personal disposition, only in the sense of the function which each group played in the realization of the promise. Paul then asks, "There is no injustice with (para—with respect to) God, is there? Absolutely not." What does all of this have to do with Israel's present unbelief? How can God's promise to Israel be harmonized with their disobedience?

All true Israel has been and still is only those who obey the covenant responsibility to God. The example speaks strongly against the covenant people as possessing the "irresistible gift of faith." There is a consistent use of the adultery metaphor for Israel's unbelief in the Old Testament (Ex. 32:12ff.; Lev. 20:5-6; Judg. 2:17; Ps. 73:27). Three of the greatest prophets in the Old Testament condemn Israel for her unfaithfulness to Yahweh by charging them with spiritual adultery. In Isa. 1:21 he asks, "How is the faithful city become a prostitute!" Jeremiah denounces Israel with these biting words, " . . . you have played the prostitute with many lovers; yet return again to me, says the Lord" (Jer. 3:1). The great co-laborer of Isaiah, Hosea, movingly pleads with Israel declaring that " . . . the spirit of whoredom has caused them to err, and they have gone a whoring from under their God." " . . . your daughters shall commit whoredom, and your wives shall commit adultery" (Hos. 4:12-13; 9:1ff.). Yahweh speaks to uprooted exiles saying, "I am broken with their whorish heart" (Ezek. 6:9; also Ezek. 16:30ff.; and 23:1ff.). Clearly from these brief references to Israel's past history of disobedience, Paul's generation is not the first to reject the promises of God.

Paul moves to show that God's justice is one with his mercy. The first example Paul employs comes from Ex. 33:19, "I will have mercy on whom I have mercy, and I will have compassion on whom I have compassion." The theme of the Exodus passage is the presence of God. This presence has been denied to rebellious Israel, but given to Joshua and Moses at the tent of meeting. As always, only a remnant of true believers have access to the presence of God. Moses then seeks a guarantee of God's presence for the people of God. God then promises Moses his presence and Israel ultimate rest in Canaan. Then Moses asks for a vision of God (33:17-23). He prays to see the glory of God. His revelation is his name proclaimed in terms of his acts to man. God's nature is defined as goodness and grace, verse 19. (For discussion of the Hebrew *tub*, "goodness," see P. Hyatt, *Exodus*, New Century Bible, 1971.) The object of God's goodness is disloyal disobedient Israel, "I will be gracious to whom I will be gracious." This Hebrew phrase can in no way imply any abrupt arbitrariness of God's act toward Israel. Though the English translation might imply this connotation, the Augustinian understanding of verse 19 as it is quoted in Rom. 9:15 cannot be sustained from either the Exodus context, or its place in Romans 9. God's promise entails only mercy, never injustice.

VII. Sovereignty, Freedom, and Responsibility

Paul's second example of God's merciful justice is Pharaoh. Paul quotes from the LXX rather than the Hebrew text in the quotation in verse 17. "For this very purpose I raised you up to demonstrate my power in you, and that my name might be proclaimed throughout the whole earth." In Ex. 9:16 the Hebrew *he èmadhtikha* literally means "caused you to stand"; rendered "maintained you alive." (See U. Cassuto, *Exodus*, p. 116; and Hyatt, *Exodus*, New Century Bible, 1971, on this verse.) The theological point in the context of Exodus 9 is God's merciful patience. This, too, is Paul's point in Rom. 9:16-18. God would have destroyed Israel in the plagues of Egypt, but he had elected them to participate in his purpose of redemption. It is very important to remember the cosmic perspective of three consecutive verses in Ex. 9:14, 15, 16, "in all the earth," "from the earth," and "in all the earth," and how the universal implications of God's sovereign power fits the contexts of Rom. 9:17-18. The LXX version of Exodus 9 quoted by Paul in Romans 9 has been used to suggest God's arbitrary fiat against Pharaoh. The passage in Exodus does not mean that God created or "raised up" Pharaoh just to show his superior might. The hardening of Pharaoh's heart in no way is to be taken to mean that God arbitrarily closed Pharaoh's heart against God's people.[11] The "hardening" is part of the total design to be accomplished and Pharaoh participates in his own hardening.

Pharaoh refuses to free the children of Israel. God pleads with him through Moses and Aaron, but he only becomes more obdurate and revengeful to the Semitic slaves. God's mercy and justice are made available to both Israel and Pharaoh, but the former accepts, the latter refuses.

Paul advances his argument by responding to an objector who supposes that the apostle regards God's act in hardening Pharaoh's heart as an overwhelming brute force which no one has resisted or can resist. Now Paul uses imagery from different periods of the history of Israel's unbelief, i.e., apostasy from covenant responsibility—Isa. 45:9-11; 64:8; 29:16; and Jer. 18:8. The English text of Rom. 9:20-22 might suggest a mechanically arbitrary relationship between the potter and the clay, which none of the Old Testament references to this image will support.

Jeremiah 18 follows a powerful appeal to rebellious Israel to repent. Trust in the Lord and return to Israel. " . . . Israel will know my power and my might, and they shall know that my name is the Lord" (Jer. 16:21). Further, God tells Jeremiah to go stand in the Benjamin Gate and commands to speak to the kings of Judah. "Take heed for the sake of your lives. . . . Yet they did not listen or incline their ear, but stiffened their neck, that they might not hear and receive instruction" (Jer. 17:21-23). If you do not heed the prophet's warnings, then you will be destroyed. These are the ringing words of the weeping prophet. Then comes the great chapter which contains the imagery employed by Paul, the potter and the clay. God has appealed to Israel, and now they respond to him, " . . . we will follow our own plans, and will everyone act according to the stubbornness of his evil heart" (Jer. 18:12).

Now comes the blow to a Calvinistic interpretation of Paul's example in Rom. 9:20-21. God asked Jeremiah to go down to the potter's house. There he tells the prophet that he is " . . . shaping evil against you and devising a plan against you. Return everyone from his evil way, and amend your ways and your doings" (Jer. 18:11). Because they will not respond to God's gracious call, judgment is inevitable. "I will show them my back, not my face, in the day of their calamity" (Jer. 18:17). Apostasy is the condition of Israel. They refuse God's gracious warning. They are committing spiritual adultery by worshipping false gods (19:1ff.). Jeremiah prophesies in the court of the Lord's house, "Behold, I am bringing upon the city and upon all its towns all the evil that I have pronounced against it, because they have stiffened their neck, refusing to hear my words" (Jer. 19:15). The same themes are present in the other scriptures where this imagery appears. Isaiah says that Israel " . . . draws near with their mouth . . . while their hearts are far from me" (Isa. 29:13). In Isa. 45:9-11, the context is of captivity and God's sovereign employment of Cyrus as liberator of imprisoned unfaithful Israelites. This great passage again affirms that men are morally responsible for their behavior; they can repent, but if they will not, then God's merciful justice will prevail in spite of their self-destructive refusal.

In the great eschatological section of Isaiah 60-66, we note again the potter-clay imagery. We hear a prayer for mercy, "You are our Father; we are the clay, and thou art our potter; we are all the work of your hand" (Isa. 64:8). In every passage in which the above imagery appears, God is calling his rebellious people to repentance. If they cannot repent, then what of the moral significance of asking them to do something which God knows they cannot do? It is most important to note that Paul implies human responsibility as he goes on to speak of God's patient endurance toward "vessels of wrath prepared for destruction" (v. 22). Many vessels of wrath, both Jews and Gentiles, repented and thus became vessels moving toward (eis—preposition meaning motion in the direction of, used of both mercy and absence of mercy in v. 21). The standard English translation "vessels of mercy" and "vessels of wrath" are not precisely what the Greek text declares because the grammar uses the preposition eis plus accusative case, and not the genitive case from which we might derive the translations "of mercy," "of wrath." The Greek word for this later translation is not *orge* but an alpha privative on the root word "mercy." The word literally means the absence of mercy. This is true because God's mercy is available only to the faithful and obedient individual, Jew or Gentile.

The doctrine of the irresistible gift of faith is not taught in this passage, or for that matter elsewhere in Scriptures. Often Eph. 2:8 is given as a proof text that faith is a gift. The gender of the Greek form of the pronoun "this" has as its antecedent "grace" rather than "faith" because the antecedents must agree in gender.

The phrase "vessels of wrath prepared for destruction" translates *skeue orges katertismena eis apoleian*. The English translation generally implies that some individuals were prepared by a sovereign act of God for destruction. At least since Augustine and Calvin this viewpoint has been widely held. But the form *katertismena* is a perfect passive or middle participle. In the perfect tense the passive and middle have the same form, only the context will determine which way the word should be translated. The context of this term is Paul's argument, which immediately stems from the three questions asked in verse 20.

The larger context has been the entire structure of Romans 9. Every example which Paul has shown stresses personal responsibility on man's part, and justice and mercy on God's part. The whole of Romans 9 is concerned with Israel's unbelief, and it is central to Paul's total argument that Israel is responsible for their rebellious attitude toward God's promise. God always judges unbelief; this is his justice. It is always possible to repent and return to the presence of God; this is his mercy. In this context, I see no justification for translating the word under consideration as passive, i.e., the subject is acted upon; rather, the translation should be "fitted themselves" for wrath. From 1:18 we learn that God's "wrath" is continually being revealed (*apokaluptetai*, pres. ind. passive—presently and not at some further event of judgment) from heaven against all ungodliness and unrighteousness of men, who suppressed the truth in unrighteousness. Paul's kinsmen according to the flesh were experiencing the wrath of God outside of God's righteousness in Christ. Rebellion against God's promised purpose has always brought his wrath, but only after calling to repentance and restoration.

There are vessels of mercy and vessels of wrath among both Jews and Gentiles. The purpose of God's patience (v. 22) was to give those who prepare themselves by unbelief for God's wrath a time to repent. "The Lord is not slow about his promise as some count slowness, but is forbearing toward you, not wishing that any should perish, but that all should reach repentance" (2 Pet. 3:9). The glory of God is his presence among his people. Paul has already set forth that Christ is our righteousness, object of our faith, and the source of the distinction between "vessels of mercy" and "vessels of wrath" (compare Rom. 8:28-30 and 9:23-24). We must be most careful in the manner in which we complete the conditional clause in verses 22-23. (This is all the more imperative because Paul's sentence dissolves into an *anacoluthon* or an erratic sentence), though the context points us to what God has actually done without discriminating between Jews and Gentiles. God has mercifully deferred his wrath from those who prepare themselves for wrath by showing his patience. Thus, God's power, even with regard to those on whom he could wish (v. 22, *thelon*—participle) to reveal his wrath, has been exercised with merciful patience and not as brute force (e.g., Pharaoh, and Israel during her many periods of unbelief). More in accord with Paul's entire development would be the conclusion (though it is not provided in Paul's Greek text as we are here dealing with a grammatical anacolution) " . . . how can you, mere man, suppose that God exercises his will in an arbitrary and capricious manner, as though it were brute force?" God's sovereign freedom does not mean that he will disregard the limited freedom of his creatures; and so we must recognize the qualitative aspects of God's power even where the rebellious unbeliever is concerned (Rom. 2:3-4).

The objector is rebuked for his insolent assumption that he has a right to challenge the power of God, especially by supposing that God's power is not graciously exercised. God's word has truly not failed, because it is his word that must be understood as a promise realized on the basis of God's free choice (9:6-13). God commits no injustice in the realization of his promise (9:14-18). God's free act is ordered to universal salvation (not universalism). Even in the case of those who fitted themselves for God's wrath (they are responsible, Rom. 2:3-5), God's freedom has been mercifully exercised.

Paul next spells out God's historically manifested mercy for Jews as well as Gentiles (9:25-33). Paul appeals to God's word through Hos. 1:10. (This quotation is not from the New Testament, nor the LXX of any known version, though it contains the awkward LXX translation in essence.) By using Hosea's great heart-rendering call to unbelieving Israel, Paul describes God's merciful call to the Gentiles. The original text contains God's appeal to Israel to repent after she had continually committed spiritual adultery. After Israel's adulterous affair with Baal, God says that she ceased to be his people. Hosea clearly reveals God's mercy and Israel's personal responsibility and freedom to repent and return to God. God condemned the ten northern tribes, but he was not unjust, because they deserved his judgment. His mercy was evident in his call to repentance; his love (*hesed*, covenant love) was visible in Hosea's maternal situation (read chs. 1-3). The promise to restore Israel was contingent on their repentance. The theology of Hosea is crystal clear: the abandonment of God meant the loss of covenant status (no Old Testament suggestions of Eternal Security). The demand of repentance emphasized Israel's moral responsibility (freedom to act and return to God), and the "remnant" theme strongly asserts that only the faithful, i.e., believers in Yahweh's promises, will return and that corporate Israel will be destroyed, as it was historically.

The theme taken from Hosea is present in Paul's argument. But in its Old Testament context, the word applies simply to Israel. Paul simply extends the "my people" to include Gentile believers, expressing the point that all true believers are God's people not merely biologico-historico Israel. The universal scope of Hosea's message as applied to Gentile believers is appropriated as proof of the actual fulfillment of the intention of God's word. The "not my people" are now called "sons of the living God." God's call of Israel must be understood as the call of a remnant in the days, " . . . but also from among Gentiles" (v. 24).

VIII. God's Promise and the Believing Remnant

God's promise is being fulfilled, even though the fulfillment deals with a remnant, a believing remnant. Paul concludes this particular defense of the efficacy of the Lord's word of promise by pointing out that its apparent failure is really the failure of some to understand God's promise. God's word has not failed (9:6, *ekpeptoken*, fallen down); rather, unbelieving Israel has stumbled over it. Paul denies that God's word has failed even in a most remote detail. From Abraham forward, God's promised blessing entails *only believers*. Israel's failure is evidenced by their false striving after righteousness according to the law. Paul quotes from Isaiah in order to emphasize both the remnant theme and the punishment of faithless Israel. In verse 27, Isa. 10:22-23 (modified LXX) is used to support the remnant motif. This remnant pericope contains the dual polarity (10:20-21; 10:22-23), "For though your people, O Israel, were like the sand of the sea, a remnant would return from them. Destruction is decreed, overflowing with righteousness" (Isa. 10:22). The remnant will be a community of faith. There is an unquestionable correlation between the leaning on Yahweh in "truth" and the demand for "faith" in 7:2-9. The reference to the "house of Jacob" (v. 20) seems to call to remembrance that those who trust in God can count upon the saving action of God and will also be the inheritors of the election promises connected with the patriarch Jacob. The name of Isaiah's oldest son, Shear-jashub, is introduced in the form of a sentence which provides a commentary on it. The idea of remnant serves to provoke hope and, at the same time, is a summons to repentance. The remnant carries the designation "Jacob" to emphasize the fact that this group of the faithful remnant will be the bearers of the election promises made to the founding father of Israel.

It is most important that we take note of the fact that the absolute election promises of Israel are conditional. The election promises are placed in direct correlation with the faithfulness of the elected ones. This is precisely Paul's claim in Rom. 9:27. Both Isaiah and Paul juxtapose *salvation* and *judgment* in order to prevent any misunderstanding of God's promise, whereby the remnant could claim to be a privileged group. The ominous tone of Isa. 10:20 seems obvious. God's promise to make Israel as the sand of sea (Gen. 22:17; 32:13) will not prevent him from bringing about a decisive end to Israel's national existence. This is the second time Isaiah refers to the Abrahamic promise in connection with the negative aspects of the remnant motif (Isa. 1:9—which Paul quotes in Rom. 9:29). In both passages the *promise* has been made *conditional*. Only true believers will inherit the promise, because the multitude is unwilling to repent and return to God. The principal emphasis in both Isaiah and Paul is for the express purpose of confuting a false reliance upon the election promise given originally to Abraham (Gen. 22:17) and repeated to Jacob (Gen. 32:13). The mere fact of a physical, patriarchal ancestry will not spare unbelievers in the future judgment. This is precisely Paul's thought in Rom. 9:27. Faith which was always so intricately connected with the remnant motif has now an explicit object.

In Isaiah it is faith in Yahweh's promise; and in Paul it is faith in Jesus Christ the righteousness of God and the fulfiller of God's promise. In verse 29 Paul refers to another reference in Isaiah—1:9 (LXX). Isaiah declares that only because of God's grace and mercy "a few survivors" (Heb. word carries connotation of *fleeing*) were left. Had it not been for the power of "Yahweh of hosts" and especially his mercy, the entire nation would have been wiped off the face of the earth as Sodom and Gomorrah had been in the time of Abraham. (Gen. 18-19. Note also that there is the remnant motif "mercy" and call to repentance in the narrative of the cities of the Plain.) Isaiah compares the city of Jerusalem with Sodom and Gomorrah because both narratives reflect on the actual historical situation. The comparison is not between the "means" but the "totality" of destruction. There was no remnant from Sodom and Gomorrah; but repentance and faithfulness to the covenant would enable even a "few survivors" to continue the historic unfolding of the promise. Israel's rebelliousness brings God's punishment for their breach of his most holy covenant (Isa. 1:4), which is God's "alien work" (Isa. 28:21). In referring to Israel's unbelief, Isaiah raises the question, will Israel understand that the time given her is but a time of probation? God extends his grace in order to give the "few survivors" another chance to return to him in faith. God preserves the seed-promise through "a few survivors."

With splendid urgency Paul suggests that this same situation hovers over his kinsmen according to flesh. Paul, as did Isaiah, clearly assumes the freedom to return to God and that individuals are responsible for their own actions. God has shown patience and mercy toward those who are "fitting themselves" for God's condemnation; the overriding perspective for understanding God's action, however, is that he prepares men for his glory. This he has done without discriminating between Jew and Gentile (9:19-24). The actualization of God's word of promise is precisely what the scriptures declare (9:25-30). What, then, are we to say to account for the fact of such paradoxical fulfillment which has entailed the blessing of Gentiles and disbelief of so many in Israel?

Paul responds to this question (9:30-31) by further explanation of the way in which God intends to fulfill his word of promise. God's promise to Abraham "in your seed shall all the nations of the earth be blessed" is being fulfilled in history. The conditions for participation in its fulfillment have always been the same—faith in the purpose of the one who made the covenant of promise with his people. In both the Old and New Testaments faith means obedience to covenant responsibility and thus the saving grace of God is always contingent. Biologico-historico Israel is our supreme example. The cause of Israel's unbelief is to be found, not in God, but in Israel itself. Israel's unbelief is its freely chosen preference. As with all human choices, man possesses a limited range of freedom to choose from among alternatives, but he is not free to determine the consequences. Paul is not really intending to place praise or blame on any group. He does not say that the Gentiles did not pursue justice, but that Israel did pursue it. Nor does he say that the Gentiles have obtained justice whereas Israel has not obtained it. He does affirm in effect that one group obtained a justice from faith; and another did not obtain justice because it sought justice by human aspiration and effort. Only the perfect can pursue a law of justice. In fact, Israel did not attain the standard set by the law itself. The defective factor was neither the law nor their striving, but as verse 32 makes clear, their nonattainment of righteousness by law stems from an improper perspective, i.e., not God's perspective of his promised intentions. God's justice is only available by faith in a person, the only one who fully explains the Father (John 1:18). Paul's gospel proclaims that in Jesus Christ alone is the goal (Rom. 10:4—*telos*) of the law and the fulfillment of the law (10:4).

IX. God's High Rock

Paul declares that Israel stumbled over the rock of ages. The rock was laid in Zion for Israel's safety. God's gracious mercy had laid the rock. But the rock became an offense, an occasion of stumbling instead of a place of security. By way of conclusion (ch. 9) and transition (ch. 10), Paul quotes a conflated text from Isa. 8:14-15 and 28:16. Christ, the living stone, serves as the basis for an edifice that will not confound the one who relies on him. Paul is the bearer of the great mystery of the divine plan of salvation. The context of Isa. 28:16 (also Rom. 10:11; 1 Pet. 2:4-6) is a call to repent for the " . . . scoffers, who rule this people in Jerusalem" who have made a covenant with death and do not believe that justice will prevail make lies their refuge and falsehood their shelter. Repent and trust the sure foundation laid in Zion because a decree of destruction has gone out from the Lord God (Isa. 28:22). In Isa. 8:14-15 Yahweh is once more warning rebellious Israel, but the warning is also a call to blessing. Whether it be blessing or curse will ultimately depend on obedient faith or disobedient unfaithfulness. This, too, is Paul's point in verse 33. Those who believe will not come to grief over it. In Romans 9 God is the sovereign who has ordered all things as he pleases. He is pleased by the gospel to save sinners (1 Cor. 1:21); he is pleased by the faith of those who diligently seek him (Heb. 11:6); he wills that all men be saved (1 Tim. 2:4); he is willing that all come to him by repentance (2 Pet. 3:9). God's promise in Christ entails universal history.

NOTES

1. A. R. Hall, *From Galileo to Newton* (N.Y.: Harper, 1963; and A. Koyré, *The Astronomical Revolution* (Ithaca, N.Y.: Cornell University Press, E.T., 1974).

2. M. Flick, *De gratia Christi* (Rome: Gregorian, 1962); J. Alfaro, *Fides, spes, caritas* (3 volumes; Rome: Gregorian, 1964); R. T. Forster, V. Paul Marston, *God's Strategy in Human History* (Wheaton: Tyndale, 1974); H. Rondet, *The Grace of Christ* (Newman Press: Glen Rock, N.J., E.T., 1966); S. J. Mikolaski, *The Grace of God* (Grand Rapids: Eerdmans, 1966, pb); James Moffatt, *Grace in the New Testament* (N.Y.: R. R. Smith, 1932); and Robert Shanks, *Life in His Son* (Westcott Pub. P.O. Box 803, Springfield, MO, 1960). *Old Testament Vocabulary for Sin*: Early vocabulary—*hattah*, miss mark (Judges 26:16); *awon*, iniquity, crookedness (Gen. 4:13; 15:16); *ra*, evil (earliest root) (Gen. 2:9). Physical calamity or violent breaking of God's orders; Patriarchial Period: two new words—*resha*, wickedness, (Gen. 18:23, root, loose, ill-regulated); *pesha*, transgression (Gen. 50:17, root rebel), 1 Kings 12:19, deliberate and premeditated—Job 34:37 speaks of adding *pesha* to *hattah*. Moses' Period—2 new terms: *ma-al*, trespass (Lev. 5:15, Num. 5:12), marital faithlessness, root, treachery, or faithlessness to covenant (1 Chron. 9:1); *awel* (or *awal*), perversity (Lev. 19:15) root, to deviate, man's deviation from right course. Moses-David. *Awen*, wickedness, root, to be tried. *New Testament Vocabulary for Sin*: Sin in the New Testament is regarded as the missing of the mark or aim (*hamartia* or *hamartema*); the overpassing of transgressing of a line (*parabasis*); the inattentiveness or disobedience to a voice (*parakoe*); the falling alongside where one should have stood upright (*paraptoma*); the doing through ignorance of something wrong which one should have known about (*agnoema*); the coming short of one's duty (*hettema*); and the non-observance of a law (*anomia*); (*adikia*), unrighteousness.

3. For theological structure on Romans see: J. Cambier, *L'Evangile de Dieu selon l'Epitre aux Romains. L'Evangile de la Justice et de la Grace*, 1967. A. Luz, *Das Geschichtsverstandnis des Paulus*, 1968. E. Pfaff, *Die Bekehrung des Ll. Paulus in der Exegesis des 20 Jhs.* (Rome: 1942, rep. 1970). Bartsch, H. W. "Die historische Situation des Romerbriefs." *Communio Viatroum*. Prague. X. Leon-Dufour. "Juif et Gentil dans l'Epitre aux Romains." *Studia Paulina Congressus* (Rome, 1969, pp. 309-315. A. Descamps, "La structure de Romains 1-11." *Studia Paulina Congressus*. 1961. *Analecta Biblica* 17 (Rome: 1963). A. Feuillet, "Le plan salvifique de Dieu d'apres l'epitre aux Romains. Essai sur la structure litteraire de l'epitre et sa signification Theologique." *Revue Biblique* 57, 1950. S. Lyonnet, "Note sur le plan de l'epitre aux Romains." *Recherches de Science Religieuse* (Paris: 1951-52). J. Dupont, "Le probleme de la structure litteraire de l'epitre aux Romains." *Revue Biblique* 62, 1955. Strack-Billerbeck, III, pp. 258-294. Paul's hermeneutical use of O.T. in Romans, esp. 9, see J. Bonsirven, *Exegese Rabbinique et exegese Paulinienne* (Paris: 1939), p. 324—"His typological method is what distinguishes him most deeply from the preachers of the synagogue. His Christian faith alone revealed to him the whole profound significance of the O.T. and its symbolic meaning." B. Lindars, *New Testament Apologetics* (Phil.: Westminster, 1961), pp. 238ff. E. E. Ellis, *Paul's Use of the Old Testament* (Grand Rapids: Eerdmans, 1957), esp. pp. 114ff.

4. Yves Congar, *The Mystery of the Temple*. Lon.: Burns Oates, E.T., 1962. Gutbrad, "Israel," *TDNT, III*, pp. 356-391. Grand Rapids: Eerdmans.

Peter Richardson, *Israel in the Apostolic Church* (Cambridge: Cambridge University Press, 1969).

5. See the following works on Proselytism: F. M. Derwacter, *Preparing the Way for Paul: The Proselyte Movement of Later Judaism* (McMillan, 1930); B. J. Bamberger, *Proselytism in the Talmudic Period* (Cincinnati: Hebrew Union, College Press, 1939); Paul Dalbert, *Die Theologie der hellenistisch judischen Missionsliteratur unter Ausschluss von Philo und Josephus* (Verlag, Hamburg, 1954).

6. A. Feuillet, *Le Christ, Sagesse de Deus* (Paris: 1966).

7. Maurer, "Suneidesis," *TDNT, VII*, pp. 898-919, esp. 914ff. J. Dupont, "Syneidesis aux origines de la notion Chretienne de conscience Morale," *Studia Hellenistica*, 5, (1948), pp. 119-153. C. A. Pierce, *Conscience in the New Testament* (Naperville: Alec Allensen, 1955).

8. H. Ljungman, *Pistis. A Study of Its Presuppositions and Its Meaning in Pauline Use.* 1964; A. Luz, *Das Geschichtsverstandnis des Paulus*, 1968. Herbert Butterfield, *Christianity and History* (Fontana Books, 1957). Arend Th. van Leeuwen, *Christianity in World History* (N.Y.: Scribners, 1964).

9. "The Origin, Development and Significance of the Concept of the Remnant in the Old Testament" (unpublished Ph.D. dissertation, Faculty of Divinity, University of Edinburgh, 1958). G. F. Hasel, *The Remnant* (Berrien Springs, Michigan: Andrews University Press, 1972, esp. pp. 216-403). R. Hoshizoki, "Isaiah's Concept of the Remnant" (unpublished M.Th. Thesis Southern Baptist Theological Seminary, Louisville, KY, 1955). B. F. Meyer, "Jesus and the Remnant of Israel," *JBL*, 84 (1965), pp. 123-30. V. Weber, *Kritsche Geschichte der Exegese des 9 Kapitels, resp. der Verse 14-23, des Romerbriefs bis auf Chrisostomus und Augustinus einschliessliche*, Wurzburg, 1889. Wilhelm Visches, "Das Geheimnis Israels, Eine Erklaruug der Kapitel 9-11 des Romerbriefs," *Judaica*, VI (1950), pp. 81-132.

10. Our brief exposition of Romans 9 precluded a technical encounter with a major alternative interpretation to the one presented in this essay, but see *Luther's Works*, Volume 25, Hilton C. Oswald, editor (St. Louis: Concordia Publishing House, 1972), pp. 371-403. *The Epistles of Paul the Apostle to the Romans and to the Thessalonians.* Edited by D. W. Torrance and T. F. Torrance (Grand Rapids: Eerdmans, 1960), pp. 190-261. John Murray, *The Epistle to the Romans* (London: Marshall, Morgan and Scott, 1970 printing). (Two volumes in one—part 2 of new edition, pp. 1-103.) As is widely known, the central problem with respect to the theological content of Romans 9-11, etc., is how are we to relate the sovereign power of our Creator-Redeemer God and a range of human freedom even in view of the Fall. To the grassroots reader it seems an insurmountable problem to intelligently relate the determining power of God and the possibility of free responsible human decision. The real issue is not is Calvinism logically coherent as a theological system, but is it biblical? In the milieu of the Old and New Testament world deterministic world views were set forth. Some examples of such systems are: (1) Democratian physics, that is, classical Greek physics. (2) Several species of Gnosticism. (3) The Dead Sea Scrolls, especially the *Thanksgiving Hodayot* (see QH 10:3-4 and 15:13-18). Rabbi Akiba states, "Everything is foreseen, but freedom is still left." In the traditions of Judaism, the Pharisees defended human liberty, but in a context in which the idea of predestination of everything, both good and bad, for individuals and nations alike was maintained. The Essenes maintained fatalism, and the Sadducees completely rejected fatalism. (4) *The Koran* teaches a strict predestination and man's possibility of free decision. In all classical forms of astrology we encounter complete determinism. This is also true in the 20th century forms. (5) We encounter the same deterministic perspective in much contemporary physical theory, psychological theory (Skinner), bio-chemical determinism, especially as a result of the work of Greek and Monad on the gene code; in social theory respecting environmental determinism. Skinner

calls us beyond freedom and dignity, but in this instance is somehow freed from the determining factors of the gene code and the environment, in order to direct us toward the brave new world. The present author will exegetically examine all the classical scriptures set forth as defense of the five points of Calvinism in his forthcoming *Theology of Promise* (Biblical Theology). Further on Election, see Barth, *Dogmatics*, II, 2, pp. 3-506, "The Election of God." Calvin, *Institutes*, III, XXI-XXIV, "Concerning the Eternal Predestination of God." E. Dinkler, *Predestination bei Paulus* (Neukirken, 1957), esp. pp. 98ff. J. I. Packer, *Evangelism and Sovereignty of God*, Inter-Varsity Press, 1961, paperback. Concerning *The Five Points of Calvinism*: Calvin's *Institutes*, *The Westminster Confession*, B. B. Warfield's essay on "Predestination"; the five points refer only to the fact that there were five Armenian points for the Synod of Dort to "Answer": (A) Total Depravity, (B) Unconditional Election (Augustine's *DeLibro Arbitrio*), (C) Particular Redemption (Limited Atonement—Extent or Effectiveness?), (D) Efficacious Call or Irresistible Grace, and (E) Eternal Security of Believers.

11. Three different Hebrew words describe Pharaoh's condition: (1) The first word is *kabed* which means "to be heavy, insensible or dull." ([1]See Ex. 7:14; 8:15, 32; 9:7, 34. Brown, Driver, and Briggs. *A Hebrew and English Lexicon of the Old Testament* [Oxford: 1952 edition, p. 457].) (2) The second word is *qasah* and carries the significance of "being hard, severe, or fierce." (In the Hif'il stem it means "making hard or difficult.") ([2]*ibid.*, p. 904. Appears in 7:3; 13:15.) (3) The third term is *hazaq* and means "to be or grow firm, strong." ([3]See 7:13, 14, 22; 8:15, 19, 32; 9:7, 34-35; 13:15 and Brown, Driver, and Briggs, p. 304.) The same term is also employed in Joshua 11:20 which relates that God " . . . hardened their (inhabitants of Canaan) hearts that they should come against Israel in battle, that he might destroy them completely. . . . "

11

The Contribution of John Wesley
to the Theology of Grace

ARTHUR SKEVINGTON WOOD

The stature of John Wesley as a theologian is being increasingly recognized today. For too long it has been assumed that the founder of Methodism was mainly a man of action and only minimally a man of constructive thought. Recent years, however, have witnessed a radical reappraisal of his theological role, which in its turn has required that the nature of his distinctive doctrinal emphasis should be taken into serious consideration.

This renascence of interest in Wesley's contribution to Christian thinking is reflected in the literature of the postwar period. In 1946 William R. Cannon examined *The Theology of John Wesley* with special reference to the doctrine of justification, and in 1960 Colin W. Williams assessed *John Wesley's Theology Today*. It was out of the conviction that Wesley's greatness could be measured not only in the fields of evangelism and church renewal, but also in theological development, that Robert W. Burtner and Robert E. Chiles compiled *A Compend of Wesley's Theology* in 1954. By 1964 a volume on Wesley, edited by Albert C. Outler, was included in the Library of Christian Thought. Numerous studies dealing with Wesley's treatment of particular doctrinal themes have appeared of late, while Martin Schmidt of Mayence has produced a theological biography on the assumption that Wesley's life can only be fully understood in relation to his apprehension of what Goethe meant by the significant, fundamental truth motivating the total personality.

Most recently of all, Bernard Semmel is prepared to claim that "certainly Methodist theology deserves the kind of attention which 17th century Calvinism has received." [1] Such an estimate must qualify the verdict of Alfred North Whitehead in 1933, when he described Methodism as "singularly devoid of new ideas" though "singularly rich in vivid feelings." [2] He appreciated the effect of the revival both on church and nation, but saw it as "the first decisive landmark indicating the widening chasm between the theological tradition and the modern intellectual world." [3] Despite the justifiable eulogies bestowed on it, the Methodist movement could "appeal to no great intellectual construction explanatory of its modes of understanding." [4] Research over the last forty years has compelled a revision of such generalized attitudes. As Semmel argues, if Wesley's theology was so regressive and repressive as some have assumed, is it conceivable that it could have produced such remarkable and indeed revolutionary effects? [5]

It must not be supposed that creative theology is necessarily marked by audacious originality. None of the major Protestant reformers were addicted to wild innovations, nor was John Wesley. He did not see himself as an inventor but as in interpreter. "This is theology's proper calling," according to John Line; "not to patent novel brands, so much as to give language and form to the unchanging gospel such as will make the witness to it presently effective. Wesley did this emphatically as few have done." [6] It is not without reason that the evangelical succession has traditionally been held to run from Paul to Wesley by way of Augustine and Luther.

Wesley's theology was practical and occasional rather than theoretical and systematic. It was hammered out on the anvil of evangelistic experience. Leisure and he had parted company —even the leisure that might have enabled him to shut himself up in his study over a lengthy period in order to produce a theological *Summa*. It is significant that the doctrinal standards of the Methodist church are enshrined, not in a confession or a set of articles, but in Wesley's exegetical *Notes on the New Testament* and in his major published sermons. Like James Denney later, Wesley had no use for a theology which could not be preached, and it is in this form that we discover it. Other sources of Wesley's teaching are found in his occasional treatises and in his controversial writings as he contended for the evangelical faith against those who rejected it, both outside the church and even within it. His position was further defined by contrast with those who pressed more extreme Calvinistic interpretations. It is with this latter feature that we are mostly concerned as we consider Wesley's contribution to the theology of grace.

It should be realized, however, that Wesley's doctrinal stance aligned him somewhat more closely with classical

Calvinism than is often supposed. Indeed, he could claim that the truth of the gospel (which was his primary concern in conducting theological investigations) lay "very near," indeed "within a hair's breadth" of, John Calvin's teaching.[7] At the Bristol Conference of 1745, Wesley proposed a pertinent question for discussion among his preachers: "Wherein may we come to the very edge of Calvinism?" The answer is reported thus: "(1) In ascribing all good to the free grace of God. (2) In denying all natural free will, and all power antecedent to grace. And (3) In excluding all merit from man; even for what he has or does by the grace of God." [8]

According to A. Mitchell Hunter, "the sovereignty of God dominates Calvin's thought and forms the citadel into which he retreats whenever hard pressed by antagonists." [9] Wesley was no less committed to a biblical insistence on this essential truth, though not in any defensive fashion. In his *Thoughts upon God's Sovereignty* (1777) he asserted that as creator God may, "in the most absolute sense, do what he will with his own." [10] On the other hand, when God acts as a governor, or rewarder, he no longer does so only by his creative authority. That is to say, his sovereignty is exercised in consonance with his justice—and a justice, moreover, that is tempered by mercy. "Whatever, therefore, it hath pleased God to do by his sovereign pleasure, as creator of heaven and earth; and whatever his mercy may do on particular occasions over and above what justice requires; the general rule stands firm as the pillars of heaven: 'The judge of all the earth will do right. He will judge the world in righteousness,' and every man therein, according to the strictest justice." [11]

The consequence of God's sovereign justice and mercy is that "he will punish no man for doing anything he could not possibly avoid; neither for omitting anything which he could not possibly do. Every punishment supposes the offender might have avoided the offence for which he is punished. Otherwise, to punish him would be palpably unjust, and inconsistent with the character of God our governor." [12] Hence, Wesley concluded, "we give God the full glory of his sovereign grace, without impeaching his inviolable justice." [13]

In Wesley's view, God's sovereignty is not isolated from the rest of his attributes. Our concept of God must be derived from Scripture and not from philosophical presuppositions. Wesley believed that only a defective and one-sided picture of God will so emphasize his sovereignty as to neglect other aspects of his nature. He challenged the premise of those who argued that if God might justly have excluded all men from salvation, then he may justly exclude some merely by a royal command. "Where is it written? I cannot find it in the Word of God. Therefore I reject it as a bold, precarious assertion, utterly unsupported by Holy Scripture." [14] He proceeded to show that those who make this supposition assume that God's power is somehow detachable from his justice and mercy. If we are to abide by the total revelation of Scripture, we "will never speak of the sovereignty of God, but in conjunction with his other attributes. For the Scripture nowhere speaks of this single attribute, as separate from the rest. Much less does it anywhere speak of the sovereignty of God as singly disposing the eternal states of men. No, no; in this awful work, God proceeds according to the known rules of his justice and mercy; but never assigns his sovereignty as the cause why any man is punished with everlasting destruction." [15]

If Wesley recognized the sovereignty of God, he equally conceded the incapacity of man. Any who may imagine that Wesley's theology was no more than a refined Pelagianism will find that the evidence provided by his own writings fails to support them. "In what sense is Adam's sin imputed to all mankind?" was a question discussed at the first Methodist Conference in 1744. Here is the answer to which Wesley lent the weight of his approval. "In Adam all die; that is, (1) Our bodies then became mortal. (2) Our souls died: that is, we were disunited from God. And hence, (3) we are all born with a sinful, devilish nature. By reason whereof, (4) we are children of wrath, liable to death eternal (Rom. 5:18; Eph. 2:3)." [16]

Man's natural condition is represented in Scripture as a deep sleep. Wesley amplified the metaphor. "His spiritual senses are not awake; they discern neither spiritual good nor evil. The eyes of his understanding are closed; they are sealed together, and see not. . . . Hence, having no inlets for the knowledge of spiritual things, all the avenues of his soul being shut up, he is in gross, stupid ignorance of whatever he is most concerned to know. He is utterly ignorant of God, knowing nothing concerning him as he ought to know. He is totally a stranger to the law of God, as to its true, inward, spiritual meaning. He has no conception of that evangelical holiness, without which no man shall see the Lord; nor of the happiness which they only find whose 'life is hid with Christ in God.' " [17]

Even when quickened and enlightened by the convicting Spirit, the natural man, now repentant and seeking release, is utterly incapable of freeing himself from the shackles of sin and obeying the commandments of God. He desires to break loose from sin and indeed begins to struggle with it. "But though he strive with all his might, he cannot conquer: sin is mightier than he. He would fain escape; but he is so fast in prison, that he cannot get forth. He resolves against sin, yet sins on; he sees the snare, and abhors and runs into it. So much does his boasted reason avail—only to enhance his guilt, and increase his misery! Such is the freedom of his will; free only to evil; free to 'drink iniquity like water'; to wander farther and farther from the living God, and do more 'despite to the Spirit of grace' " [18]

Wesley believed that in the natural man the image of God is completely forfeited. By this expression, he understood man's moral capacity. It "consisted eminently in righteousness and true holiness." [19] Man retains the natural and political image of God, though in an impaired form. He still possesses the qualities of personality and has responsibility for exercising a degree of dominion over the rest of creation. "In this respect Wesley finds a certain continuity between man's life before and after the fall," Lindström explains. "Yet it is a circumstance which in no way alters his idea of natural man. From the point of view of salvation natural man has no resources of his own whatsoever. He is sinful through and through, has no knowledge of God and no power to turn to him of his own free will." [20]

When Dr. John Erskine implied that Wesley's understanding of natural free will was at variance with his firmly Calvinistic interpretation, Wesley insisted that they were precisely of one mind on this matter. "I believe that Adam, before his fall, had such freedom of will, that he might choose either good or evil; but that, since the fall, no child of man has a natural power to choose anything that is truly good. Yet I know (and who does not?) that man has still freedom of will in things of an indifferent nature. Does not Dr. E. agree with me in this? O why should we seek occasions of contention!" [21]

It is not without significance that Wesley's longest theological treatise, running to more than two hundred and fifty pages in Jackson's edition of his *Works*, dealt with *The Doctrine of Original Sin* (1757), in reply to a unitarian treatment of the same subject by Dr. John Taylor of Norwich. The substance of his argument from Scripture, reason, and experience (a typical combination in Wesley's writings) was that "man in his natural state, is altogether corrupt, through all the faculties of his soul: corrupt in his understanding, his will, his affections, his conscience, and his memory." [22] Wesley saw here a fundamental distinction between heathenism and Christianity. The former may indeed allow that men have many vices. "But here is the *shibboleth*. Is man by nature filled with all manner of evil? Is he void of all good? Is he wholly fallen? Is his soul totally corrupted? . . . Is 'every imagination of the thoughts of his heart only evil continually'? Allow this, and you are so far a Christian. Deny it, and you are but an heathen still." [23] As Williams has reminded us, Wesley was making the same point as Kierkegaard later crystallized in his famous statement that there is great "edification implied in the thought that against God we are always in the wrong." [24] Recognition of man's unmitigated bankruptcy and incapacity in his alienation from God constitutes the essential prelude to Wesley's doctrine of grace. He anticipated Rudolf Bultmann's analysis of Pauline anthropology in terms of man prior to the revelation of faith, and man under faith, with the former envisaged from the standpoint of the latter.[25] "If we were not ruined by the first Adam, neither are we recovered by the second. If the sin of Adam was not imputed to us, neither is the righteousness of Christ" [26]

It has been claimed that Wesley's conception of grace is basic to his idea of free will.[27] It might also be argued that his conception of free will underlies his idea of grace. Certainly the two themes are closely interrelated and, as in Scripture, the one must be permitted to control our understanding of the other. If man still retains any inherent ability to meet the righteous demands of God, then grace is no longer either full or free. What, in fact, is the extent of this fullness and freedom? That was the theme of Wesley's crucial sermon on "Free Grace," which Semmel rates as "a superb proclamation of the doctrine of universal redemption," and Luke Tyerman considered to be in some respects "the most important sermon that he ever issued." [28]

After announcing his text from Rom. 8:32, Wesley embarked on a brief but moving introduction. "How freely does God love the world! While we were yet sinners 'Christ died for the ungodly.' While we were 'dead in sin,' God 'spared not his own Son, but delivered him up for us all.' And how freely with him does he 'give us all things'! Verily, FREE GRACE is all in all!" [29] Having thus indicated the unlimited scope of divine grace, Wesley proceeded to present his basic affirmation. "The grace or love of God, whence cometh our salvation, is FREE IN ALL, and FREE FOR ALL." [30] What did Wesley mean by these twin insistences?

The first rules out any suggestion of salvation by works. God's grace is free in all to whom it is given. "It does not depend on any power or merit in man; no, not in any degree, neither in whole, nor in part. It does not in anywise depend either on the good works or righteousness of the receiver; not on anything he has done, or anything he is. It does not depend on his endeavors. It does not depend on his good tempers, or good desires, or good purposes and intentions, for all these flow from the free grace of God; they are the streams only, not the fountain. They are the fruits of free grace, and not the root. They are not the cause, but the effects of it. Whatsoever good is in man, or is done by man, God is the author and doer of it. Thus is his grace free in all; that is, no way dependent on any power or merit in man, but on God alone, who freely gave his own Son, and 'with him freely giveth us all things.' " [31]

In this Wesley was simply summarizing the definitive insights of the Protestant reformers. "By grace alone" was their watchword as it was his. When, as Sugden put it, he "blew the first trumpet call of the Evangelical Revival" in his sermon before the University of Oxford from the pulpit of St. Mary's on June 11, 1738, Eph. 2:8 was his text. "By grace are ye saved through faith." [32] "All the blessings which God hath bestowed upon man are of his mere grace, bounty, or favour; his free, undeserved favour; favour altogether undeserved; man having no claim to the least of his mercies"—so the discourse began. "For there is nothing we are, or have, or do, which can deserve the least thing at God's hand. 'All our works, thou, O God, hast wrought in us.' These, therefore, are so many more instances of free mercy; and whatever righteousness may be found in man, this is also the gift of God." [33]

There is, however, another and more profound meaning to Wesley's expression "free in all," as Cannon brings out.[34] It is expounded elsewhere in Wesley's sermons and writings. Although man is born a sinner and corrupt in every part of his being, he is at the same time a recipient of prevenient grace, or the grace that goes before. "There is no man, unless he has quenched the Spirit, that is wholly void of the grace of God. No man living is entirely destitute of what is vulgarly called *natural conscience.* But this is not natural. It is more properly called *preventing grace.* Every man has a greater or lesser measure of this, which waiteth not for the call of man." [35] As Umphrey Lee maintained, in Wesley's thinking the "natural man is a logical abstraction." [36] Alongside the fact that man is "dead in trespasses and sins" (Eph. 2:1) must be set the prevenient grace of God at work in all. The corollary of this doctrine is underlined by Wesley: "No man sins because he has not grace, but because he does not use the grace which he hath." [37]

Whatever theological problems may arise from Wesley's approach, Williams is nevertheless justified in maintaining that he broke the chain of logical necessity by which the Calvinist doctrine of predestination appears to flow from the doctrine of original sin.[38] The way was prepared for Wesley's further and more radical assertion that grace is not only free in all but also free for all. God's salvation may be extended to all because his grace is already incipiently at work in all.

Wesley's insistence that divine grace is free for all, or to all, as well as in all is ultimately grounded on God's redemption of mankind in Christ's death on the cross. "Nothing in the Christian system is of greater consequence than the doctrine of the atonement," he told Mary Bishop. "It is properly the distinguishing point between Deism and Christianity." [39] For him, the universality of grace was bound up with the universality of salvation. If Christ did indeed die for all, then all *may* be saved. Wesley recognized that not all *would* be saved, for it is possible to resist the proffered grace of God. But he fixed his foot against the suggestion that any are excluded from the benefits of the cross because of some prior consideration in the divine purpose.

In *Predestination Calmly Considered* (1752), Wesley vigorously countered what he regarded as the specious and unscriptural arguments of those who limited the scope of the atonement to the predetermined elect, and denied that the love of God in Christ was extended to the reprobate. "If this were true, we must give up all the Scriptures together; nor would the infidels allow the Bible so honourable a title as that of a 'cunningly devised fable.' But it is not true. It has no colour of truth. It is absolutely, notoriously false. To tear up the very roots of reprobation, and of all doctrines that have a necessary connexion therewith, God declares in his word these three things, and that explicitly in so many terms: (1) 'Christ died for all' (2 Cor. 5:14), namely, all that were dead in sin, as the words immediately following fix the sense. Here is the fact affirmed. (2) 'He is the propitiation for the sins of the whole world' (1 John 2:2), even of all those for whom he died. Here is the consequence of his dying for all. And, (3) 'He died for all, that they should not live unto themselves, but unto him which died for them' (2 Cor. 5:15), that they might be saved from their sins. Here is the design, the end of his dying for them." [40] Wesley challenged those who defended a restricted atonement to produce scriptures which repeal or even modify such unambiguous declarations as those he had quoted.

At this point Wesley appealed to the judicious reasoning of Isaac Watts. "It is very hard indeed, to vindicate the sincerity of the blessed God or his Son, in their universal offers of grace and salvation to men and their sending ministers with such messages and invitations to accept of mercy, if there be not at least a conditional pardon and salvation provided for them. His ministers, indeed, as they know not the event of things, may be sincere in offering salvation to all persons, according to their general commission, 'Go ye into all the world, and preach the gospel to every creature.' But how can God or Christ be sincere in sending them with this commission, to offer his grace to all men, if God has not provided such grace for all men, no, not so much as conditionally?" [41]

For Wesley, as for Watts, unless grace is free for all as well as free in all there is no effective gospel to proclaim. If some are already consigned to condemnation by an arbitrary decree, how can it be said that God loves them or that his grace reaches them? Wesley concluded that, on such a monstrous theory, all that meets such unfortunates is not saving grace, since that is reserved for the elect, but what can only be described as damning grace.[42] It is not merely such in the event, but even more damagingly in the intention. "Thou receivedst it of God for that very end, that thou mightest receive the greater damnation. It was given, not to convert thee, but only to convince; not to make thee without sin, but without excuse; not to destroy but to arm the worm that never dieth, and to blow up the fire that never shall be quenched." [43] After thus apostrophizing the hypothetical victim of such speculative theological determinism, Wesley asked: "Is not this such love as makes your blood run cold?" [44]

Wesley declined the immediate responsibility of labelling salvation as either conditional or unconditional. "I declare just what I find in the Bible, neither more nor less; namely, that it is bought for every child of man, and actually given to every one that believeth. If you call this conditional salvation, God made it so from the beginning of the world; and he hath declared it so to be, at sundry times and in divers manners; of old by Moses and the prophets, and in later times by Christ and his apostles. 'Then I never can be saved; for I can perform no conditions; for I can do nothing.' No, nor can I, nor any man under heaven—without the grace of God. 'But I can do all things through Christ strengthening me.' So can you; so can every believer. And he has strengthened, and will strengthen you more and more, if you do not wilfully resist till you quench his Spirit." [45]

Wesley was careful to distinguish between almighty grace and irresistible grace in the matter of salvation.[46] By almighty grace he meant the power through which all things are possible. But he was not prepared to concede that this power can never be resisted by the obdurate will of man. There may be occasional instances where God appears to work irresistibly for the time being. "Yet I do not believe there is any human soul in which God works irresistibly *at all times*,"

Wesley added. "Nay, I am fully persuaded there is not. I am persuaded that there are no men living that have not many times 'resisted the Holy Ghost,' and made void 'the counsel of God against themselves.' Yea, I am persuaded, every child of God has, at some time, 'life and death set before him,' eternal life and eternal death; and has in himself the casting voice." [47] Wesley then quoted the dictum of Augustine: "He who made us without ourselves, will not save us without ourselves." [48] The issue was put in a nutshell as Wesley enquired why it should be thought more for the glory of God that man should be saved irresistibly, rather than as a free agent by such grace as he might either concur with or reject.[49]

Wesley's concept of grace forbade him to regard it as irresistible or to restrict its application to the elect. He parted company from the more thorough-going Calvinists of his time in refusing to attribute reprobation to the primary will of God. Many moderate Calvinists among the 18th century evangelicals were in agreement with him. Wesley preferred to adhere to a positive account of election as he found it in the Scriptures. Hence he could speak categorically about "the unchangeable, irreversible, irresistible decree of God" as contained in Mark 16:16, "He that believeth shall be saved; but he that believeth not shall be damned." [50] In other words, "God decrees, from everlasting to everlasting, that all who believe in the Son of his love, shall be conformed to his image; shall be saved from all inward and outward sin, into all inward and outward holiness." [51] Such a statement of the case was calculated to avoid the extremes both of hyper-Calvinism and of antinomianism.

Wesley discovered that, in Scripture, election may mean one of two things. "First, a divine appointment of some particular men, to do some particular work in the world. And this election I believe to be not only personal, but absolute and unconditional." [52] Cyrus was chosen to facilitate the rebuilding of the temple and Saul of Tarsus to preach the gospel, along with the twelve. But this has no necessary connection with final salvation. Judas was elected to apostleship, yet his lot is with the devil and his angels (cf. John 6:70).

Wesley held that election means, secondly, "a divine appointment of some men to eternal happiness. But I believe the eternal decree concerning both is expressed in the words 'He that believeth shall be saved; he that believeth not shall be damned.' And this decree, without doubt, God will not change, and man cannot resist. According to this, all true believers are in Scripture termed elect, as all who continue in unbelief are so long properly reprobate, that is, unapproved of God, and without discernment touching the things of the Spirit." [53]

The decree of grace is associated with the covenant of grace. Wesley was unable to trace in Scripture any covenant by which the Son agreed with the Father to suffer and die so that a certain limited number of souls might be saved as a recompense, while the rest were inevitably condemned. "The grand covenant which we allow to be mentioned therein, is a covenant between God and man, established in the hands of a mediator 'who tasted death for every man,' and thereby purchased it for all the children of men. The tenor of it is this: 'Whosoever believeth unto the end so as to show his faith by his works, I the Lord will reward that soul eternally. But whosoever will not believe, and consequently dieth in his sins, I will punish him with everlasting destruction." [54] God's covenant is thus eternal and yet conditional. His promised blessings are for those who believe and continue to do so. "God is the Father of them that believe so long as they believe. But the devil is the father of them that believe not, whether they did once believe or no." [55] Belief is no static condition: it is the active exercise of faith. So far as foreknowledge was concerned, Wesley attempted to cut the Gordian knot by the recognition that, since his being is beyond time, there is no before or after with God, but simply an eternal now.[56]

Wesley claimed that, with respect to the central Protestant doctrine of justification, he concurred entirely with the teaching of Calvin, and did not differ from him even by a hair's breadth.[57] "I believe justification by faith alone, as much as I believe there is a God," he declared.[58] It was, in fact, by employing this basic doctrine as a yardstick that, like Arminius before him, Wesley felt compelled to question the more exaggerated forms of Calvinistic ideology. He did so in the name of the reformation itself, by appealing to Scripture. To his logical mind, the issue was crystal clear. Is salvation by an absolute decree or is it essentially by grace through faith? Or, to carry the argument a stage further, is Christ an effective or merely an instrumental Savior?

Wesley interpreted the doctrine of predestination in terms of the controlling biblical principle of justification. He realized that to do otherwise is to circumscribe the freedom of grace and thus to jeopardize the universality of Christ's saving act on the cross. He was genuinely puzzled by the fact that, when he repudiated the notion of salvation by prescriptive election or decree, he was accused by his more rigidly Calvinistic friends of condoning salvation by works. His perplexity persisted until, as he explained, "a thought shot across my mind, which solved the matter at once. 'This is the key: those who hold, Everyone is absolutely predestinated either to salvation or damnation, see no medium between salvation by works and salvation by absolute decrees.' It follows, that whosoever denies salvation by absolute decrees, in so doing (according to their apprehension) asserts salvation by works." [59] The assumption that the rejection of unconditional predestination is considered to imply a retrogression to conditional work-righteousness, indicates that, in fact, both these attitudes are contrary to the scriptural insistence that, in the undeserved favor of God, salvation is offered in Christ to all who believe.[60] For Wesley, the gospel itself was at stake. Unless he could assure all who flocked to hear him that the Savior had died explicitly for them, and that they too might enter into life by repenting and trusting in the merits of Christ's death, then he felt he had no general good news to announce.

NOTES

1. Bernard Semmel, *The Methodist Revolution* (New York: Basic Books, 1974), p. 5.

2. Alfred North Whitehead, *Adventures of Ideas* (Cambridge University Press, 1933), p. 27.

3. *Ibid.*

4. *Ibid.*

5. Semmel, *op. cit.*, p. 5.

6. John Line, "The Theological Mission of Methodism," in *London Quarterly and Holborn Review*, January 1947, p. 42.

7. *The Works of the Rev. John Wesley*, 3rd edition, ed. Thomas Jackson, 14 Vols. (1829-1831), Vol. VIII, p. 284 ("Minutes of Some Late Conversations").

8. *Ibid.*, p. 285.

9. A. Mitchell Hunter, *The Teaching of Calvin* (London: J. Clarke, 1950 [2]), p. 51.

10. Wesley, *Works*, Vol. X, p. 361.

11. *Ibid.*, p. 363.

12. *Ibid.*

13. *Ibid.*

14. *Ibid.*, p. 217 ("Predestination Calmly Considered").

15. *Ibid.*, p. 220.

16. *Ibid.*, Vol. VIII, p. 277 ("Minutes of Some Late Conversations").

17. *Wesley's Standard Sermons*, ed. Edward H. Sugden, 2 Vols. (London: Epworth Press, 1955-56), Vol. I, pp. 181-182 (Sermon IX, "The Spirit of Bondage and of Adoption").

18. *Ibid.*, pp. 188-189.

19. Wesley, *Works*, Vol. IX, p. 381 ("The Doctrine of Original Sin").

20. Harald Lindström, *Wesley and Sanctification* (London: Epworth Press, ET 1946), p. 45.

21. Wesley, *Works*, Vol. X, p. 350 ("Some Remarks on 'A Defence of the Preface to the Edinburgh Edition of *Aspasio Vindicated*' ").

22. *Ibid.*, Vol. IX, p. 443; cf. Wesley, *Sermons*, Vol. I, pp. 155-156: "Know that corruption of thy inmost nature . . . that thou art corrupted in every power, in every faculty of the soul; that thou art totally corrupted in every one of these; all the foundations being out of course" (Sermon VI, "The Way to the Kingdom").

23. Wesley, *Sermons*, Vol. II, p. 223 (Sermon XXXVIII, "Original Sin").

24. Colin W. Williams, *John Wesley's Theology Today* (London: Epworth Press, 1960), p. 47; cf. Søren Kierkegaard, *Either-Or* (London: Oxford University Press, 1944), Vol. II, p. 287.

25. Rudolf Bultmann, *Theology of the New Testament* (New York: Scribner, 1951-55), Vol. I, p. 191.

26. Wesley, *Works*, Vol. IX, p. 428 ("The Doctrine of Original Sin").

27. *A Compend of Wesley's Theology*, ed. Robert W. Burtner and Robert E. Chiles (New York: Abingdon Press, 1954), p. 109.

28. Semmel, *op. cit.*, p. 91; Luke Tyerman, *The Life and Times of the Rev. John Wesley*, 3 Vols. (Hodder & Stoughton, 1870-71), Vol. I, p. 317.

29. Wesley, *Works*, Vol. VII, p. 373 (Sermon CXXVIII, "Free Grace"). It was the publication of this discourse which drew a considered reply from George Whitefield and sparked off the Calvinistic controversy of 1741. Wesley addressed this explanation to his readers: "Nothing but the strongest conviction, not only what is here advanced is 'the truth as it is in Jesus,' but also that I am indispensably obliged to declare this truth to all the world, could have induced me openly to oppose the sentiments of those whom I esteem for their work's sake: at whose feet may I be found in the day of the Lord Jesus!" (Cf. Irwin W. Reist, "John Wesley and George Whitefield: A Study in the Integrity of Two Theologies of Grace," in *The Evangelical Quarterly*, Vol. XLVII, No. 1 [January-March 1975], pp. 26-40.)

30. Wesley, *Works*, Vol. VII, p. 373.

31. *Ibid.*, pp. 373-374.

32. Wesley, *Sermons*, Vol. I, p. 36 (Editor's introduction to Sermon I, "Salvation by Faith").

33. *Ibid.*, p. 37.

34. William R. Cannon, *The Theology of John Wesley* (New York: Abingdon Press, 1956), p. 100.

35. Wesley, *Works*, Vol. VI, p. 512 (Sermon LXXXV, "On Working out our own Salvation").

36. Umphrey Lee, *John Wesley and Modern Religion* (Nashville, Cokesbury, 1936), p. 124.

37. Wesley, *Works,* Vol. VI, p. 512.

38. Williams, *op. cit.*, p. 44.

39. *The Letters of the Rev. John Wesley*, Standard Edition, ed. John Telford, 8 Vols. (London: Epworth, 1931), Vol. VI, pp. 297-298 (To Mary Bishop, 7th. February, 1778).

40. Wesley, *Works*, Vol. X. p. 225. cf. Reist, *op. cit.*, p. 34: "The difference between Wesley and Whitefield is not about the source of salvation, which is grace, but its mode of operation. For Wesley grace is operative positively on all men; for Whitefield it is applied redemptively only to the eternally elect in Christ." Of course, for Wesley, saving grace is effectual only in those who believe.

41. Wesley, *Works*, p. 226.

42. *Ibid.*, p. 229.

43. *Ibid.*

44. *Ibid.*

45. *Ibid.*, p. 254.

46. *Ibid.*

47. Wesley, *Works*, Vol. VI, p. 281 (Sermon LXIII, "The General Spread of the Gospel").

48. *Ibid.* Augustine, *Sermones de Scripturio Novi Testamenti*, CLXIX.xi.13.

49. Wesley, *Works*, Vol. X, p. 231 ("Predestination Calmly Considered").

50. *Ibid.*, Vol. VI, p. 227 (Sermon LVIII, "On Predestination").

51. *Ibid.*

52. *Ibid.*, Vol. X, p. 210 ("Predestination Calmly Considered").

53. *Ibid.*

54. *Ibid.*, p. 239.

55. *Ibid.*, pp. 297-298 ("Serious Thoughts upon the Perseverance of the Saints").

56. *Ibid.*, Vol. VI, p. 226 (Sermon LVIII, "On Predestination").

57. Wesley, *Letters*, Vol. IV, p. 298 (To John Newton, 14th May, 1765).

58. Wesley, *Works*, Vol. X, p. 349 ("Some Remarks on 'A Defence of the Preface to the Edinburgh Edition of *Aspasio Vindicated*' ").

59. Wesley, *Works*, Vol. XI, p. 487 ("Thoughts on Salvation by Faith"); cf. Mildred B. Wynkoop, *Foundations of Wesleyan-Arminian Theology* (1967), p. 102. See *Theology of Love; Dynamic of Wesleyanism* (Kansas City: Beacon Hill Press, 1972).

60. Wesley came to the conclusion that an "unconditional decree excludes faith as well as works; since, if it is either by faith or works foreseen, it is not by unconditional decree. Therefore salvation by absolute decree excludes both one and the other; and, consequently, upon this supposition, salvation is neither by faith nor by works" (*Works*, Vol. XI, p. 488).

12

Jacob Arminius' Contribution
to a Theology of Grace

DONALD M. LAKE

This volume of essays would certainly be incomplete without a chapter on Jacobus Arminius, sometimes referred to as James Arminius. Few leaders in the Christian Church have been more neglected than this 16th century theologian and pastor. Although Caspar Brandt's Latin biography, written in 1724-1725, was finally translated into English in mid-19th century and although two other works on Arminius appeared before 1926,[1] it was not until 1971 that Carl Bangs offered English readers a thorough study of Arminius' life and an introduction to his theology. Ironically Arminius' works appeared first as a collected three volume set in English. To date no complete edition of Arminius' works in Dutch, German or French exists![2] No doubt the relatively unfamiliar Dutch language and the fact that Arminius' works originally were written in Latin have helped to obscure their significance, just as the Danish originals of Søren Kierkegaard's works kept him in obscurity for more than fifty years after his death.

In the light of two recent studies on Arminius and his contribution to theology and after a reexamination of his major writings, I want to suggest that his importance for Christians living in the last half of the 20th century lies in three major areas. First, he was a theologian who lived out his faith in the day-to-day struggles of the church. Second, his faith and theology led him to participate in, rather than withdraw from, the socio-political issues of his own day. And finally, his personal life, marked as it was with personal tragedy, misunderstanding and controversy, provides a model for every Christian, and especially for the theologian and professor of theology.

In the pages that follow, no attempt is made to give an

abbreviated biography of Arminius' life. The reader whose curiosity and appetite for such a biography is hereby whetted will best be served if he reads Carl Bangs' *Arminius: A Study in the Dutch Reformation*. What this essay attempts to show, however, is that an examination of Arminius' theology can be extremely beneficial to those who seek for some direction in living the Christian faith in the 20th century. Like us, Arminius lived in one of the most turbulent eras of history! The old order was collapsing and a new one was being shaped. The issues were complex, the stakes high, and the intensity of the struggle is illustrated by the slaughter, confusion and conflict of The Thirty Years War fought between 1618 and 1648. Jacobus Arminius was born about 1559 and died in 1609, but the issues he raised far outlived him. And the controversy surrounding his teachings helped to bring about the Synod of Dort, 1618-1619. The fact that The Thirty Years War begins as the Synod of Dort concludes is less than coincidental. Ideologically some historians see Arminianism as the beginning of the modern era characterized by a more liberal attitude in theology; whereas, these same historians see The Thirty Years War as the end of the Reformation Era and the beginning of the modern age. Humanism and secularism certainly are the major characteristics of our age; however, I would challenge the conclusion that Arminius and his views are directly responsible. On the other hand, the doctrinal rigidity of *Protestant Scholasticism* had indeed spent its force by the beginning of the 17th century, and it was soon to be challenged on every side.

Personally, Arminius illustrates one of the contrasting elements of theology as it moves toward the end of the 20th century. One theological trend currently in vogue is the theology of hope, but the current crises threatening the peace of mankind leads one to question the somewhat optimistic assumptions of this theological fad. And this is particularly true when such a theology of hope is tied to a 19th century Marxist utopianism and a theology of liberation and revolution. If history has a permanent lesson beyond man's ability under the grace of God to survive, it is that history itself offers us little hope! A reexamination of the life and theology of Jacobus Arminius will not lead us, I am convinced, to a more optimistic perspective about our own age. If any biblical text appropriately fits the life and work of Arminius, it is Phil. 1:29-30.

> For it has been granted to you that for the sake of Christ
> you should not only believe in him but also suffer for his sake,
> engaged in the same conflict which you saw and now hear . . .

And we should remember that Rom. 15:4 applies to all of

church history and not simply biblical history.

> For whatever was written in former days was written for our instruction . . .

I. Arminius: Pastor of Christ's Church

Tradition has it that Arminius was born on October 10, 1560, but more recent historical research has proven this tradition wrong. Since his father died sometime between 1553 and 1559, it is unlikely that he was born any later than this latter date. His real name had been Jacob Harmenszoon, meaning "Jacob the son of Harmen," but "according to the custom of scholars of the time, he latinized his name to Jacobus Arminius." The name Arminius came from a first-century Germanic chieftain remembered for having resisted the Romans.[4] After the death of his father, a local priest of somewhat Protestant sympathies acted *in loco parentis* for young Arminius. One authority relates that this priest, Theodore Aemilius, "charged himself with his education; and as soon as his tender age was thought capable of receiving the elements of learning, he had him carefully instructed in the rudiments of the Latin and Greek languages, and his mind imbued with principles of religion and virtue."[5] Since Aemilius resided in Utrecht, Arminius himself probably did not reside long in his birthplace, Oudewater. It is possible that in Utrecht, he attended the famous *Hieronymusschool*, known as the famous St. Jerome School. Bangs in his biography relates the excellence of this school and its academic program.[6] Arminius was to spend the first fourteen or fifteen years of his life under the influence of this godly priest.

After the death of Aemilius, Arminius received a new benefactor, Rudolphus Snellius, a linguist and mathematician from the University of Marburg, Germany. But his stay in Marburg was to be a year or less. In 1575, the Spanish invaded the town of Oudewater, destroying most of the city and its inhabitants. Upon hearing of the massacre, Arminius journeys the 250 miles between Marburg and Oudewater on foot only to discover that all that remained of his family had been slain! He probably returned to Marburg, but only briefly, for as soon as the new university of Leiden opened, he enrolled there. Here he studied and mastered mathematics, logic, theology and Hebrew. Here too he came into contact with a mixed Calvinistic theology, hearing both the staunch Calvinism of Professor Danaeus as well as the milder form presented by pastor-professor Coolhaeus. It was also during these early years of the new university that she became embroiled in controversy over Peter Ramus' attack upon Aristotelian logic.

Arminius was to become an exponent of Ramism.[7]

When Arminius finally finished his studies at Leiden, he was granted a continuing scholarship which enabled him to pursue his theological studies further: first at Geneva, then in Basel where he was offered the Doctor of Theology degree because of his brilliance—an honor he rejected because he felt he was too young, then to Geneva again, and finally spending a few months in Italy studying at the University of Padua under the renowned professor of philosophy Zabarella. The trip to Italy not only gave him a firsthand exposure to the Roman Catholicism of his day, but also raised questions back in Amsterdam about his theological soundness! Even during his student days, Arminius had created controversy in Geneva when he challenged the established Aristotelianism by his own endorsement of Ramism. As his formal studies came to an end, his benefactors in Amsterdam were ready for him to return home and assume the role of city pastor. Consequently in 1587, he returned to Amsterdam where in a few short weeks he was officially received as one of the ministers of the Reformed Church of that city.

> Arminius was the first Dutch pastor of the Dutch Reformed Church of the greatest Dutch city, just when it was emerging out of its medieval past and bursting into its Golden Age. His relationship to Amsterdam began only three years after its Reformation.[8]

So began a career as one of Amsterdam's leading clergymen, a career to last fifteen years. It was here too that he married into one of the leading families of the city. He began his pulpit ministry officially on Sunday evening, February 7, 1588, as a *proponent*—a preacher on trial. According to one of his contemporaries, he was one of the most popular preachers of the day, and he consistently drew large crowds whenever it was known that he would be the preacher of the day.[9]

During these years as pastor, Arminius' pulpit ministry centered on the book of Romans. Although other biblical books from both Testaments occasionally attracted his attention and he sometimes deviated from this basic epistle to devote his attention to some pertinent theme, it was however from these expository sermons on Romans that he began to develop a modified Calvinistic view on such matters as predestination and the nature of the human condition. And it was as a result of his preaching on Romans 7 and 9 that his real troubles began in Amsterdam, troubles that would follow him to his deathbed. But preaching was only one of his many activities during those fifteen years in Amsterdam. We have records of his visitations with the sick and the erring as well as his performances at holy matrimony. On one occasion during the bubonic plague of 1601 when an estimated 20,000 persons in Amsterdam died, he endangered his own life by entering an afflicted household in order to give a drink of water to each of its inhabitants! [10]

Arminius seems always to have been at the center of controversy, but the reasons are not always clear. His writings reveal so little of his personality and he speaks so seldom about himself that one is tempted to think that the reasons lie somewhere other than his personality. On the basis of the cogency of his arguments, we may rightly assume, I think, that his concern for truth led him to question all. Nothing was so sacred that one should not reexamine the basis upon which it was founded. While others were content perhaps to buy the commonly accepted interpretations of the day, Arminius always begins at the beginning. His analysis of Romans 7 and 9, for example, are not only exegetical and logical but also historical. He calls every major theologian and church father to testify in his behalf! I am convinced that it was this aspect of Arminius' methodology that irritated his co-laborers. His first real problems began in 1591 over his interpretation of Romans 7; however, he was able to gain the support of the city fathers, and so triumphed over his opponents. It should also be pointed out that a staunch Calvinism had not as yet been able to establish itself in Amsterdam. Some have accused Arminius of having been influenced by Luther, but there is little in his writings to reveal this. He was commissioned to reply critically to the Anabaptists who were finding sanctuary in Holland, but this was an assignment which he never finished. Probably because he may have found some of their views more scriptural than their opponents. One thing is clear from these events: he never stooped to cheap vulgarities as Luther was often proned to do; his arguments were never vindictive, nor did he take advantage of his opponent's weaker argument by degrading him! [11]

When the plague of 1601 and 1602 took the life of theological professor Lucas Trelcatlus, Arminius was immediately recommended by several as the likely successor; however, Arminius was reluctant to accept the position. He modestly claimed that others were more worthy and more qualified, but his real hesitation was caused by his devotion to the pastorate.

> He has a number of objections. One is the close mutuality which exists between himself and the church in Amsterdam. "You know likewise," (he writes to his friend Uitenbogaert) "the amazing difference between the intense affection which sheep evince towards their shepherd who is always with them

and that temporary affection which even the most virtuous of students manifests towards a man who is their instructor only for a few years." There is also the "personal sanctification" which cannot but come to a man who sincerely carries out the holy offices of the pastoral ministry. Already in Amsterdam he has been hindered in exercises contributing to private holiness by the investigation of difficult theological topics. "What will become of me," he asks, "when I shall have dedicated myself to that employment which prefers far larger demands for the contemplation and discussion of difficult topics?" [12]

Arminius' love for his people and their mutual esteem and affection for their pastor reflects a relationship too seldom found in the church. This is particularly true when one remembers that he had been there fifteen years!

II. Arminius: Christian Citizen

One does not have to agree with the particular views espoused by Jacobus Arminius to appreciate his personal participation in the political and economic life of 16th and 17th century Holland. During this turbulent era most of the major European countries shifted political positions and many changed their religious alignment. At midpoint in the 16th century, Holland was still threatened by Spanish control. It was, in fact, the Spanish who invaded Oudewater and massacred several thousand persons, including Arminius' mother, his sister and brother. But the defeat of the Spanish and the transition to Protestant loyalties during the 1570's brought little real unity to Holland. Even the Thirty Years War found Holland torn between Protestant and Roman Catholic armies before she finally settled into the hands of Protestant forces.

One specific issue to which Arminius lent his support concerned the role and authority of the state. Generally speaking it was the issue of "states' rights" as over against a strong nationalism. In the debate, Arminius stood with the leader of the patrician, older and wealthier merchant classes, Johan van Oldenbarnevelt. Opposing Oldenbarnevelt was Maurice of Nassau. The states' rights party had come to support a somewhat mixed political-ecclesiastical theory. On the one hand, Arminius and Oldenbarnevelt favored toleration for those holding deviant theological views, but also supported state control over the church in ecclesiastical matters at least at the local and regional level. Maurice and the stricter Calvinistic school favored a national synod to decide church controversies, such as would be the case at the Synod of Dort. Arminius felt, however, that the magistrate could best protect the church from a clericalism that was too close and too similar to the hierarchicalism of Roman Catholicism.

Maurice and Oldenbarnevelt, each in his way, were realists. Maurice never abandoned his goal of military conquest, but he quietly consolidated his political power with the goal of establishing himself as a royal sovereign in the north. Oldenbarnevelt, suspecting that the south could never be captured, was willing to entertain the idea of a truce with Spain. The new commercial interests in the seaport towns, anxious to get on with world trade, watched the issue from a financial perspective: which course would be good for business? The clergy asked many questions, each to his own preference. What would be good for the nation? What would do the greatest harm to the Spanish agents of the papal Antichrist? While Maurice and Oldenbarnevelt quietly moved under the surface to undercut each other, all these issues began to coalesce. There would be a war party, militaristic, staunchly Clavinistic and anti-Catholic, predestinarian, centralist, politically even royalist, and ecclesiastically presbyterian. There would be a peace party, trade-minded, theologically tolerant, republican, and Erastian. The first would support the war and fight Arminianism; the second would support a truce and fight Calvinism.[13]

So toleration, regional ecclesiastical autonomy, and the rule of the magistrate in matters ecclesiastical became the primary features of the states' rights party with which Arminius was identified. And when later theological issues over strict Calvinism were raised, these same divisions separated the Remonstrants from the strict Calvinists. It was Arminius' identification with Oldenbarnevelt that helped to secure the position at the University of Leiden.

What needs to be observed here is that Arminius carried his theological views into the arena of politics. And while he advocated toleration for the Anabaptists, he had no sympathy for their views of political isolationism. It is, however, also important to note that Arminius' participation in the political struggles of the day was not a cheapening of his own theological convictions. The evidence is not as abundant as the historian would like, but there is sufficient grounds to argue that Arminius participated in these issues because of principle: *the principle that the Christian life and Christian theology ought not to be divorced from the mainstream of human life and its social, economic and political consequences.*

We cannot predict how Arminius would have viewed later religious and political problems, but in principle he certainly would not have advocated a *laissez faire* attitude toward political involvement. His consistent defense of religious toleration at the expense of coercion and religious persecution would make him one of the better examples of a religious liberalism that has consistently characterized later Arminianism. It should be pointed out here that terms such as *"conservative"* and *"liberal"* have meaning only when the point of reference is clearly understood. He was nevertheless a defender of religious freedom, and in terms of the rigidity of 16th and 17th century Calvinism, this was a dangerous liberalism!

III. Arminius: Biblical Theologian

The works of Arminius in the English three-volume edition now number more than 1700 pages. For one whose professional career as a professor of theology lasted only six years, this is a tremendous legacy. Interestingly enough, most of his writings come from his years as pastor. How much has not been preserved, only the Lord knows! I have felt it wise here to list Arminius' works with some brief notes as to contents and time of composition.

VOLUME ONE

1. *"The Priesthood of Christ."* 35 pages; this was Arminius address upon the reception of his Doctor of Divinity degree in July, 1603; a good example of his style of biblical and theological exposition.

2. *"Four Orations on the Nature of Theology."* 94 pages; in these four orations, he deals with the object, author, end and certainty of theology. The first three orations were part of Arminius' introductory lectures on theology given at the University of Leiden in 1603. The fourth oration deals with the problem of reconciling religious dissensions and was given in 1606 when issues of theological differences were splitting the church.

3. *"Declaration of Sentiments."* 71 pages; here is the heart of Arminius' controversial theology, presented before the States of Holland at The Hague in October of 1608, just one year before his death. This document deals with the topics of predestination, divine providence, the freedom of the will, the grace of God, the divinity of the Son of God, and the justification of man before God. If one were to read only one small section of Arminius' writings, here is the proper place to begin!

4. *"Apology Against Thirty-One Defamatory Articles."* 105 pages; Arminius' enemies had secretly circulated certain articles which accused him of being unorthodox and unbiblical with regard to the nature and origin of saving faith, the perseverance of the saints, the nature of the heathen and other related topics. In some cases, he admits that his critics have stated his position correctly, but the charges were often poorly worded or distortions of what he had actually said and taught; first published in 1609.

5. *"Nine Questions Exhibited for the Purpose of Obtaining*

an *Answer from Each of the Professors of Divinity, and the Replies which James Arminius gave to them: with other Nine Opposite Articles."* 7 pages; November, 1605.

6. *"Twenty-Five Public Disputations."* 280 pages! These theses were discussed between 1603 and 1609 in Arminius' classes on divinity at Leiden, but the nearest thing Arminius wrote to a systematic theology, and they deal with subjects as diverse as biblical authority as well as idolatry and civil government. This work along with the *"Declaration of Sentiments"* ranks among his more important works theologically.

VOLUME TWO

1. *"Seventy-Nine Private Disputations."* 184 pages; the subtitle of this work is revealing: "On the principal articles of the Christian religion, commenced by the author chiefly for the purpose of forming a system of divinity." Exact date is unknown, but probably written during his years at Leiden; first published in 1610.

2. *"Dissertation on the True and Genuine Sense of the Seventh Chapter of the Epistle to the Romans."* 258 pages! Extensive exegetical and historical analysis of this chapter; see discussion later in this article.

3. *"A Letter to Hippolytus a Collibus."* 25-page letter, written in April, 1608 to the Ambassador of the Elector of the Palatine to the United Dutch Provinces. The letter deals with five specific issues: the divinity of the son of God, the providence of God, divine predestination, grace and free will, and justification. Arminius' theological position had been attacked at the University of Heidelberg, and this letter is an attempt to defend his views.

4. *"Certain Articles to be Diligently Examined and Weighed."* 30 pages; no date; deals with controversial articles of Protestantism and particularly Calvinism.

5. *"A Letter on the Sin Against the Holy Ghost."* 26-page letter, addressed to John Uytenbogaert, one of Arminius' later defenders and lifelong friend. March, 1599.

VOLUME THREE

1. *"Epistolary Discussion Concerning Predestination Between James Arminius, D. D. and Francis Junius, D.D."* 256 pages, about 1596.

2. *"Appendix: Theses of Dr. Francis Junius."* 16 pages of theses set forth by Junius at the University of Leiden in 1593.

3. *"An Examination of a Treatise Concerning Order and Mode of Predestination and the Amplitude of Divine Grace by Rev. William Perkins."* 245 pages; written in 1602 as a reply to the views of Perkins, the noted Calvinistic theologian at Christ's College, Cambridge.

4. *"Analysis of the Ninth Chapter of the Epistle to the Romans."* 38 pages; written in 1593 and addressed to Gellius

Snecanus, a minister in West Friesland. Snecanus had expressed some agreement with the view of Arminius about this chapter; see my later discussion.

What is Arminius' uniqueness? What is his distinctive contribution to theology? What is or are his heresy or heresies? The modern reader will probably be impressed with two facts about the writings of Arminius: his theological works involve an intricate logical style and his views do not seem unusual or even problematical, let alone heretical. The logical and syllogistic style of his theological works strikes the modern reader as being somewhat dry! There is, however, a precision about his works that reveals a keen mind and sensitive perception about the issues of the day. Perhaps the controversy and antagonism surrounding Arminius are to be attributed partly to the soundness of Arminius' style of theological writing. As one reads only Arminius' side of the controversy and hears the logical nature of his position, one wonders how his opponents could stand against the powerful persuasion of his arguments. It is to be observed, however, that many theological debates are not won or lost on the basis of logical soundness or even biblical soundness!

There is neither time nor space here to review all of Arminius' theological writings. The silent gaps in his writings indicate how orthodox he was in most points of his theology. This also helps to explain why most of his extant writings are of such a controversial nature: he spent the major part of his life defending those positions found to be most unacceptable to his critics. There are major areas of theology where we know little or nothing about his views, e.g. eschatology. He was in most points a mild Calvinist. He did not like nor use the term Trinity, but his view on the nature of the Godhead was certainly orthodox in intention. His discussions about the sacraments and the church as well as the relationship of the church and state represent a traditional Calvinistic position, with the possible exception that he was more Erastian than Calvin.[14] He was certainly closer to Calvin than he was to Luther, Zwingli or the Anabaptists. And except for the fact that he refused to use a term *autotheos*, which was being used to describe the essential deity of the second person of the Godhead, his views on the diety of Christ were essentially orthodox. He did give greater place to the subordinate redemptive role played by the Son in the drama of redemption than some of his contemporaries like, but the objective 20th century reader will see little, if anything, unorthodox about his Christology. It is, however, in the areas of human responsibility, grace, predestination, the extent of the atonement and the perseverance of the saints that Arminius' contribution lies.

(1) *Exegetical theology: Romans 7 and 9.* Both of these chapters had a standard Calvinistic interpretation in the 16th century. Romans 7 was understood as a description of the continuing conflict between the Christian's Adamic nature and the new regenerative nature. Arminius, on the other hand, argues that the man in Romans 7 is a man under law and therefore unregenerate. But what is his purpose in so interpreting the passage? It is not as his critics charged, to support freedom of the will or a Pelagian view about man's moral ability. Arminius' purpose is to show that the rigid Calvinistic interpretation being proposed is not exegetically sound nor has it been universally accepted in the history of theology. It illustrates, I think, the way in which Arminius did his *homework* when he prepared his sermons: he begins at the beginning, nothing is to be assumed and all is to be reexamined in the light of the text but always with a heart to the history of interpretation. His exegesis of Romans 7 confirms his general contextual impression that this passage is dealing with a man before regeneration. And although he does show that the fallen man, dramatically described by Paul in this chapter, is certainly not without some apprehension of the law of God, he does not drive that conclusion farther than the text of Romans 7 warrants. At the same time he attacks a complacent attitude toward Christian sanctification, often defended by an appeal to this passage. Later as a professor, Arminius would have to deal with the charge of teaching perfectionism, but this much is clear: his view of grace and human fallenness is as *high* and *low*, respectively speaking, as his Calvinistic opponents! Since the spiritual defeat described in Romans 7 belongs to the unregenerate unbeliever, the human will is, therefore, in complete bondage to sin, and the sinner has no power at all to deliver himself from this inherited bondage. It is strange that Arminius should be accused of being Pelagian.[15]

The interpretation of Romans 9 was equally important and equally controversial in the 16th century, but Arminius' challenge probably had less historical support than his interpretation of chapter 7. And Arminius' examination of Romans 9 takes only a little more than 38 pages, whereas he devotes more than 225 pages to the earlier chapter. He begins his analysis by admitting the great difficulties, but he believes that he has found a clue to the proper meaning of the text. He says:

In the first place, the scope of the chapter is the same with that of the whole epistle: *That the Gospel, not the law, is the power of God unto salvation, not to him that worketh, but to him that believeth, since, in the Gospel the righteousness*

> *of God is manifested in the obtainment of salvation by faith in Christ.*[16]

Arminius' examination is based primarily upon this theological and exegetical assumption. This chapter is, therefore, dealing with two types or two routes to salvation: those who seek the righteousness of God by faith and those who seek it by works. "Nothing," says Arminius, "is more plain in the Scripture, than that sinners, persevering in their sins against the long suffering of God, who invites them to repentance, are those whom God wills to harden." [17]

One of the keys in Arminius' analysis of the chapter deals with the question of the meaning of the term *lump* in verse 21. He attacks the view set forth by Beza and other contemporary Calvinists that the passage supports a *supralapsarian* view of the order of the divine decrees. Beza and the supralapsarians had argued that the *lump* refers to mankind not yet created and not yet corrupted by the Fall; hence, God arbitrarily chose some to salvation while rejecting or passing by others without regard to anything they might have done. Arminius' rebuttal, however, returns to the general note of the epistle and the chapter: the children of the promise are those who believe, not those who trust in the flesh. It is interesting that Arminius sees nothing of a distinction in this passage between an *election to salvation* and an *election to vocation*. (In my judgment, such an interpretation is demanded by the basic issue of chapters 9, 10 and 11: on what basis did God choose Israel as the medium of revelation and redemption and is God now finished with his people? The answer is that God chose Israel on the basis of grace, but that does not imply that all Israel is the Israel of faith!) The instruments and vessels of wrath, according to Arminius, are those who belong to that group of mankind who trust in the flesh. Those who trust in the flesh are those whom God has destined to be vessels of wrath, but the origin of that divine decree does not lie in a hidden secret will of God decreed even before man was created and fell. On the contrary, the decrees to redeem and reprobate are predicated upon the prior decrees of creation and the permissive will of God to allow man to sin.

(2) *Human sin and freedom of the will.* The historical sources reveal that Arminius was the victim of malicious charges designed to malign his character and ministry both as a pastor and as a teacher. One can only conjecture as to the psychological and personal motivations behind these vicious attacks, but it is my own suggestion that certain periods of history lend themselves to an aura of suspicion and mistrust. And there is a pathological distrust that usually results when

people are insecure about the positions or views they hold. Holland was attempting to achieve a new national unity, and she was being threatened in the process by the military conquests of Spain to the South, and she was still haunted by the ever present ghost of Roman Catholicism from her past. Internally, she had become a haven for Anabaptists and the disinherited from the British Isles. It is not incidental, therefore, that some of the charges levelled against Arminius were that he was soft on the Catholics, that he secretly advocated Catholic views in theology and that he was not rigorous enough in his attacks upon the Anabaptists. Bangs' investigations support this claim. He points to the attacks of one of the leading Roman Catholic theologians of the day, Robert Cardinal Bellarmine (1542-1621).

> Robert Cardinal Bellarmine may well have touched it off when he attacked the Reformed doctrine of predestination. Here he found the soft underbelly of the Protestant enemy, and his jabs hit home. It was partly to offset these Jesuit attacks that the Theological College had been established at Leider Then, when someone else, especially a Reformed professor of theology, took his own jabs at the underbelly, it was regarded as a defection to the arch-enemy of the true faith, a sell-out to the papal Antichrist. This very charge would soon be made about Arminius. It was in this context that tales about his having kissed the Pope's toe in Rome were circulated. All this served to make predestination a touchy issue, for it seemed to strike at the very foundation of both the Reformed religion and the national struggle for independence. How could the church tolerate someone who joined Bellarmine in rejecting Beza's supralapsarianism? [18]

It is difficult to see how Arminius' critics missed the position of Arminius, a position which he set forth with such clarity. (What a contrast with some contemporary theologians whose style so obscures their doctrinal intention that the reader is never quite sure what they want to say!) His concise, clear statement on the issue of human depravity and freedom of the will are set forth often in his writings, but representative is this statement taken from "The Declaration of Sentiments".

> This is my opinion concerning the Free-will of man: *In his primitive condition* as he came out of the hands of his Creator, man was endowed with such a portion of knowledge, holiness and power, as enabled him to understand, esteem, consider, will, and to perform THE TRUE GOOD, according to the commandment delivered to him. Yet none of these acts could he do, *except through the assistance of Divine Grace.* But in his *lapsed and sinful state,* man is not capable, of and by himself, either to think, to will, or to do that which is really good; but it is necessary for him to be regenerated and renewed in his intellect, affections or will, and in all his powers,

by God in Christ through the Holy Spirit, that he may be qualified rightly to understand, esteem, consider, will, and perform whatever is truly good. When he is made a partaker of this regeneration of renovation, I consider that, since he is delivered from sin, he is capable of thinking, willing and doing that which is good, but yet *not without the continued aids of Divine Grace.* [Italics in the original translation, but I do not know if they indicate some emphasis stressed in the Latin original.][19]

In his letter to Lord Hippolytus a Collibus, written in 1608, he restates his position. "Concerning grace and free will," writes Arminius, "this is what I teach according to the Scriptures and orthodox consent: Free will is unable to begin or to perfect any true and spiritual good, without grace. That I may not be said, like Pelagius, to practice delusion with regard to the word 'grace,' I mean by it that which is the grace of Christ and which belongs to regeneration." [20]

It is to be noted that his position on the freedom of the will as regards the believer's condition after regeneration eventually raised the question of perseverance of the saints. Arminius' mature opinion on this subject is stated in "The Declaration of Sentiments" delivered before the States of Holland, at The Hague, in 1608. It is topic five in The Declaration and too lengthy here to quote in full, but his concluding paragraph is worth citing.

Though I here openly and ingenuously affirm, I never taught that *a true believer can either totally or finally fall away from the faith, and perish*; yet I will not conceal, that there are passages of Scripture which seem to me to wear this aspect; and those answers to them which I have been permitted to see, are not of such a kind as to approve themselves on all points to my understanding. On the other hand, certain passages are produced for the contrary doctrine [of unconditional perseverance] which are worthy of much consideration.[21]

A careful reading of Arminius' works indicates that he was, in no significant way, in disagreement with the Calvinistic tradition on the issue of freedom of the will. As to the complete loss of the *imago Dei* or the image of God, his analysis of Romans 7 led him to affirm that even fallen man stands qualitatively above the lower species! The image of God has not been completely lost as Calvin claims in the *Institutes*, but this does not imply any moral ability.

(3) *Divine foreknowledge, faith and predestination.* The contemporary reader may not fully agree with Arminius' interpretation of the Bible with regard to the subject of predestination; however, what does puzzle the contemporary observer is the way in which the *Belgic Confession* and *Heidelberg Catechism*—the two standards of 16th century Dutch Cal-

vinism—were subjected to a rigid interpretation. Arminius defends himself well when it comes to an examination of these confessional standards. In support of his views, he turns to the 14th Article of the confession:

> Man knowingly and willingly subjected himself to sin, and consequently, to death and cursing, while he lent an ear to the deceiving words and impostures of the devil.

He argues that "from this sentence I conclude, *that man did not sin on account of any necessity through a preceding decree of Predestination*: which inference is diametrically opposed to that doctrine of Predestination against which I now contend." [22] Furthermore, the 20th question of the catechism states that

> Salvation through Christ is not given to all who had perished in Adam, but to those only who are engrafted into Christ by true faith, and who embrace his benefits.

Arminius observes that "from this sentence I infer, *that God has not absolutely predestinated any men to salvation; but that he has in his decree considered [or looked upon] them as believers*." [23] He continues with an examination of the 54th article of the catechism, but we need not pursue this line of argument farther. The point is obvious: *both the creed and the catechism were ambiguous enough to allow for considerable latitude in interpretation*. To exclude the Arminian or Remonstrant Party from the church as was done after the Synod of Dort in 1618-1619 was unjustified upon the very grounds claimed by the strict Calvinistic party!

Arminius' own constructive position can be easily stated:

I. The FIRST absolute decree of God concerning the salvation of sinful man, is that by which he decreed to appoint his Son, Jesus Christ, for a Mediator, Redeemer, Savior, Priest and King, who might destroy sin by his death, might by his obedience obtain the salvation which had been lost, and might communicate it by his own virtue.

II. The SECOND precise and absolute decree of God, is that in which he decreed to receive into favor *those who repent and believe*, and, in Christ, for HIS sake and through HIM, to effect the salvation of such penitents and believers as persevered to the end; but to leave in sin, and under wrath, *all impenitent persons and unbelievers*, and to damn them as aliens from Christ.

III. The THIRD divine decree is that by which God decreed to administer *in a sufficient and efficacious manner* the MEANS which were necessary for repentance and faith; and to have such administration instituted (1.) according to the *Divine Wisdom*, by which God knows what is proper and becoming both to his mercy and his severity, and (2.) according to Divine Justice, by which He is prepared to adopt whatever his wisdom may prescribe and put it in execution.

IV. To those succeeds the FOURTH decree, by which God decreed to save and damn certain particular persons. This decree has its foundation in the foreknowledge of God, by which he knew from all eternity those individuals who *would*, through his preventing grace, *believe*, and, through his subsequent grace *would persevere*, according to the before described administration of those means which are suitable and proper for conversion and faith; and, by which foreknowledge, he likewise knew those who *would not believe and persevere*.[24]

Arminius then draws twenty conclusions from these four major articles. I wish that space permitted the full text of these conclusions since he shows how this particular view magnifies the grace of God and belittles it not a degree!

Arminius has made foreknown faith the basis for God's elective decree and the absence of faith the basis for God's neglecting decree, the former to save and the latter to allow for man's own exclusion from the kingdom of God. But his critics were quick to notice one of the major weaknesses of his position: if the prevenient grace preceding saving faith is available to all, how does he distinguish this prevenient grace from a Pelagian natural moral ability? Arminius' reply to this charge was simply that one was of grace and the other was of human effort! What he does not clearly answer, to my satisfaction at least, is the reason why some men come to saving faith and others do not, although all share equally God's prevenient grace. Here, I think, his analysis of Romans 7 as well as a more precise interpretation of the *imago Dei* might have assisted him. Arminius might have suggested that a unique *State of Conviction* exists between the *State of Bondage*, in which man is in bondage to sin, his corrupted nature, the devil and the demonic forces in the world, and the *State of Grace and Redemption*, in which man is now under the new power of the risen Lord Jesus Christ. In this *State of Conviction*, man is freed by the prevenient grace of God so that his response to the saving work of Christ is free and undetermined. I have advocated this position in another place and so has Ethelbert Stauffer in the article on ἐφ' ᾧ in *The Theological Dictionary of the New Testament*.[25] If this position is accepted, then the essential nature of the *imago Dei* is understood as creativity. Certainly man's creativity is blighted by the Fall, but under the illumination of the Law and Gospel, it is possible for man once more to be free, but free not in the sense of being able to do good or evil, but free in the sense of creatively responding to the offer of divine grace. Arminius himself, however, does not seem to have contemplated this approach to the problem. For Arminius the problem was: *is man's response to the grace of God in Christ free or determined?* Total mystery is not removed, but the negative consequences of making God responsible for evil are avoided.

IV. Legacy: Arminius and Arminianism

The English edition of Arminius' works is now out of print (although I am presently encouraging the original printer in America to re-issue these important volumes), and few theological students know much about Arminius. Ironically, however, we still hear much about *Arminianism*. And this particular position is usually set in contrast to the old *five points of Calvinism*, sometimes called the T.U.L.I.P.: total depravity, unconditional election, limited atonement, irresistible grace, and the perseverance of the saints. In the hundred years or so after the death of Arminius, his theological descendants moved toward what may rightly be called "a more liberal position." So much so that today most people view Arminius and Arminianism through either the theology of John Wesley and the Methodists or that more liberal tradition which eventually came to be known as unitarianism and universalism. And not a few have read these latter positions back into Arminius!

One finds repugnant the claim of Louis Berkhof, a Reformed theologian, that "the views of Arminius himself, in regard to the five points, were formed under Lutheran influences, and do not differ essentially from those of the Lutheran Church."[26] This viewpoint can hardly be sustained on the basis of historical evidence! Let me cite another illustration from Berkhof's *Systematic Theology* in which the confusion between the views of Arminius and Arminianism are confused, and no distinction is acknowledged. In discussing the relationship between foreknowledge and predestination, Berkhof observes that "the Arminian will of course say that he does not believe in a foreknowledge based on a decree which renders things certain, but in a foreknowledge of facts and events which are contingent on the free will of man, and therefore indeterminate."[27] In his *History of Christian Doctrine*, Berkhof very often combines Arminianism with Semi-Pelagianism or Socinianism. J. L. Neve, a Lutheran historian, in his *A History of Christian Thought* quotes approvingly a statement by Meusel on Arminianism:

> According to its whole genius (*Geistesrichtung*) it gradually made dogma second to ethics; it saw in Christ pre-eminently a new lawgiver, not the redeemer. In the dogma of the Trin-

ity it inclined to the subordination of the Son and the Holy Spirit to the Father. Original sin was taken as an inborn weakness. The image of God in man was not seen in a righteousness and holiness given him at the creation, but was taken to consist merely in the dominion over the creatures, as with the Socinians. In the receiving of divine grace (in conversion) there was taken to be a co-operation of many by virtue of an inborn moral freedom. The substitutional atonement of Christ and His fulfilment of the law was denied to have been sufficient in itself, but was merely a free act of love which was accepted as sufficient. For this reason there can be no justification of the sinner as an imputation of Christ's merit in the sense of a forensic justification. The sacraments have only a ceremonial significance. Baptism was the ceremony of an admission of believers into the Church. Infant baptism had little favor, because children cannot believe. The Lord's Supper offers only a moral strengthening of faith and love.[28]

One hardly recognizes Arminius from the above description!

There is, I think, a more accurate description of Arminius' legacy. In the small volume of essays edited by Gerald O. McCulloh, entitled *Man's Faith and Freedom: The Theological Influence of Jacobus Arminius*, is a more balanced appraisal by Lambertus Jacobus van Holk. He writes:

In conclusion, let those who feel inspired by the spirit of Arminius share the rich inheritance that has come through him by repeated investigations of his theology and the unity and diversity of Arminianism. As these studies are made, it would seem that the following aspects merit special attention:

1) The belief in the universal grace of God as it has been revealed in the gospel of Jesus Christ as the common basis of all men. This encourages Christians in the missionary spirit inherent in the gospel, as they acknowledge the share in truth and salvation that belongs to non-Christian religions as a result of this universal grace.

2) The persuasion that, in discussing the scope of Christian freedom, emphasis should be placed upon present personal and social responsibility rather than upon the predestinational controversy as such. If this is done, the grace of God and the freedom of man do not seem to be two separate items, but rather understood as two integral parts of a permanent dialogue.

3) The belief that Arminius' pleas for peace, moderation, and love in the Church is by no means antiquated but is needed now more than ever before on the national, racial and class levels.

4) The feeling that the study and exegesis of the Bible should be as impartial and objective as possible, using the best methods available. This will provide for the development of a dynamic, prophetic dialogue between the Church and the world.

5) The emulation of Arminius' open-minded appreciation

of ancient civilizations. This will insure a similarly open-minded awareness of both the treasures and failures of all cultures, regardless of their age or their nature.[29]

Obviously there are overtones of an Arminianism that even Arminius himself might not recognize in the above remarks of van Holk; nevertheless, I think the substance of Arminius' contribution is to be found in the five points listed above. Certainly this volume of essays, dedicated as it is to an exoneration and appreciation of the free grace of God, can look with gratitude upon the life and works of Jacobus Arminius.

> A noble army, men and boys,
> The matron and the maid,
> Around the Saviour's throne rejoice,
> In robes of light arrayed:
> They climbed the steep ascent of heaven
> Through peril, toil, and pain;
> O God, to us may grace be given
> *To follow in their train.*[30]

NOTES

1. See A. H. Harrison, *The Beginnings of Arminianism to the Synod of Dort* (London: University of London Press, 1926).

2. Carl Bangs, *Arminius: A Study in the Dutch Reformation* (Nashville, Tenn.: Abingdon Press, 1971), p. 18.

3. See James H. Nichols, *History of Christianity 1650-1950* (New York: The Ronald Press Company, 1956), pp. 3ff.

4. Bangs, 25.

5. *The Works of James Arminius, D.D.*, 3 vol. (Auburn and Buffalo: Derby, Miller and Orton, 1853). Vols. 1 and 2 contain the translations by James Nichols; Vol. 3 is translated by Bagnall. Hereafter cited as *Works*. See Vol. I, 17; Bangs, 25-44.

6. Bangs, 34-36.

7. See Bangs, 37-38, 55, 56-63, 71, 73, 247, 257.

8. Bangs, 19.

9. Bangs, 113.

10. Bangs, 110-137, 153-175.

11. Bangs, 138-152, 186-227.

12. Bangs, 131-132.

13. Bangs, 274-275; see also Gerrit Jan Hoenderdaal, "The Life and Struggle of Arminius in the Dutch Republic," in *Man's Faith and Freedom* edited by Gerald O. McCulloh (Nashville, Tenn.: Abingdon Press, 1962), pp. 11-26.

14. The term *Erastian* takes its name from one Thomas Erastus (b. 1524) who advocated the supreme rule of the State in ecclesiastical matters.

15. *Works*, II, 217-452.

16. *Works*, III, 528.

17. *Works*, III, 550.

18. Bangs, 273.

19. *Works*, I, 252-253.

20. *Works*, II, 472.

21. *Works*, I, 254.

22. *Works*, I, 220.

23. *Works*, I, 221.

24. *Works*, I, 247-248.

25. Gerhard Kittel, ed., *Theological Dictionary of the New Testament.* Translated and edited by Geoffrey W. Bromiley (Grand Rapids, Mich.: Wm. B. Eerdmans Publishing Company, 1964). Volume II, 358-362. See also Donald M. Lake, "The Pauline Concept of Man's Will and How Affected by Sin." Unpublished Master's Thesis. Wheaton College, Wheaton, Illinois; 1960.

26. L. Berkhof, *Systematic Theology* (Grand Rapids, Mich.: Wm. B. Eerdmans Publishing Company, 1939), p. 100.

27. Berkhof, 107.

28. J. L. Neve, *A History of Christian Thought*, 2 vols. (Philadelphia, Pa.: The Muhlenberg Press, 1946). Volume II, 24.

29. Lambertus Jacobus van Holk, "From Arminius to Arminianism in Dutch Theology," in *Man's Faith and Freedom*, edited by Gerold O. McCulloh, p. 45.

30. Reginald Heber, "The Son of God Goes Forth to War."

13

A Puritan in a Post-Puritan World— Jonathan Edwards

JAMES D. STRAUSS

The two hundredth anniversary of Jonathan Edwards' death[1] was celebrated in 1958. In 1957, Yale University Press began publishing a new edition of the works of "the greatest philosopher-theologian yet to grace the American scene," *Freedom of the Will*. His controversial contribution continues to challenge all thinking people, Christians as well as non-Christians, to clarify the fundamental philosophical and/or theological issues entailed in the vexing problem of the relationship between determinism[2] and man's moral responsibility.

Jonathan Edwards was born in 1703. He finished Yale in 1720. During his second year at Yale he read and was greatly influenced by John Locke's *An Essay Concerning Human Understanding*.[3] In 1727, Edwards was installed at Northampton as a colleague of his grandfather, Solomon Stoddard. Difficulties with the congregation eventually brought his ministry there to a close in 1750. During the period from 1750-1758, before he was called to be president of what would become Princeton University, he was actively witnessing among the Indians. During this missionary period, he produced the *Freedom of the Will* in 1754, and *Original Sin* in 1758.

I. The Demise of Classical Calvinism

Edwards brilliantly stated the Calvinistic position against overwhelming odds. His most aggressive opponents were the Arminians, Thomas Chubb (1679-1747), Daniel Whitly (1638-1726), and Isaac Watts (1674-1748). (*Freedom of the Will*, pp. 66, 81-118). But other influences, especially Deism and Unitarianism (Conrad Wright, *The Beginnings of Unitarianism in America* [Boston: Starr King Press, 1955]), were ultimately gaining the allegiance of the New England religious mind (Smith and Jamison, editors, *The Shaping of American Religion* [Princeton University Press, Volume I, pp. 232-321; and Volume IV, pp. 976-1169]); and F. H. Foster, *A Genetic History of New England Theology* (New York: Russell and Russell, reprinted, 1963). The intellectual and spiritual demise of classical Calvinism left an enormous vaccum to be filled, but not for long. Eighteenth and nineteenth century science was ultimately to remove God and his grace from nature. Science claimed the power, in principle, to completely quantify nature; thus nature becomes only a cosmic machine which cannot only be controlled but modified by man's creative freedom and the scientific method.

Hardly a generation beyond Edwards would pass until classical Christian assumptions would be replaced by the presuppositions of classical liberalism. Four basic assumptions dominate intellectual Zeitgeist: (1) The Inevitability of Progress; (2) The Inherent Goodness of Man; (3) Total Uniformity of Nature as a Cosmic Machine; and (4) The Animality of Man, who was completely immersed in graceless nature. (See C.F.H. Henry, *Remaking of a Modern Mind*, reprinted in 1972 by College Press: Joplin, Mo. See the author's bibliographical essay included in this reprint.) The mechanistic model of the Newtonian world machine appeared to many 18th century Calvinists, especially Jonathan Edwards, to be a paradigm for the "theological determinism" implicit in the Calvinistic system of theology. Scientific developments in the 19th and 20th centuries appear to many to have only reenforced Edwards' profound evaluation. The entire intellectual *Sitz im leben* of 20th century western man is oriented around a cosmic determinism. Both genetic and environmental determinism are basic presuppositions of contemporary physical, biological (bio-physic and molecular biology), and behavioral sciences.

Edwards claims that his entire argument in *Freedom of the Will* rests upon two correlating truths, that of *reason* and *revelation*. He encourages all readers to determine "whether these things are agreeable to scripture, let every Christian, and every man who has read the Bible, judge; and whether they are agreeable to common sense, let everyone judge, that have human understanding in exercise" (*Freedom of the Will*, p. 326). However, this author does not share Edwards' evaluation regarding the relationship of God's foreknowledge and the certainty of future events. (Read and compare Edwards' position expressed on pages 239-256 in *Freedom of the Will* with this author's essay in this present volume on "God's Promise and Universal History"—Theology of Romans 9.[4])

It must be realized at the outset that Edwards' theme is not "the freedom of the will" as such. Perhaps the original title will provide the clue to his intentions. What Edwards brilliantly analyzes in his *Freedom of the Will* is clearly stated as: *A careful and strict inquiry into the modern prevailing notions of that freedom of the will which is supposed to be essential to moral agency, vice and virtue, reward and punishment, praise and blame.* By "modern prevailing notions," Edwards means the Arminians. He said that "I proceed to consider the Arminian notion of the freedom of the will, and the supposed necessity of it in order to moral agency, or in order to anyone's being capable of virtue or vice, and properly the subject or command or counsel, praise or blame, promises or threatening, rewards or punishments; or whether . . . the thing meant by liberty in common speech, be not sufficient, and the only liberty, which makes, or can make, anyone a moral agent, and so properly the subject of these things" (*Freedom of the Will*, p. 171). Edwards not only destroys the Arminian notion of self-determination, but his own "moral agency" thesis as well.

In Edwards' Calvinistic interpretation of freedom and responsibility the prior question is the nature and effect of sin (and ultimately God's irresistible grace); therefore, one should be acquainted with the content of Edwards' work on *Original Sin* before encountering his *Freedom of the Will*. The controversy between the Arminians and Edwards centers around this problem: Does God's absolutely certain knowledge of the future act of a human agent destroy man's freedom? If Edwards' God is absolutely sovereign and man is dominated by the enslaving power of "original sin," how is Edwards going to work out with systematic consistency a harmony between God's sovereignty and man's moral responsibility of his actions? Edwards' Calvinistic interpretation required an assertion of necessity, and a denial of what he believed was the Arminian view of the freedom of the will. He believed that by establishing the doctrine of "moral necessity," the Calvinists would have a firm basis from which to confute Arminian objections to the doctrines of total depravity and efficacious grace, absolute, eternal, and particular election, and the perseverance of the saints.

II. Edwards' Definition of Will

Before proceeding to examine Edwards' arguments in favor of this doctrine, perhaps a brief word concerning the freedom of the will from the fountainhead of Arminianism would be enlightening.

"The will is the proper, adequate and immediate cause of sin, and has two motives and incentives to commit sin, the one internal, the other external. The internal, which lies in man himself, is the love of himself and a concupiscence of lusting after temporal things, or of the blessings which are visible. The external motive is an object moving the appetite or desire; such objects are honors, riches, pleasures, life, health, and soundness. . . . But these motives do not move the will so efficaciously that the will is necessarily moved; for, in this case, the will would be excusable from sin; but they move the will through the mode of persuasion and enticement" (*Writings of James Arminius* [Grand Rapids, Mich.: Baker Book House, 1956], Volume II, pp. 525-526).

The hypothesis of the self-determined sinful nature of each man, and his ability at any given moment to choose to sin or not to sin is the assumption which Edwards seeks to refute. He does distinguish between freedom before and after the fall of man. Before the fall, man had the ability either to sin or not sin; after the fall, man has had liberty to sin, but not to do good. "When man sinned, and broke God's covenant, and fell under his curse, these superior principles (spiritual, holy, righteousness), . . . entirely ceased; the Holy Spirit, that divine inhabitant, forsook the house" (*The Great Christian Doctrine of Original Sin Defended*, pp. 476, 477). Edwards maintains a distinction between the self-determing power of an agent and a free will. An agent is self-determined because he is the author of his own acts and that he is the origin of his own determinations. (Note this is central to Edwards' theorical efforts to harmonize God's sovereignty and man's moral responsibility.)

Both Edwards and the Arminians agree on two fundamental issues: (1) Man is a free moral agent (we will consider what this means in Edwards' theory later); and (2) A free agent is the author of his own acts. In order to evaluate what Edwards means by these claims, it is imperative that we understand how God's foreknowledge is related to his solution. For Edwards, God's foreknowledge renders an event absolutely certain. The central issue centers around an event being certain; and that certainty must be admitted, or else suppose that "free acts" are uncertain and not known to an omniscient God. "If God certainly knows the future existence of an event which is wholly contingent, and may possibly never be, then he sees a firm connection between a subject and predicate that are not firmly connected; which is a contradiction" (*Original Sin*, p. 265). Edwards concludes his argument from the Scriptures by noting that foreknowledge supposes certainty, that foreordination determines it, and that providence effects it. "Indeed, such an universal determining providence, infers some kind of necessity of all events; such a necessity as implies an infallible previous fixedness of the futurity of the event. . ." (*Original Sin*, p. 431).

His doctrine that the will is determined and not self-determined is involved in the rational character of our acts. Edwards' understanding of free agency is removed from a "mechanical necessity," which precludes the possibility of responsibility from a theory of contingency which assumes that an act, in order to be free, must be uncertain; and from a self-determined will, which acts independently of reason, conscience, inclinations and feelings. Edwards,[6] in contrast to Kant, struggles with the idea of freedom *within* a determinate order, a world order of which it is a part; therefore, he does not deny the "determination of the will," only the Arminian theory of the same. Men choose, and choose freely, but their choices are in the midst of a world which their choices did not make.

III. Freedom of the Will and Moral Inability

"Tis easy to see how the decision of most of the points in controversy, between Calvinists and Arminians depends on the determination of this grand article concerning the freedom of the will requisite to moral agency; . . ." (*Freedom of the Will*, p. 431). Edwards' basic thesis is "the freedom of the will requisite to moral agency." But as a Calvinist theologian, Edwards is committed to hold that ". . . as to freedom of the will dying in the power of the will to determine itself, there neither is any such thing, nor any need of it, in order to virtue, reward, commands, counsels, etc." (*Ibid.*, p. 436). In order to counter the Arminian theory of "self-determination" as necessary for moral agency and prequisite to the moral judgment of man, Edwards both denies "self-determination" and sets forth a brilliant, if futile, account of the true "determination of the will." His account must show the consistent relation of the ordinary language account of moral responsibility and praise or blame, i.e., moral judgment with the Calvinistic doctrines of total depravity, election foreknowledge, and irresistible grace. Edwards' position must mediate between an absolute determinism and the Arminian theory of "self-determination" which he does attempt with his thesis of "moral inability."

Edwards clearly deliniates the nature and implications of "moral inability" in his *Freedom of the Will*. "The things which have been said, obviate some of the chief objections of Arminians against the Calvinistic doctrine of the total depravity and corruption of man's nature, whereby his heart is wholly under the power of sin, and he is utterly unable, without the interposition of sovereign grace, savingly to love God, believe in Christ, or do anything that is truly good and acceptable in God's sight. For the main objection against this doctrine is, that it is inconsistent with the freedom of man's will, consisting in indifference and self-determining power; . . . Now this doctrine supposes no other necessity of sinning, than a moral necessity; which, as has been shewn, don't at all excuse sin; and supposes *no other inability* to obey any command, or perform any duty, even the most spiritual and exalted, but a moral inability, which, as has been proved, don't excuse persons in the non-performance of any good thing, or make 'em not to be the proper objects of commands, counsels and invitations. And moreover, it has been shewn, that there is not, and never can be, either in existence, or so much as in idea, any such freedom of will, consisting in indifference and self-determination, for the sake of which, this doctrine of original sin is cast out; and that no such freedom is necessary, in order to the nature of sin, and a just desert of punishment.

"The things which have been observed, do also take off the main objections of Arminians against the doctrine of efficacious grace; and at the same time, prove the grace of God in a sinner's conversion (if there be any grace or divine influence in the affair) to be efficacious, yea, and irresistible too, if by irresistible is meant, that which is attended with a moral necessity, which it is impossible should ever be violated by any resistance." (*Freedom of the will*, pp. 432, 33; also see the chapter, "Original Sin and Enlightenment" by Clyde A. Holbrook, pp. 142-165 from *The Heritage of Christian Thought*, edited by Robert E. Cushman and Egil Grislis, Essays in Honor of Robert L. Calhoun.)

IV. Edwards' Definition of Will

Understanding the nature of the will and its determination is basic for comprehending the issues involved in moral agency and responsibility. "When a thing is from a man, in that sense, that it is from his will or choice, he is to blame for it, because his will is in it; so far as the will is in it, blame is in it, and no further. Neither do we go any further in our notion of blame, to inquire whether the bad will be 'from' a bad will: there is no consideration of the original of that bad will; because according to our natural apprehension, blame originally consists in it" (*Ibid.*, pp. 427-428). Decision or choice is good or bad ". . . not so much because they are from some property of ours, as because they are our properties" (*Ibid.*, p. 428). "Will" in Edwards' thought, is the man as a moral agent. Where there is a will there is a moral agent, and where there is a moral agent, there is a will. Will is not an autonomous category of man for Edwards, as it is in the Arminian theory of "freedom of the will."

V. Shades of Locke—Edwards on the Nature and Power of Will

While a student at Yale, Edwards came under the influence of Lockean philosophical psychology, as set forth in chapter xxi, "Power in Human Understanding" (Oxford University Press, 1960 reprint, pp. 135-150). Edwards brilliantly modifies Locke's insights concerning the power of the will. "The faculty of the will is that faculty or power or principle of mind by which it is capable of choosing: an act of the will is the same as an act of choosing or choice" (*Ibid.*, p. 137).

Edwards' definition of choice is very ambiguous; therefore, crucial argument based on too broad a definition ultimately jeopardizes Edwards' systematic argumentation. "'. . . whatever names we call the act of will by choosing, refusing, approving, disapproving, liking, disliking, embracing, rejecting, determining, directing, commanding, forbidding, inclining or being averse, or being pleased or displeased with all may be reduced to this of choosing. For the soul to act voluntarily is evermore to act electively" (*Ibid.*). Each of these "acts" have antecedent causes; therefore, the "will" cannot possibly be "free," i.e., be autonomous or outside of a causal chain of events. Edwards claims that man's moral responsibility is grounded in the fact that ". . . a man never, . . . wills anything contrary to his desires, or desires anything contrary to his will" (*Ibid.*, p. 139).

Edwards' attempts to show that ordinary language usage of "freedom of the will" means that ". . . a man's doing as he wills and doing as he pleases, are the same thing. . ." (*Ibid.*). Freedom is power . . . that power and opportunity for one to do and conduct as he will. . . ," and this is all that is implied by freedom or liberty (*Ibid.*, p. 164). Freedom does not belong to an act, according to Edwards, because each act as defined by him is part of a causal chain of events. The consequences of a man's acts are "free," when a man does as he pleases, and to do as one pleases is to perform an act which is caused by an act of choice. Free choice to Edwards is to do as one pleases; it is not a consideration of the prior determination of the will. But Edwards specifically and clearly sets forth his understanding of prior determination: "To talk of the determination of the will, supposes an effect, which must have a cause. If the will be determined, there is a determiner" (*Ibid.*, p. 141). Edwards' "grand inquiry," what determines the will, thus becomes the central question. Acts of the will are caused by motives, but what are motives?

VI. Motives Cause Acts

"The will is always determined by the strongest motive, or by that view of the mind which has the greatest degree of previous tendency to excite volition" (*Ibid.*, p. 148). Edwards must correlate this understanding of the causal connection between motives and acts of volition. He wants to establish the necessary correlation of moral necessity and determination of the will. "If every act of the will is excited by a motive, then that motive is the cause of the act of the will. . . . Thus it is manifest, that volition is necessary, and is not from any self-determining power in the will: the volition which is caused by previous motive and inducement, is not caused by the will exercising a sovereign power over itself, to determine, cause, and excite volitions in itself" (*Ibid.*, pp. 225-6). "Moral necessity" is upon us, once the implications of Edwards' terminology is accepted. There is no place for "self-determination" in a causal chain of motives and acts of volition. The will is morally unable to will anything but the necessary consequences of antecedent causes.

VII. Motivation, Causation and Moral Inability

If the will is morally incapable of breaking the causal chain of will-act, then man's acts are worthy of moral praise or blame because they are his acts. Man's moral inability consists in the "strength of his evil inclination" (*Ibid.*, p. 309). Man has a moral will (but it is evil, stemming from original sin), else man could not be praised or blamed for his acts which he chooses. He is morally incapable of good will (contra Kant's theory of good will) because every act has antecedent causal connection with evil, i.e., moral inability. Neither original sin nor moral inability excuses man. (Compare the interpretation of Ramsey in his Introduction of *Freedom of the Will* and A. E. Murphy's "Edwards on the Free Will," *Philosophical Review*, 1959, pp. 181ff. The present author concurs with Murphy against Ramsey's interpretation.)

VIII. Freedom of the Will—Real or Imagined?

Historically, students of Edwards' theory of will have accepted at face value his claim that he was concerned only with rejecting the Arminian notion of the freedom of the will. Ramsey's Introduction continues this interpretation. Ramsey maintains that for Edwards, "Freedom of the will pertains to those acts of volition in which a man is 'free from hindrance in the way of doing, or conducting in any respect, as he wills' " (p. 13 in Introduction to *Freedom of the Will*). But the passage Ramsey quotes is discussing freedom as the power to do as one pleases (*Freedom of the Will*, p. 163). This is not a freedom of acts of volition, but in acting as one chooses. In Edwards' theory voluntary action is the effect of willing with the act of volition, which is the antecedent cause of such consequences. Edwards is never primarily concerned with the question of the cause of voluntary actions. They are worthy of praise or blame because they are free as effects of "acts of will." But acts of will are not voluntary acts (see *Freedom of the Will*, section 2, Part IV, "Definition of Action and Agency," pp. 337ff.). "If a man does something voluntarily, or as the effect of his choice, then in the most proper sense, and as the word is most originally and commonly used, he is said to act: but whether that choice or volition be self-determined, or no, whether it be connected with foregoing habitual bias, whether it be the certain effect of the strongest motive, or some extrinsic cause, never comes into consideration in the meaning of the word" (*Ibid.*, p. 347).

Clearly Edwards is not presenting a phenomenological analysis of the determination of the will itself, as Ramsey claims. Edwards holds, instead, that ". . . the thing meant by liberty in common speech (the liberty to do and conduct as one chooses) is . . . sufficient, and only liberty which makes, or can make anyone a moral agent" (*Ibid.*, p. 171), while ". . . as to freedom of will lying in the power of the will to determine itself, there neither is any such thing, nor any need of it, in order to virtue, reward, commands, counsels, etc." (*Ibid.*, p. 436).

Though Ramsey, in his *Introduction*, reveals some confusion in his interpretation of Edwards' account of the determination of the will, there is actually a very serious ambiguity in Edwards' discussion (see "Concerning the Determination of the Will," pp. 141ff.). "To talk of the determination of the will supposes an effect, which must have a cause" (*Ibid.*, p. 141). Elsewhere, Edwards asserts that ". . . it is that motive, which, as it stands in the view of the mind, is the strongest, that determines the will" (*Ibid.*). Motive, ". . . an intelligent and voluntary agent (is always) apparent good" (*Ibid.*, p. 147-8). Good means "most agreeable or 'pleasing' to the mind." Logically, Edwards' definition of choosing, willing, being pleased or displeased with, and of free act as acting as we please, is clearly a tautology, i.e., it is true by definition. Then only those definitions declared true by virtue of their tautological form are "strictly necessary." The will is determined by the greatest good. (Note the analytic/synthetic debate since Kant; also the implications of all forms of apriorism since Einstein.) In fact, a central fallacy, if not a lethal fallacy, in Edwards' argument is the ambiguity of his definition of the determination of the will. He sums up his thesis by declaring that ". . . the will is always determined by the strongest motive, or by that view of the mind which has the greatest degree of previous tendency to excite volition" (*Ibid.*, p. 148). In Edwards' "attack" on the Arminian argument concerning freedom of the will, he holds that acts of will are necessary ". . . with a necessity of consequence and connection; because every act of the will is in some way connected with the understanding and is as the greatest apparent good is, in the manner that has already been explained" (*Ibid.*, p. 217).

The central thrust of Edwards' cause for "moral necessity" appears to be that ". . . certain connection between motives and volitions. . . ." reduces, on critical analysis, to the irrefutable logic that "men choose what they choose or prefer what they prefer" (Murphy, "Edwards on Free Will," *Philosophical Review*, 1959, p. 194). Edwards' analysis of the will is simply that the will is the strongest motive, or most powerful inclination of the mind. But what causes a given "inclination of the mind" to be stronger than another? The causation of such motives is not a causally connected series of acts of the will by motive, yet a necessary connection between "acts" and "motives" is central to Edwards' argument. Edwards has not demonstrated the "necessity" of the connection between acts and motives but rather has committed the definitional fallacy by his apriori, i.e., tautological definition. Thus, Edwards connects determination of the will with moral agency. As a moral agent, man must be capable of being influenced by warnings, exhortations, admonitions, etc., and these are the motives for man's "willed behavior." But can Edwards logically correlate being influenced by motives, in the above sense, to being "determined" to volitional acts by causal antecedents? "And besides, if the acts of the will are excited by motives, those motives are the causes of those acts of the will: which makes the acts of the will necessary; as effects necessarily follow the efficiency of the cause" (*Ibid.*, p. 328).

But is this description not in logical tension with Edwards' own account of the identification between strongest motives and acts of will? Though Edwards' account lacks logical consistency, his "moral inability" thesis (based on the thesis of original sin) is brought in to sustain his argument. But if his argument cannot stand, on its own inner logic, can an *ad hoc* factor save his overall attack on freedom of the will? We think not. Even his insistence that his definitions of necessity, freedom, etc., flow from ordinary language and common-sense meaning will not sustain the weight he places on it.

IX. Edwards' Moral Agency—Fact or Fiction

Edwards' attack is sufficient to liquidate his 18th century Arminian opponents' views concerning the "self-determination" of the will, but does not Edwards demolish his own "moral agency" argument along with the "determination of the will" thesis? The entire structure of *Freedom of the Will* is committed to the defense of the thesis that only "moral agents" are properly "the subjects of moral treatment." Yet, what can Edwards mean, given his account of the determination of the will, by the claim that the will can be "influenced by moral inducements"? Surely, such inducements must be classified as "motives," if they are to move the will. For motives to "influence the will" is for them "to bring it into subjection to the power of something extrinsic, which operates upon it, sways and determines it, previous to its own determination" (*Ibid.*, p. 357).

There is plainly no place for both "being influenced by moral inducements" and any agency of the self in the determination of moral quality, of its actions, yet, it is for this and only this "moral agency" that the agent can be morally exonerated or condemned. Once a given motive (inducement) is strongest (it is not by choice that this is done), it causes a given bodily movement. But is this moral agency? How would Edwards' argument fare in the hands of Creek, Monod, or Skinner? Edwards' "moral inability" thesis necessarily entails moral incapacity and moral judgment upon any given activity, where such inability is a necessary factor in the human condition, is a gross injustice, because man's actions are inevitably fixed or determined by antecedent conditions. Edwards' specie of theological determinism must defend a theory of "causation of voluntary acts," which, as I have already briefly suggested, he cannot do with internal consistency. Edwards' massive and brilliant efforts actually generates a *reductio ad absurdum* of the claim that "moral agency" is logically reconcilable with any form of radical determinism.

In conclusion, I maintain that Edwards' thesis can be responded to by three very important arguments for man's ability to transcend a radically determined universe: (1) Man is not reducible to a machine model as Gödel's theorem proves; (2) Chomsky's transformational grammar strongly supports the claim that thought and language cannot be reduced to machine translation, even in principle; and (3) Mackay's models of freedom of choice.

X. Freedom, Human Transcendence and Gödel's Theorem

Gödel argued for the difference between the abilities of the human mind and of formal systems of which machines are obvious embodiments. Knowing whether or not man is a machine is crucial for the possibility of freedom toward transcendence. See E. Nagel and J. R. Newman, *Gödel's Proof* (New York, 1958); Stanley L. Jaki, *Brain, Mind, and Computers* (New York: Herder and Herder, 1969), pp. 197-251; K. M. Sayre and F. J. Crosson, eds., *The Modeling of Mind* (Notre Dame: University of Notre Dame Press); K. M. Sayre, *Consciousness: A Philosophic Study of Minds and Machines* (New York: Random House, 1969); J. J. C. Smart, *Philosophy and Scientific Realism* (London: Routledge and Kegan Paul, 1963). If Gödel's argument is irrefutable, then freedom is a reality.

Gödel's proof states that even in elementary parts of arithmetic there are propositions which cannot be proved or disproved in that system. These propositions are concerned with relations between whole members and thus seem to confine themselves solely to mathematics. In proposition VI of Gödel's proof, he sets forth a corollary in which the argument moved into "meta-mathematics." The meta-mathematical statement of corollary I of proposition VI consists in the recognition of the fact that when an arithmetic proposition "a" is specified as one which is undecidable within the system, this indecidable statement is not mere arithmetic but a meta-mathematical assertion.

Since machines are formal systems and need no meta-mathematical proofs to work efficiently, it can be argued that Gödel's theorem amounts to declaring a basic, insurmountable difference in kind, not merely degree, between the abilities of the human mind and of formal systems of which computers are paradigm. A machine can have only a finite number of components and it can operate only on a finite number of initial assumptions, though it could operate on a randomizing device. Gödel's theorem suggests that it is the limitation of all mechanical systems, whether existing only on paper as theorems of arithmetic or mechanically implemented, they have to rely on a system extraneous to them for their proof of consistency. Gödel's proof cuts the ground from under all known efforts to completely parallel the capacity of the human mind and machines. For defense of Gödel see J. R. Lucas, "Mind, Machines, and Gödel," *Philosophy*, (1961), pp. 112-127; for opposing view, see I. J. Good, "Logic of Man and Machine," *The New Scientist* (1965), pp. 182-183. Machines must be finite and definite, and as such, would not contain their proof of consistency. Since machines are constructed of physical and chemical components, it follows that the human mind cannot be fully explained in terms of physics and chemistry, nor by adding neurophysiology before performing a reduction to mathematical equations, then to a machine model. Freedom does have scientific justification if Gödel's proof is intact.

XI. Freedom, Thought, Language and Transformational Grammar

Chomsky's theory of transformational grammar entails linguistic universals and intentionality, neither of which can be adequately machine translated, even in principle. Until Chomsky has been refuted by linguistic data, those who operate philosophically with defective understandings of the nature of language, e.g., Edwards, Wittgenstein, Heidegger, et. al., must not be allowed to direct our linguistic ventures regarding the relationship of language, truth, logic, and ontology. Chomsky's theory of the relationship between linguistics and semantics also strongly resists the reduction of the mind to the brain. (*Aspects of the Theory of Syntax* [Cambridge: The M.I.T. Press, 1965]; "Explanatory Models in Linguistics" in E. Nagel, P. Suppes, and A. Tarski, Logic, *Methodology and Philosophy of Science* [Stanford, Cal.: Stanford University Press, 1962; and his Cartesian Linguistic.) Chomsky's theory of semantics can be stated and defended independently of any form of Cartesian epistemology.

XII. Mackay's Model of Freedom of Choice

The developments in science from Galileo and Newton to the Popper-Carnap-Kuhn debates have surely taught us that many things are predictable but not necessarily inevitable. There are both *reasons* and *causes* for behavior. One may get out of bed by falling out (cause), but one can also intentionally set the alarm for a given time and get out of bed (reason). In discussing the causes (note contemporary discussion in scientific philosophy of jointly sufficient condition and necessary and sufficient conditions) of a given event is there an alternative between "absolute universal causation" (machine model), Marxian freedom (no individual free until everyone is free), and Sartrean ontological freedom (which is insanity)? Are there conditions under which particular future tense descriptions of human agents became self-invalidating for particular individuals? The answer is yes—if Mackay's arguments are valid.

Edwards' analysis of contingency would apply to the contemporary theory of chance as expressed by Jacques Monod. "Pure chance, absolutely free but blind, . . . is the basis of man's cosmic homesickness because . . . neither his destiny nor his duty have been written down" (*Chance and Necessity* [London: Collins, 1971, pp. 110-167]). God's foreknowledge stands in unmodifiable conflict with Monod's chancism. But it does not follow that God's knowledge, which is his basis of predicting future events, makes future events inevitable. Scientifically, knowledge is imperative for predictive power, but no one surely would say that the knowledge, which enables scientists to predict future events, "causes" future events. Scientifically, no fully determinate specification of results already exists. This does not necessarily imply that God is limited, rather that his loving merciful sovereignty over all of creation does not absolutely specify every detail which occurs in the space-time spectrum.

Before exploring Mackay's insights, let us assert three things: (1) It is not self-evident that Edwards' Calvinistic interpretation of election, predestination, foreknowledge is biblically sound. (2) It is not self-evident that Edwards' use of Locke's philosophy of mind represents a true model. (3) It is not self-evident that Edwards' telling arguments against his Arminian opponents also hold for new possibilities, such as Gödel, Chomsky, and Mackay.

Mackay deliniates between two possible models of freedom of choice: (1) A choice which is unpredictable by "everyone." (2) A choice which is both free and predictable, and consistent with human responsibility. A choice is free if there is no ". . . determinate specification that is binding on (valid and definitive for) everyone, including the agent, before he makes up his mind" (D. M. Mackay, *Freedom of Action in a Mechanistic Universe* [New York: Cambridge University Press,1967], p. 17; contra Edwards' thesis of God's foreknowledge of the volitions of moral agents—*Freedom of the Will*, p. 239). By human responsibility, we mean an intentional choice (goal directed which requires transcendence for goal determination. Note the significance of contemporary extentional, i.e., behavioristic, and intentional, i.e., non-behavioristic *Theories of Logic*). Freedom of the whole man (not will) does not entail uncontrolled randomization in thinking. But a comprehensive view (either/both scientific/theological) must account for all of the data. An adequate explanation must entail all available information, such as the state of mind when "anyone" decides to do what has been predicted of his or her behavior.

Does God's foreknowledge entail a description of inevitable future events in every situation? This question may "... sound strange to those of us who have been accustomed to suppose that the doctrine of divine predestination meant just this—that there already exists *now* a description of us and our future, including the choices we have not yet made, which is binding upon us, if only we knew it, because it is known to God. But I hope it is now clear that we should do God no honour by such a claim; for we should merely be inviting ourselves to imagine him in a logical self-contradiction. At this moment, we are unaware of any such description; so if it existed it would have to describe us as *not believing it*. But in that case we would be in error to believe it, for our believing it would falsify it! On the other hand, it would be of no use to alter the description so that it describes us *as believing it*; for in that case it is at the moment false, and therefore, although it would become correct if we believed it, we are not in error to *dis*believe it! Thus the divine 'foreknowledge' of our future, oddly enough, has no unconditional logical claim upon us, unknown to us.

"This, I believe, demonstrates a fallacy underlying both the theological dispute between Arminianism and Calvinism, and the philosophical dispute between physical or psychological determinism (in the technical scientific sense) and libertarianism in relation to man's responsibility. What I am suggesting is that even God's sovereignty over every twist and turn of our drama does not contradict (i.e., offers no valid alternative to) our belief that we are free, in the sense that no determining specification already exists which if only we knew it we should be correct to believe and in error to disbelieve, whether we liked it or not." (Donald M. Mackay, *The Clock Work Image* [London. InterVarsity Press, October, 1974, first American printing, pp. 81, 82]).

The three pivotal arguments of Gödel, Chomsky, and Mackay enable us to speak of man's freedom and responsibility, and effectively respond to Edwards' efforts at correlating theological determinism and man's moral agency. Jonathan Edwards was a brilliant artisan of argumentation. We thank God that he continues to challenge us to state the Christian case for man's moral agency in a fallen and "structured" universe. We do not share the enthusiasm of many for the validity of Edwards' arguments in *Freedom of the Will*, but we share his concern for deliniating how God can be a sovereign creator-redeemer, and man can be a responsible sinner in need of his healing help.

Jonathan Edwards was indeed a Puritan in a post-Puritan world, and we are Christians in a post-Christian world. In order to recover powerful Christian witness, we must recover the sovereignty of God from the immanent sovereignty of our contemporary neo-Hegelian-Marxian Promethius. Our technological Promethius must be bound once more, not by radical determinism, but by truth which has both its own transcendent and immanent power!

NOTES

1. Jonathan Edwards (general editor, Perry Miller), *Freedom of the Will*, edited by Paul Ramsey; *Religious Affections*, edited by John E. Smith; *Original Sin*, edited by Clyde A. Holbrook; *The Great Awakening*, edited by C. C. Goen (Yale University Press: New Haven and London). *The Philosophy of Jonathan Edwards from His Private Notebooks*, edited by Harvey G. Townsend (Eugene, Oregon, 1955); W. P. Jeanes, "Jonathan Edwards' Conception of Freedom of the Will," *Scottish Journal of Theology*, 14:1-41, Mr., 1961; A. E. Murphy, "Jonathan Edwards on Free Will and Moral Agency," *Philosophical Review*, 68: 181-202, April, 1959; A. N. Prior, "Limited Indeterminism," *Review of Metaphysics*, 16: 55-61, Sept. 1962 (cf. also 16: 366-79, December, 1962). H. G. Townsend, "The Will and the Understanding in the Philosophy of Jonathan Edwards," *Church History*, 16: 210-20, December, 1947. *Jonathan Edwards on Evangelism*, reprinted 1958 ed., 825 ISBN-0-8371 6588 - 1 Greenwood. Jonathan Edwards (son of J. Edwards), *Dissertation Concerning Liberty and Necessity* (continuous discussion of his father's *Freedom of the Will*), B. Franklin reprinted. T. H. Johnson, *The Printed Writings of Jonathan Edwards—1703-1758. A Bibliography* (Princeton University Library Publication, Princeton, N.J., 1940), reprinted Burt Franklin, Lenox Hill Publishers and Distribution Corporation, N.Y.). C. H. Faust and T. H. Johnson, editors, *Jonathan Edwards: Representative Selections*, revised edition 1962 (best handbook); N. R. Burr, *A Critical Bibliography of Religion in America*, Volume 2, pp. 976-87, 1961; D. J. Elwood, *The Philosophical Theology of Jonathan Edwards* (1960), stresses Platonic and Augustinian influences; C. Cherry, *The Theology of Jonathan Edwards: A Reappraisal* (1966); *Calvin's Works*, especially his Magnum opus *Institutes of the Christian Religion* (various Latin editions of the Institutes are in opera, I-II Latin edition 1559; French translation, 1560. For textual criticism of Latin and French texts see Marmelstein, *Etude Comparative des textes Latins et Francais de l'Institutes*, 1921. Doumerque, Emile. *Jean Calvin, L'Homme et les choses de con Temps* (7 folios 1899-1927; also the work of Jacques Panneir). B. B. Warfield, *Calvin and Calvinism* (Presbyterian Reformed, reprinted from 1931 edition).

2. Contemporary Philosophic Discussion of Free Will and Determinism: Berofsky, B., editor. *Free Will and Determinism* (Harper and Row, 1966); C. V. Borst, editor, *Mind-Brain Identity Theory* (Macmillan, 1970); C. A. Campbell, *In Defense of Free Will and other Philosophical Papers* (Allen

and Unwin, 1967); K. Campbell, *Body and Mind, Problems of Philosophy* (Macmillan, 1971); G. Dworkin, *Determinism, Free Will and Moral Responsibility* (Prentice-Hall, 1970); A. Farrer, *Freedom of the Will* (second edition enlarged, A. & C. Black, 1963); H. Feigl and M. Scriven, editors. *Foundations of Science and Concepts of Psychology and Psychoanalysis* (Minnesota University Press, 1956); H. Feigle and G. Maxwell, editors, *Concepts, Theories and the Mind-Body Problem*, Studies in Philosophy of Science 2 (Minnesota University Press, 1958); R. L. Franklin, *Freewill and Determinism* (Routledge, 1968); P. T. Geach, *Mental Acts, Their Content and Their Objects* (Routledge, 1957); H. C. Longuet-Higgins, C. H. Waddington, J. Lucas, and A. Kenny, *Nature of Mind*, Gifford Lectures (Edinburgh University Press, 1973); J. R. Lucas, *Freedom of the Will* (Oxford University Press, 1970: J. MacMurray, *Self as Agent*, Gifford Lectures (Faber, 1953, 1957); N. Malcolm, *Problems of Mind: Descartes to Wittgenstein, Essays in Philosophy* (Allen & Unwin, 1972); A. I. Melden, *Free Action* (Routledge, 1961); O'Connor, *Free Will Problems of Philosophy* (MacMillan, 1972); P. Ricoeur, *Freedom and Nature, Voluntary and Involuntary*, trans. E. V. Kohak (Northwestern University Press, 1966); SPEP; Spakovsky, A. V. *Freedom, Determinism, Indeterminism* (Nijhoof, 1963); E. W. Straus, and R. M. Griffith, editors, *Phenomenology of Will and Action*, the Second Lexington Conference on Pure and Applied Phenomenology (Nauwelaerts, 1967). C. A. Van Peursen, *Body, Soul, Spirit: A Survey of the Body-Mind Problem*, trans. H. H. Hoskins (Oxford University Press, 1966); R. M. Zaner, *Problem of Embodiment: Some Contributions to a Phenomenology of the Body* (Phaenomen, 17 Nijhoff, 1964).

If consciousness is "explained" as "natural phenomenon suited to being described by and dealt with by the body of the laws and methods of physical sciences," then the defense of a comprehensive mechanistic philosophy is feasible. If man is describable in the terms of pure physics, i.e., in terms of a mechanistic model, then there is no qualitative distinction between man and an artificial mind. The first automatic computer began operation in 1944 and created the computer revolution (E. C. Berkeley, *The Computer Revolution* [Garden City, N.Y. 1962, pb], p. 20). The cybernetics revolution demanded a drastic revision of all classical discussions of the significance of words like "intelligence," "thinking," and "thought." If there is even a modicum of plausibility in the thesis that the human brain has an analogue in the computer, then man is reducible to a machine and the universe becomes exhaustively describable in quantification terms. As Plotinus asserted centuries ago, if we know who we are, i.e., the nature of man, the solution would embrace all other questions (*The Enneads*, Tractate VII of the Sixth Ennead).

A. *Democritus* (ca. 460-360 B.C.). God in Exile. The culturally disruptive influences of Democritus' world machine was most apparent in Greek society, as is the social, political, legal implications of genetic and envirnomental de‌‌ Aristotle replaced the mechanistic model of Democritus.

B. *Lucretius* (95-52 B.C.). The thesis of an atomistic view of the mind and its functions are set forth in his book, *De rerum natura*, especially books three and four. The logical consistency of his psychology breaks against the existential rocks of attempting to give the power to choose and to think to agglomeration of mind-atoms.

C. *Galileo* (1564-1641). The method suggesting that reality could be quantified found fruition in Newton's *Two New Sciences*

D. *Hobbes* (1588-1679). He maintained that only matter and motion exist. He identified man as a "living organism" in terms of a machine model. He objected to Descartes' *Philosophical Work*, Vol. III, p. 65. *Leviathan*. Part I, ch. 5.

E. *Descartes* (1596-1650). *L'Homme* was the first major total mechanistic physiological model of man in modern times. (*Meditation on the First Philosophy*, found in Vol. I of *The Philosophical Works of Descartes*, especially page 196. Also see Locke's work, *An Essay Concerning Human Understanding*, book 4, chp. 3; Leibniz's *Selection*, pb., pp. 390ff.)

F. *Newton* (1642-1727). The modern mechanistic explanation of the universe reached its zenith with the scientific revolution of Newton. He was cautious regarding the ability to provide total explanatory power by the psychiophysical model of the brain (*Principia*, ed. Cajore, Berkeley, 1934).

G. *De la Mettrie* (1709-1751) and *D'Holbach* (1723-1789). The former's *L'homme machine*, and the latter's *Systeme de la nature* were the results of wholesale reductionism, i.e., moving from physics to biology to psychology with a total naturalistic explanation of the universe, both macro and micro cosmic. If physics is viewed as an unchanging set of truths, then a mechanical model of man is hardly avoidable.

H. *Charles Babbage* (1792-1871). The founder of computers considered that his calculating machines were illustrations of the existence of an infinite intellect, or creator. In his *Ninth Bridgewater Treatise* one of his objectives was to show that the power and knowledge of the great creator of matter and mind are unlimited. Babbage differs from Edwards in that he defended human free will in his model. If the universe is in fact a machine, then freedom is precluded in any form, verbal or otherwise. Contemporary microscopic physics has underminded the mechanical model of reality in that the principle of isomorphism, i.e., the mind mirrors the image of the sum total of sense experience and conceptual content, is not a defensible explanation of how the mind contacts the empirical world, then some range of freedom is a part of the actual state of affairs. Isomorphism maintains that even without a functioning intellect, sense experience would eventually order itself into an intelligible pattern. Chancism stems from the fallacy that there is no difference between intelligent intentional actions and mechanically caused events. If there is a difference, freedom is a necessary but not a sufficient condition for responsible human actions. The language of sense data and the language of the mind cannot be considered as isomorphic. This means that the relationship of the respective roles of senses and reason in the cognitive process are all scientifically indefensible. If this thesis is defensible, then we can show that the mind is unique and part of its uniqueness is that it is free to transcend the dimensions of total determinism within the structure of reality. Indeterminacy forecloses a reduction of thought processes to the methods of physics.

3. *John Locke—Esaays on the Law of Nature* (in Latin, first English edition in 1954); *An Essay Concerning Human Understanding* (1690), many editions since); Jans O. Christophersen, *A Bibliographical Introduction to the Study of John Locke* (N.Y., 1930); R. I. Aaron, *John Locke* (3rd edition, 1971); J. Gibson, *Locke's Theory of Knowledge and Its Historical Relations* (1917); J. W. Yolton, *John Locke and the Way of Ideas*, 1956).

4. *Freedom of the Will* (Schmidt, *TDNT*, III, "Thelō," pp. 44-64; Schrenk, I, "Boulomai," pp. 629-37).

A. *Aristotle* (384-322 B.C.). He uses *will* less frequently than terms such as wish, purpose, desire, appetite, or choice, but he generally employs the term "will" in signifying power which turns thought into actions. Man has a range of freedom in Aristotle's philosophy. (*Metaphysics*, Book IX, ch. 5; *Soul*, Book III, ch. 7; *Ethics*, Book VI, ch. 2; *Great Books Syntopicon*, Vol. IV, pp. 1071-1101. Indispensable source book.)

B. *Augustine* (354-430 A.D.). He defines will as "Voluntas est anim motus, cogente nullo, ad aliquid vel non amittendum vel adipiscendum," *De Duabus Animabus* X, 14; for the significance of this definition for Augustine's view of original sin see *Retractionae* I, 15, 2. This issue is fundamental to the concern of this essay. The will's action on the whole man is exercised through the mediation of the ideas and images over which it has control. In Augustinian psychology the will binds the "ideas" together; it does not generate them. Will applies our powers of intellect, imagination, etc., to actions toward decision not to overtly act, which is in itself an act. See *De Trinitate*, XI, 7, 12). Augustine's theory of the will as effected by "original sin" is fundamental for understanding the Calvinistic theory which finds expressions in Jonathan Edwards' *Freedom of the Will*.

C. *Aquinas* (1224-1274). He deliniates three acts of will with respect to ends: (1) enjoyment and use; (2) volition and consent, and (3) intention and choice. For the will the end or purpose comes first in order of intention; but in the actual execution action is initiated by the means. Clearly there is a freedom of the will which makes human responsibility a morally significant predication (*Aquinas: Summa Theologia*, Part I, Q, 14; Q 54; Q 75; Q 80; Q 83; Q 87; Part I-II, Q 50; Q 62; Q 77, etc.).

D. *Hobbes* (1588-1679). His materialistic philosophy rationally precludes any non-material factor such as will. Yet, he distinguishes between "vital motion," e.g., heartbeat, blood flow, etc., and voluntary motion which always depends on internal beginning (of course his materialism cannot logically support the distinction between internal and external) of all voluntary motion" (*Leviathan*, Part I, 61a-cff., Part III 165c.).

E. *Descartes* (1596-1650). Freedom of the will is identified with the power of choice, according to Descartes. This concept is clearly announced in his statement that "the faculty of the will consists alone in our having the power of choosing to do a thing or choosing not to do it, . . . we act so that we are unconscious that any outside force constrains us in so doing." Will is self-caused according to his view. (See his *Meditations* III, 82d-83aff., IV 89a-93a.) According to Descartes, God's omnipotence lies in the supremacy of his will in its absolute independence, yet he does not maintain that the human will is independent of . . . "the knowledge of understanding, . . . " Being free does not entail indifference in Descartes' theory of will. (Spinoza' panentheism directly attacked Descartes voluntarism.)

F. *Locke* (1632-1704). Jonathan Edwards drank deeply from Locke's empirical psychological well while yet a young student. Locke often speaks of willing as though it were an act of thought, though he distinguishes between the understanding as passive, and willing as active. Locke's explanation of the power of will is in terms of thinking of the deed to perform or an action to be taken. We cannot explain how one body moves another, let alone know how bodies are moved by the will, according to Locke. (This is similar to William James' "ideo-motor action.") (See Locke's *Civil Government*, ch. VI—57-63; *Human Understanding*, Book II, chs. 6, 7, 21.)

G. *Kant* (1724-1804 and *Hegel* (1770-1831). Both hold to a concept of the will as an activity grounded in reason. For Hegel, freedom is the essence of will. "Will without freedom is an empty word, while freedom is actual only as will, as subject." (See his *Philosophy of Right*, Introduction; *Philosophy of History*, Introduction, 163a-164a.) This view of will is completely at variance with the view of Jonathan Edwards, as it is the direct expression of autonomous self-determining man.

H. *Freud* (1856-1940). Freud does not use the term "will," but he does attribute to what he calls "the ego" the same power which Locke attributed to the will.

The preceding survey of theories of the will in relationship to freedom suggests at least two basic concerns which are important for this study: (1) Modern theories, e.g., Hegel, et al., hold that man has a free will and is self-determining. (2) Man is free, but we cannot explain how "will" causes bodies to move. Jonathan Edwards takes Locke's insights and adds his Calvinistic reinterpretation, and concludes that the explanation of how the will moves bodies is grounded in the sovereign will of God, which causally holds the universe together. Edwards also employs Newton's (1642-1727) theory of absolute universal causation to explain his Calvinistic interpretation of predestination. The central problem regarding any investigation of freedom of the will is how its acts are "caused," and how it causes the free or voluntary effects it produces. Historically, two factors are vital for our understanding the demise of "freedom of the will" talk along with faculty psychology. Free will was progressively endangered by the physical theory that every event must have a cause. Voluntary acts are no less determined than involuntary acts. According to Locke and Jonathan Edwards, a man acts freely when he carries out what he himself has decided to do. Is there any way to speak meaningfully of freedom in a world dominated by universal causation?

5. *Freedom in the New Testament*—2 Cor. 3:17, "Where the Spirit of the Lord is, there is freedom," D. Nestle, *Eleutheria. Studien zum Wesen der Freiheit bei den Griechen und im N.T.* (Bd. I Die Griechen, 1967); S. Lyonnet, *Liberte Chretienne et loi de l'esprit selon St. Paul* (Rome, 1954); J. Cambier, "La liberte Chretienne selon s. Paul," in *Studia Evangelica*, II (Berlin, 1954), pp. 315-353; R. N. Longnecker, *Paul, Apostle of Liberty* (N.Y., 1964); L. Cerfaux, "Condition Chretienne et liberte selon saint Paul" in *Structures et liberte* (Etudes carmelitaines, Bruges, 1958), pp. 244-252. M. Pohlenz, *La liberte grecque: nature et evolution 'd'un ideal* (Paris: French translation, 1956); D. Amand, *Fatalisme et Liberte dans l'antiquite grecque* (universite de Louvain: Louvain, 1945); compare with A. D. Nock and A-J. Festugiere, *Corpus Hermeticum*, I (Paris: 1945), especially pp. 193-195; C. Spicq, *Charite et liberte dans le Nouveau Testament* (Paris, 1961); R. Bultmann, "Die Bedeutung des Gedankens der Freiheit fur die abendlandische Kultur," Glauben und Verstehen Volume 2 (Tübingen, 1952, pp. 274-293). *Augustine*—Works, translated in Nicene and Post-Nicene Fathers, Volumes 108; T. van Bavel, *Repertoire bibliographicque de S. Augustin* (1950-60), 1963; R. Bernard, *La predestination de Christ total selon S. Augustin*, 1965; J. Chene, *La Theologie de S. Augustin Grace et Predestination*, 1962; M. T. Clark, *Augustine Philosopher of Freedom*, 1958; H. Jonas, *Augustin und das paulunishce Freiheitsproblem*, 1965; D. Lenfant, *Concordantiae Augustinianae*, reprint 1938, 2 vols.; N. S. Merlin, *Augustin et les dogmes du peche originel et de la grace*; G. Nygren, *Das Pradestinationsproblem in der Theologie Augustine*, 1956; L. Smits, *S. Augustin dans l'Oeuvre de Jean Calin*, 2 vols., 1957-1958; J. Goette, *Preliminary Studies for the Interpretation of St. Augustine's Concept of Providence* (N.Y.: Moroney, 1953); A. Niebergall, *Augustin's Anschauung der Gnade* (Gottingen: Vandenboeck, 1951); Joseph van Gerven, *Liberte humaine et Providence d'apres S. Augustin* (Louvain Ph.D. Thesis, 1955); C. Boyer, "Le systeme de S. Augustin sur la grace," *Recherches de Science Religieuse*, 20 (1930), pp. 481-505. Plinval, G. de, "Aspects du des Etudes Augustiniennes I" (1955), pp. 345-378. G. Nygren, "The Augustinian Conception of Grace," *Texte und Untersuchungen*, 64 (1959), pp. 257-269. *Pelagius and Pelagianism* (condemned at Council of Carthage). The heart of Pelagianism is the absolute independence of human freedom, unlimited power for good as well as for evil. Degrees of freedom—grace of Christ. Pelagius' *Commentary on Romans* has been restored by Souter, editor, *Texts and Studies* (Vol. 9, 1922-26), p. 48—grace in Romans 5:20). G. de Plinval, *Pelage, ses e'crits, sa vie et sa reforme* (Lousanne: Payot, 1943); *Saint Augustin et les dogmes du peche originel et de la grace* (Paris, 1931); (If moral choice depends on a cause extrinsic to the will, can man still be responsible for his choice? Pelagius got the idea of freedom from Stoicism. Will cannot be free if it needs God's help (De Plinval, p. 94. Scriptures used by Pelagius—emphasis clearly voluntaristic).

A. *The Augustinian-Pelagian Controversy:* The heart of the Pelagian system is the absolute independence of human freedom. His idea of freedom is largely stoic in nature. Stoicism could not produce a consistent view of freedom because of its atomistic-deterministic world view, though it did speak of free choice, but it did so at the expense of logical consistency. For the Pelagians, God need only give man the moral law and free will (shades of Locke and the classical liberal tradition). The Pelagians used grace in an equivocal sense, applying it to nature, free will, Christ's example, moral law, etc. Augustine maintained that man's freedom was derived from grace, and apart from the salvic grace of Christ, man is in bondage to sin. Augustine responded to Pelagius' *De natura* with his *De natura et gratia*. Augustine's theology of predestination and freedom must also be seen in the context of the fatalistic determinism of the Manicheans. In his *City of God* (XXI, 12), Augustine set forth his view that God saves some and abandons others to the consequences of their sin; therefore, salvation is a gift of God's infinite mercy, thus an optimism of grace.

B. *The Semi-Pelagians on Grace and Freedom:* Pelagianism was condemned but Semi-Pelagianism rejected Augustinian predestination and determinism of grace; the limited salvic will of Augustinianism stands in direct opposition to Paul's theology of the universal salvic will.

C. *The Thomistic Synthesis of Grace and Freedom:* Ultimately, Aquinas is as radical as Augustine on the consequences of "original sin." The historians of medieval thought have not been mistaken on this point. Aquinas maintained that the preparation for grace demands not only a supernatural providence, but an interior help in the will. But Thomas does not admit an irresistible grace, anymore than does Augustine. Grace does no violence to freedom; it presupposes freedom. God could not justify man without man's cooperating in his justification.

D. *Luther and Augustinian Nominalism:* Luther saw Aristotle as the fabulator who distorted the Christian faith and Augustine as its all but perfect defender. Luther reacted to the latent Pelagianism in nominalism he espoused. But nominalism controlled his interpretation of both Paul and Augustine. The ultimate conclusion regarding the relationship of grace and freedom in the mature Luther becomes visible in the tension between his theological determinism and religious individualism. But the two theses which came into particularly sharp relief are: the impotence of free will and the subjective certitude of justification. Luther's lively debate with Erasmus brought grace and free will into sharp tension. Erasmus' *De libero arbitrio* represents reason's emancipation from revelation and salvation in Christ and his church. Luther's *De servo arbitrio* (1525) ultimately generated a heated battle over theological determinism, and the debate over "synergism."

E. *Calvin's Systematic Logic:* Calvin considers reprobation and predestination before discussing Adam's sin. He does not link the question of predestination with that of so-called original sin. "Man is now stripped of free will and pitifully subjected to every evil." For Calvin, God acts through irresistible grace in the hearts of those whom he leads to salvation. Freedom is thus identified with spontaneity.

F. *Grace:* Freedom, Grace, Theology of Will—God/Man. Predestination, Justification, Election, Glorification, Sanctification in Biblical Theology. Kittel article—*xapis*; W. T. Whitley, ed., *The Doctrine of Grace* (London, 1932); *Charis*—Greek Fathers, pp. 89-105, N. Gloubokovsky; *Recherches de science religieuses*, 1928, pp. 87-104; P. Rousselot, "La grace d'apres saint Jean et d'apres saint Paul," *Ibid.*

6. Conrad Wright, "Edwards and the Arminians on the Freedom of the Will," *Harvard Theological Review*, Vol. 35, No. 4, October, 1942. H. G. Townsend, "The Will and the Understanding in the Philosophy of Jonathan Edwards," *Church History*, Vol. 16, 1947. Arthur E. Murphy, "Jonathan Edwards on Free Will and Moral Agency," *Philosophical Review*, 1959.

7. D. M. McKay, "The Sovereignty of God in the Natural World," *Scottish Journal of Theology*, 21 (1968), pp. 13-36. D. M. McKay, "Choice in a Mechanistic Universe," *British Journal of Philosophy of Science*, 22 (1971), pp. 275-285. D. M. McKay, "The Logical Indeterminateness of Human Choices," *British Journal of Philosophy of Science* (1973), pp. 405-408. D. M. McKay, *Room for Freedom and Action in a Mechanistic Universe* (Cambridge: Cambridge University Press).

DATE DUE			
3.24.91			
APR 8 '98			
DEC 2 07			
R-F 06			
LFD			
R-F-08			
LFD			
R-F 09			
LFD			